Reb

# The Archaeology of Identity

*The Archaeology of Identity* presents an overview of five of the key areas that have recently emerged in archaeological social theory: gender, age, status, ethnicity and religion. This book reviews the research history of each of them, and the different ways in which they have been investigated, as well as offering potential ways forward. Emphasis is placed on exploring the ways in which material culture is structured by these aspects of individual and communal identity, with a particular stress on social practice.

A wealth of scholarship is brought together in this book, which provides an integrated approach to identity not commonly found in similar studies. This book is suitable for students and readers interested in issues of identity, as well as social scientists dealing with similar aspects in sociology, anthropology and history.

**Margarita Díaz-Andreu** is Senior Lecturer in Archaeology, University of Durham.

**Sam Lucy** is Post-Excavation and Publications Officer, Cambridge Archaeological Unit, University of Cambridge.

**Staša Babić** is Assistant Professor, Department of Archaeology, University of Belgrade.

**David N. Edwards** is Lecturer in Archaeology, School of Archaeology and Ancient History, University of Leicester.

# The Archaeology of Identity

Approaches to gender, age, status, ethnicity and religion

**Margarita Díaz-Andreu, Sam Lucy,
Staša Babić and David N. Edwards**

Routledge
Taylor & Francis Group

LONDON AND NEW YORK

First published 2005
by Routledge
2 Park Square, Milton Park, Abingdon, Oxon OX14 4RN

Simultaneously published in the USA and Canada
by Routledge
270 Madison Ave, New York, NY 10016

*Routledge is an imprint of the Taylor & Francis Group*

© 2005 Margarita Díaz-Andreu, Sam Lucy, Staša Babić and David N.
Edwards

Typeset in Garamond by RefineCatch Ltd, Bungay, Suffolk
Printed and bound in Great Britain by
The Cromwell Press, Trowbridge, Wiltshire

*British Library Cataloguing in Publication Data*
A catalogue record for this book is available from the British Library

*Library of Congress Cataloging in Publication Data*
A catalog record for this book has been requested

ISBN 0–415–19745–7 (hbk)
ISBN 0–415–19746–5 (pbk)

# Contents

# Acknowledgements

This book has taken a very long time to write. Two of the authors of the book started to write it in parallel with teaching an undergraduate module at the University of Durham with the same title, 'The Archaeology of Identity'. Initial drafts of three of the chapters were ready in 1998 but, because of various circumstances, the book could not be finished. This has finally been possible thanks to the kind involvement of Staša Babić and David N. Edwards, alongside much rewriting of the earlier drafts. We are extremely grateful to Routledge for their immense patience as well as their encouragement as various deadlines slipped away.

We would like to express our appreciation to the many colleagues who have shared their research and ideas with us, both in person and in print; we hope that all inspiration has been appropriately acknowledged, and we all have people to whom we owe a particular debt. We are grateful to Marie-Louise Stig Sørensen and Margarita Sánchez Romero for their comments on the chapter on gender. For those on age and ethnicity thanks to Marie-Louise Stig Sørensen (again!), J.D. Hill, Becky Gowland, Jo Sofaer, Pam Graves, Simon James and Geoff Harrison for help and discussion at various stages of what turned out to be a rather lengthy writing process. Many thanks to Zorica Ivanović, Daša Duhaček, Ivana Radovanović and Aleksandar Palavestra for their comments and sound advice in relation to the chapter on status. Needless to say the kind patience of all the people mentioned above does not, of course, render them responsible for our flaws. We are also indebted to the various cohorts of Durham undergraduates who took the module; they were stimulating to teach, and helped us to refine many of our ideas, both through the teaching process, but also through their lively (and sometimes challenging!) discussions.

This study is obviously not the last word on archaeology and identity. We hope that we are offering readers a useful starting point from which to explore further the issues raised in the volume. We have focused here on five main types of identity – gender, age, status, ethnicity and religion – and left aside others that could have merited some thought such as disability, occupation and present identities. Although we could have kept on writing, and we were keen to explore the connections between various different types of identity, the book had to have some form of structure imposed on it, and this one seemed to work well in terms of the division of labour.

Finally, we would like to thank our families. During the course of writing this book, several children have been produced; watching them grow and learn to interact and express themselves has only served to deepen our belief that identity is not a thing, but a process. This book is dedicated to Anna, Ella and Jakov.

# List of figures

# 1   Introduction

*Margarita Díaz-Andreu and Sam Lucy*

## What is identity?

'Identity' is a term that may seem self-explanatory as it gets used in a number of different ways. A cursory look through any library's catalogue under the keyword 'identity' shows that this term is mostly used in connection with ethnic studies – to the extent that 'ethnicity' is sometimes absent from the title – followed by gender and nationalism, and occasionally religion, age and class/status. All this diversity is found in archaeology in books such as, to cite just two of the many examples, Shennan's (1989a) *Archaeological Approaches to Cultural Identity* and McCafferty and McCafferty's (1998 [1991]) article on 'Spinning and weaving as female gender identity in Post-Classic Mexico'. Despite the popularity of the term, definitions of identity are hard to find. This may be related to the ambiguity with which the term has been used. This is acknowledged by the anthropologists Barnard and Spencer (1996: 292), who explain that anthropological uses of 'identity' are ambiguous, as they can refer both to individual identity (as in 'self-identity') and to group identity. It is the first meaning that is favoured by some lexical dictionaries. In the *Collins English Dictionary*, for example, identity is defined as 'the individual characteristics by which a person or thing is recognised' and as 'the state of having unique identifying characteristics held by no other person or thing'. In this volume the latter definitions will not be followed, as we will refer to them using the concept of 'personality'. Rather, collective identities and the role of the individual within them will be the focus (for further discussions on the relation of 'personhood' to such collective identities see Fowler 2004). In this and the following chapters 'identity' will be understood as individuals' identification with broader groups on the basis of differences socially sanctioned as significant.

The definition of identity we are using in this volume has many implications that are further explained below as well as in the various chapters. Briefly we will try to introduce them by saying that identity, as we understand it, is inextricably linked to the sense of belonging. Through identity we perceive ourselves, and others see us, as belonging to certain groups and not others. Being part of a group entails active engagement. Identity, therefore, is not a static thing, but a continual process (literally, that of identification, cf. Hall 1996). Identities are constructed through interaction between people, and the process by which we acquire and maintain our identities requires choice and agency. Through agency we define who we are. We are potentially able to choose the groups we want to identify with, although this selection is always constrained by structures beyond our control such as boundaries and our own body. The active role of the individual leads to identities being historical, fluid, subject to persisting change. They are also socially mediated, linked to the broader cultural discourse and are performed through embodiment and action. The concept of identity deployed in this volume, therefore, is not an essentialist, but a strategic and positional one. Identities can be hybrid or multiple and the intersection between different types of identities is one of the most enriching aspects of this new field of study.

## Identity before: a glimpse to the history of twentieth-century archaeological thought

We cannot claim that archaeological discussions of identity have only arisen recently. Yet, there are major differences in the way that the concept was used in the past (and still is by many archaeologists all over the world) and how it is understood in the most recent developments in the social sciences in general and archaeology in particular. In this section some of these differences will be explained as a way of contextualising this book. The main difference lies in the fact that traditionally archaeology has not seen identity as subjective and contingent, but as objective, inherent and primordial. The relationship between material culture and identity was perceived as unproblematic and this is something that has now been challenged. The key to understanding these differences is the role of the individual in past societies within archaeological interpretation.

From the early decades of the twentieth century, archaeologists did not see individuals as their concern, but rather archaeological cultures. Childe excellently illustrated this point when, discussing the archaeology along the river Danube, he said: 'whether these Moravian peasants actually came themselves up the Danube is immaterial; their culture did' (Childe 1927: 85). In practice, cultures were treated and perceived as individuals: cultures were born, developed and flourished and were eventually transformed into something else (another archaeological culture) and/or died. This affected the way in which identity was thought of; more than anything else, this deeply influenced perceptions of the key identity then at the heart of archaeological study: ethnic identity. Archaeological cultures were equated with ethnic groups. To start with, this equation was openly acknowledged. The renowned archaeologist Pere Bosch Gimpera, for example, explicitly identified archaeological cultures with ethnic groups in his booklet 'Endeavouring to Reconstruct the Prehistoric Ethnology of the Iberian Peninsula' (1922). As he put it:

By identifying [archaeological] cultures with ethnic groups we refer to peoples in the historical meaning of the word. We do not mean peoples in the pure anthropological sense [i.e. we are not talking about races]. One has always to take into account similarities due to proximity and trade and distinguish them from that which is based on the peoples' personality. Historical peoples are the result of many factors. However, once they have managed to form their personality, to destroy it will take as long as was needed to build it.

(ibid.: 4–5, our translation)

After the Second World War the correlation between the terms became implicit and was then, in effect, forgotten by new generations. The equation between archaeological cultures and ethnic groups became naturalised.

The perception of cultures as individuals not only had implications for how ethnic identity was portrayed, but also for other identities such as gender. Following general convention successful cultures should be thought of as male and failed ones as female.[1] This explains how someone as socially minded as Gordon Childe could state that 'the hill country of western Bohemia, Bavaria and Wurtemburg was already occupied by *virile* pastoral tribes interring their dead under barrows' (1928: 40, our emphasis), thus leaving us wondering how he imagined the women of the group. Archaeologists were well aware of the association of individuals of different genders and ages with distinct subsets of material culture. Yet, the understanding of that variability was unsophisticated, and made only at a descriptive level, often drawing on prevalent assumptions in contemporary Western society: 'As potters the women [of the Peterborough culture] were not highly skilled', conjectured Jacquetta Hawkes (in Hawkes and Hawkes 1943: 66). One can only think that it was the crudeness of the pottery and the assumption that women are universally less skilled than men that led the author to infer the sex of the maker in this scenario. In any case, as the aim of archaeology was primarily to date the origin and spread of cultures identified through diagnostic types whose importance was related to their degree of masculinity, objects associated with women, as well as children, were largely excluded from archaeological interests.

The selection of diagnostic types for defining a culture also led to an imbalance in the importance given to valuable objects in the definition of cultures. This is due to archaeologists' predisposition to look for objects that are exceptional in terms of their quality or perceived high value, a trend that can be explained as a lasting trait of antiquarianism. Cultures thought of as individuals tended to be defined by the objects perceived as being of high status, and not by those used by the whole population. This does not mean that archaeologists never dealt with them at the individual level. They did in particular cases such as in the analysis of cemeteries when discussing deposits in graves. In such analyses, however, a direct relationship between the objects and the deceased was inferred and tacit assumptions were made directly linking social prestige to economic benefits. With regard to religion, archaeologists simplified prehistoric belief systems into large groupings, too rough to encompass the variability of ritual and religious practice in non-state societies. The contemporary Judaeo-Christian doctrine entirely determined how more complex religions were understood.

The revolution in archaeological thought that started in the 1950s mainly affected archaeology in the English-speaking countries, beginning with functionalism, which was then transformed in the 1960s into the radical New Archaeology or processual archaeology. This revolt did not greatly affect the way in which identity was analysed, although it certainly paved the way for later developments. To start with, however, the relationship between the individual and society continued to be thought of in a very similar way to that of the culture-historical perspective. The individual was very much part and parcel of the group, passive and obedient to its norms and pressures. There was little recognition that people could have ambitions and desires that were contradictory to those of the social group. The aim of New Archaeology was to develop understandings of the formation of the archaeological record and to refine approaches to inferring past behaviour from observations of that record, which led to a growing interest in, for example, site formation processes, ethnoarchaeology and the use of analogy. There was thus an emphasis on the use of a rigorous hypothetico-deductive method (involving the testing of models and the use of inferential generalisations about the past). Within this perspective, the focus on culture was maintained, but the term was radically redefined as a system of interrelated components (Binford 1968: 16–23). It was, however, later to be criticised, in the same way that functionalist anthropology was, for its rather fixed views of human behaviour.

Processual archaeology became engaged with neo-evolutionary theory (Fried 1967; Service 1962, 1971), which envisaged human societies passing through a sequence of egalitarian, ranked and stratified societies. While this was criticised for its emphasis on evolution, it led to an emphasis on status in archaeology (e.g. Renfrew and Shennan 1982). These processual ideas about status tended, however, to be rather descriptive, and were better at explaining stasis than dynamic change (which had to be accounted for by internal or external stimuli, rather than being inherent in the theoretical model). An explicitly quantitative approach was fostered, expressing certain elements of the archaeological record in measurable terms, especially in the case of funerary assemblages, from where status of the buried was inferred (Binford 1972; Saxe 1970; Tainter 1978). The processual approach was also criticised for the straightforward way in which it interpreted material culture. For example, the biggest settlement in a given area was assumed to be the most important, while burial evidence was assumed to directly reflect the roles and status of the deceased in life.

## Rethinking the link between the individual and society: recent developments in the study of identity

Over the last three decades sociology, anthropology and archaeology have engaged in a pivotal debate on the relationship between individuals and the societies of which they form part. This debate has had enormous implications for the study of identity. In contrast with the image so far held by social sciences of the passive individual, anthropologists such as Pierre Bourdieu and sociologists such as Anthony Giddens have proposed that society should be viewed as something that cannot exist independently of the people of whom it is comprised; it is through their actions and practices (which themselves are largely governed by the social expectations of others) that society is constituted and carries on existing. Parallel to Giddens' concept of *practical consciousness* (Giddens 1979, 1984), Bourdieu (1977) used the term *habitus* to mean people's understanding of how the world operates, an understanding that was not based on explicit rules, but on principles that governed practice.[2] It is through practice that the individual moves, acts, lives. It is a pre-conscious way to go on in the world. In this context *agency* is understood as the ability to act or perform an action. Through agency, through people's engagement with its social and institutional structures, the world is transformed. The structuring principles of social institutions (the 'rules' governing behaviour in a temple or school, for example) are seen as both the medium and outcome of their reproduction through human action. Within this model of society, people are neither entirely free agents, nor helpless drones: they have a certain amount of knowledge about how their particular society works, and they may use that information in order to try to achieve their personal goals, but their knowledge may be imperfect, or their actions may have unintended consequences. The impact of power relations within any given society is also taken into account; for while the individual can always choose not to do something (at whatever personal cost to themselves), their actions are usually constrained by other individuals.

Following the same line of thought initiated in anthropology and sociology, of considering the individual as key in the understanding of society, several archaeologists mainly based in English-speaking countries initiated a new direction in archaeological enquiry. These were initially grouped around Cambridge in the UK under the direction of Ian Hodder, whereas other archaeologists in the USA such as Mark Leone followed a similar path (Leone 1973, 1984). Hodder's early work, under what became known as post-processual archaeology, is discussed below, as his work fully engaged in the study of identity. In a more general theoretical field, concepts such as the 'field of discourse' proposed by John Barrett (1988) directly linked with what was being proposed by Giddens and Bourdieu, but were specifically developed as a way of interpreting archaeological remains. Barrett argues that rather than consider such remains as a direct reflection of anything in the past, they should be seen as the residue of past material conditions that structured, and were organised by, past social practice. In practices, (unequal) relation-ships between people are reproduced at the same time that food and things are produced, utilised, appropriated, exchanged and consumed; the economy or relations of domination, for example, cannot be separated out from other aspects of the reproduction of society. This approach fits well with the view of identity as maintained and reproduced as part of a social process. While people are reproducing the material conditions of their lives, they are both reproducing their society and their personal and group identities. It is because of this that archaeologies of practice are ideally suited to interpret-ations of identity in archaeology (cf. Dobres and Robb 2000; Sørensen 2000; though see Meskell 1999: 8–52 for a critique).

## Ethnicity in a new light

In archaeology, the rise of the individual as an active member of society led archaeologists to turn to issues of identity. Ethnicity and gender were the first identities to attract scholars' attention. A renewed interest in ethnicity can be traced back to the late 1970s, when both Steven Shennan (1978) and Ian Hodder (1978) wondered about the nature (and indeed about the very exist-ence) of archaeological cultures, worrying that the boundaries of various dis-tributions of artefacts did not coincide in the case studies they examined (see also Binford 1965; Clarke 1968). Drawing on anthropological and socio-logical work, such as that of Barth (1969, see chapter 5) they both came to see ethnicity as a self-ascribed identity. Alongside this debate was a similar one, critiquing ideas of 'peoples' in the past, their nature and existence. Continu-ing his interest in ethnicity, a major break with the processual paradigm occurred in the early 1980s, with the publication of the seminal book *Symbols in Action* (Hodder 1982b).[3] In it, material culture was depicted as active in creating social relationships, and the need to find ways of interpreting its meaning was stressed. Much emphasis was placed here on the importance of context, as giving objects much of their 'meaning'. The major aim of this body of research was the study of living cultures 'in order to shed some light on the analysis and interpretation of cultures in prehistoric archaeology' (ibid.: 1). Interestingly, this latter study originated from an overtly proces-sual hypothesis, which was to test the relationship between resources, inter-action and cultural similarity (ibid.: 8), and it was assumed that cultural similarity would 'reflect' degrees of interaction (ibid.: 9). However, observa-tions made during the ethnographic fieldwork found that while the use and distribution of certain items such as drinking cups, wooden eating bowls and stools followed the expected patterns, those of others such as spears and calabashes did not. Hodder concluded that 'the extent to which cultural similarity relates, for example, to interaction, depends on the strategies and intentions of the interacting groups and how they use, manipulate and negotiate material symbols as part of those strategies' (ibid.: 185). These interacting groups could be ethnic (tribal), but other subgroups within those societies, such as younger men and women, were also observed to follow their own strategies in their relations with the dominant older men. Hodder stressed the need for archaeologists to understand structures of beliefs, as without this, archaeology would be unable to interpret the archaeological patterning (ibid.: 211). Particular emphasis came to be placed on 'ideology' as a means of denying social conflict caused by unequal power relations; as a way of imposing the interests of a subgroup on those of a whole community; and as a way of making inequalities seem natural (ibid.: 209). Despite this earlier emphasis on status, this promising new path of enquiry was subsequently dropped as research interest mainly turned towards discussions of the implications of present power relations and the ideological setting of archaeological research. Developments in the archaeology of ethnicity thereafter are described in chapter 5.

## Gender and age

The main impetus to studies of identity in archaeology has come from the spheres of gender and feminist archaeology. The early practitioners of feminist archaeology in Scandinavia and Anglo-American academia emphasised the lack of women in standard accounts of the past, and also focused on the contemporary position of women in the archaeological profession. This highlighted a major gap in understanding, and problematised the 'common-sense' ways in which sex and gender were being dealt with in archaeology. Part of the impetus came from feminist anthropology, which also touched on aspects of the interpretation of material culture. In the 1980s, several of these anthropologists such as Ortner (Ortner and Whitehead 1981) and Collier (Collier and Rosaldo 1981; Collier and Yanagisako 1987) had started to make use of 'practice theories' in the interpretations of other societies and the ways that they functioned. Henrietta Moore (1986), for example, with *Space, Text and Gender*, an anthropological study of an East African society that investigated the relationship between gender organisation and social space, highlighted a strong gender ideology that structured the division of space within the settlement, including where certain materials were disposed of and where different genders were buried on death.

Awareness of the importance of age came out of this feminist and gender work (see works in Moore and Scott 1997). There was a realisation that in order to understand the operation of gender relations in the past, those who needed caring for were also fundamental. Although this can now be seen to be a slightly lopsided view of children, the elderly and the disabled (i.e. as people whose sole function is to interfere with female adult freedom), they did start to be considered, a point from which they could start to be studied in their own right. While research into archaeological aspects of old age and disability has not progressed as far as one would like, there is now a substantial body of work on children. One interesting angle, in particular, that has emerged recently is a focus on children as producers and consumers of material culture, and through this as the perpetuators of social identities, which they have the ability to transform in the process (cf. Sofaer Derevenski 1994a). It is through studies of children that resolution of the stasis/change dichotomy may possibly come. Discussions about the potential of the study of gender and age in archaeology are further discussed in chapters 2 and 3.

Gender and age are identities that illustrate well the restrictions impinging on identity. These can both be in terms of what identities a society will countenance, in general, and also in terms of whether individuals can choose at will whatever identities they wish. Gender and age, as well as some ethnicities (one could also include some aspects of disability, which we do not explicitly discuss in this volume), are identities that can be termed 'embodied'. This means that the fluidity with which identity operates as one of the aspects in the relationship between the individual and society has limitations that are related to biology. Thus, there is no chance of acceptance for a child who might wish to be viewed as an adult, or a white person who might wish to be viewed as black.

## *The handmaiden of recent developments: status and religion*

The two identities of those discussed in this book that have been the worst treated by post-processual archaeologists are undoubtedly status and religion. Status as an aspect of identity has been rather neglected of late, perhaps due to its popularity during the heyday of processual archaeology during the 1960s and 1970s. With the gradual rejection of these approaches, status as an archaeological identity seems to have slipped out of view. However, there are ways of interpreting status differences in archaeology without recourse to functionalist and essentialist views of the past, as will be demonstrated in chapter 4. Religion has been barely dealt with as an aspect of identity in archaeology, despite a flurry of interest during the 1980s in aspects of ideology, and specific focus on ritual and religion by authors such as Bourdieu (1977). Indeed, it is noticeable that the few archaeologists who have worked on religion in the past two decades are mainly medieval archaeologists, often rooted in feminist and gender approaches themselves (Gilchrist 1994; Graves 1989). Despite recent attention raised by religious practices such as shamanism, archaeology does not seem to have taken into account developments in the anthropological study of religion (Díaz-Andreu 2001a). It is also noticeable that archaeologists that have taken them on board have focused on architectural interpretation, rather than related aspects such as burial, settlement archaeology or dress. It is only very recently that religion is starting to be dealt with in a critical way, as an aspect both of personal and group identity (see chapter 6).

*Identity and material culture: the specifics of the archaeological gaze towards identity and ways forward*

In contrast with other social scientists who rely on living individuals in their enquiries about identity and are able to chart their interpersonal relations and reactions in certain situations, archaeologists are most usually constrained by lack of knowledge about specific individuals. The main body of material that archaeologists work with is material culture. Through its expertise at dealing with material culture, and interpreting it in a contextual way, archaeology is ideally placed to add the material dimension so often lacking in other social sciences. Through looking at cultural items such as dress, spatial layout and architecture and considering them as the media through which many social relationships and interactions are negotiated, archaeology can detail how the material world both engages, and is engaged in, the articulation of social identity, both of the individual and of the group. Unique among other social sciences, the long time-span archaeologists usually work on makes archaeology ideal to offer a chronological perspective on aspects of identity in the past. This can serve to challenge entrenched stereotypes such as the arguments over the relative contributions of men and women to the 'agricultural revolution' (see chapter 2).

Despite some early studies (see below), most archaeological analyses of identity have mainly centred on only one of either gender, age, ethnicity, status or religion. Yet, there is an increasing inclination to move away from attempting to look at specific types of identity in isolation. Once identity is thought of as something that becomes articulated through social relationships, all the aspects of those social relationships have to be taken into account. As in sociology, where one needs to look at ethnicity, class *and* gender in order to understand, for example, migrant women's strategies of coping and resistance in Australia (Vasta 1991), archaeology has to take into account the intersections between several identities. There is in fact a growing literature on this in the field of archaeology. The most frequent identity combination looked at in archaeology has been that of gender and status (Connell 1987; Hodder 1982b; Yanagisako and Collier 1987; etc. amongst the earliest published). The relationship between gender and age has also received particular attention (see Moore and Scott 1997). Other studies have focused on ethnicity and gender (Hodder 1982b; Lustig 1997; Meskell 2001; Mitchell and Plug 1997; etc.), and others on gender and status (Sweely 1999b). This is the way we believe that archaeology should move forward.

## Present identities matter

There has been an increasing realisation that today's identities matter in how identity is studied, not only in the present, but also in the past. It has been argued that theoretical shifts in the last few decades have been the result of wider social changes, such as the growing questioning of authority in the wake of long-lived peace in Western Europe, continuing industrial growth and the rapid globalisation of culture (Boissevain 1994: 43–4). These shifts also prompted a growing interest in rituals and symbols in the wider world. Alongside this, increasing movement of people is argued to have stimulated struggles for identity and for the control of social and cultural boundaries, with growing tourist interest in some areas fostering awareness of local cultures (ibid.: 46–9). Similarly, Prout and James (1990: 15) have charted the growing importance of what they term 'interpretative' perspectives in the social sciences: examination of the everyday prompts one to see that social reality is not fixed, constant or unitary, and social life should be seen as constantly created through the activities of social actors. One word that has been widely used to convey this image of a society constantly recreating itself in its own image is 'reproduction'. As Jenks (1993: 5) stresses, though, it is important not to see this as merely 'replication'; it should be viewed just as sexual and biological reproduction is: as positive and vibrant, offering possibilities of change and new combinations of existing features.

The past twenty years have seen a rise of interest, both within academia and the wider world, in issues of identity, focusing mainly on aspects of gender (and more recently age), on ethnicity, nationalism and religion, and on class and status. Much of this interest can be linked to current social transformations in terms of these identities, with academics seeking to explain the changes they see in the world around them (and, in turn, having their own impact on those changes). In recent years, one of these major social transformations has been seen in gender identity. Drastic shifts in male and female employment patterns, changing ideologies of parenthood, and differing emphasis by the state on what gender roles should be are all having major effects. Men and women are not what they were twenty years ago: patterns of gender identity have altered markedly. Living through these changes, archaeologists – and feminist archaeologists in particular – have wondered whether relations between men and women might also have varied in the past. New questions asked of archaeological evidence have led to a revolutionary picture of past gender relations. At the same time, by rewriting the history of gender, archaeologists have further contributed to the shift in Western gender ideologies.

Gender identity has not been the only one to go through an adjustment in the modern world. In both Western countries and in other areas of the world, issues of ethnicity, nationalism and religion have also become matters for action and debate. Ethnicity, especially, has become a byword for conflict in certain regions, with the neologisms 'ethnic cleansing' and 'ethnic hatred' summing up the unfortunate direction in which one articulation of this form of identity has gone. Yet, at the same time, ethnicity can be seen to be taking on a more positive meaning, as Western states witness the emergence of vibrant and innovative traditions from 'ethnic minorities', especially in fields of contemporary culture. The emergence of new ways in which to define oneself in ethnic terms, the increasing use of 'Black British', for example, highlights the fluid and contingent nature of ethnicity. Academics are increasingly seeing ethnic groups as created through self-ascription and ascription by others (cf. Barth 1969), with a more recent dimension being that ethnic groups are no longer seen as monolithic entities but that in many cases the same person can feel that they belong to several different ethnic identifications, depending on the situation in which they find themselves (Díaz-Andreu 2001b; Jenkins 1997). This multiple and situational character of ethnicity is only just starting to be taken into account in archaeology, and incorporating it into studies of the past promises to provide radically different interpretations. This, in turn, will contribute further to the understandings of ethnicity in the present.

Likewise the continued attention given to national identities can be seen in the drastic political reorganisation of the former USSR and Yugoslavia with the gaining of independence by some or all of their former territories, as well as in more peaceful reorganisations such as devolution of power to Scotland and Wales within the UK. The past has played a role in all these transformations. As spectators and, in some cases, active participants in these shifts, many archaeologists have felt it necessary to examine critically the role of archaeology in the formation of national identities in the last 200 years. A completely new body of research has resulted from these investigations, and as a result a new and insightful understanding of the history of our discipline has arisen (Atkinson *et al.* 1996; Díaz-Andreu and Champion 1996; Díaz-Andreu and Smith 2001; Kane 2003; Kohl and Fawcett 1995; Meskell 1998).

Meanwhile, until September 11th 2001 religion and status were, for the West, supposedly becoming less important as arenas for the creation and articulation of identity: 'we're all middle-class now', despite the fact that the gap between rich and poor is ever-widening. Or are we? What exactly does it mean now to belong to a class? Is it a question of imagined communities (cf. Anderson 1991)? How should power be understood in relation to class/status identities? Moreover, religious beliefs make people experience themselves and the world in different ways and it may not be a coincidence that new thoughts about religion are coming from an archaeologist working on Islamic archaeology (Insoll 2004).

Identities clearly matter in the present, as they did in the past. They help define who we are, who we are not, what we can do, where we can go, how we dress, and a myriad other things. Often, we do not notice aspects of identity until they are out of context, so innate are they: the six-year-old girl dressed in her mother's clothes and high heels; the husband in his wife's dress. It is this very 'naturalness' of social identity that has been increasingly challenged by certain social sciences in the past two decades: a number of anthropologists have turned some of their analytical perspectives onto our contemporary societies, highlighting how contingent our social practices and attitudes are, through comparison with other cultures. Alongside this comparative approach has come a historical one, showing how attitudes towards, for example, gender, sexuality, age and religion have changed in the run-up to the present. Our identities are not inevitable, neither is our behaviour in accordance with those identities, and much of the interest lies in investigating how they can so strongly bind people's actions to other people's expectations. This curiosity about identity is gradually permeating archaeology. With the realisation that identity in the present is fluid and contingent (within certain constraining structures) comes the realisation that identities in the past may have been very different from the ways in which they have been constructed.

## Notes

1 For example in 1872, W. Turley in the journal *The Dark Blue* implored for support for masculinity by relating nationhood, gender and appropriate activity. His argument was that 'a nation of effeminate enfeebled bookworms scarcely forms the most effective bulwark of a nation's liberties'. He backed a vigorous, manly and English nation (Dodd 1999: 91). Another example is that of Gustav Klemm, who in the first half of the nineteenth century proposed the separation of humanity into two major races: one 'active', culturally advanced and masculine, and the other 'passive', innately inferior and feminine, subsuming all non-Indo-European peoples (Bunzl 1996: 44).
2 Curiously, the term 'habitus' appeared in the literature much earlier. It can be found in Spengler (1991 [1918–22]). Oswald Spengler used the term to refer to an indefinable feeling that was reflected in religion, politics, society and economics, and which could not be translated into fixed concepts.
3 Discussions were, however, well underway by then, as many of the contributions to *Symbolic and Structural Archaeology* (Hodder 1982) show; as stated in the preface of this book, 'the idea for this volume grew out of a series of graduate seminars in Cambridge in the academic year 1979–80' (ibid.: vii).

# 2   Gender identity

*Margarita Díaz-Andreu*

## Introduction

Of all the identities discussed in this book, gender is possibly the one that has received most attention in recent years. As a concept, gender first appeared in the literature in the late 1960s. It was forged in the field of psychoanalysis (Oakley 1972; Stoller 1968), spreading to other social sciences such as anthropology in the mid 1970s (Rubin 1975) and reaching archaeology in the 1980s. The reason for the late arrival in archaeology has been related to a large extent to archaeology's reluctance to knock down the bastion of archaeological objectivity and the emphasis on macroscale analyses (Wylie 1991). The potential of gender studies was only acknowledged after the publication of Conkey and Spector's article on 'Archaeology and the study of gender' (Conkey and Spector 1984), although it still took a while to filter through to archaeologists' interests. In this article and in those that followed, especially from the early 1990s, tribute was paid to a previous foundation of feminist research especially strong from the 1970s and developed both in Europe – Scandinavia and Britain in particular – and in the USA. Although the link with feminism is still predicated by some (Engelstad 2001) and assumed by many, alternatives such as masculinism (Knapp 1998) and queer theory (Dowson 1998) have also been put on the table and are gaining momentum. The criticism has also been raised that on occasions feminist scholars involved in developing gender archaeology have shown a strong loyalty and need for solidarity that has tended to exclude critique from within (Sørensen 1992). This is a reflection of the 'growing pains' (as Sarah M. Nelson and Myriam Rosen-Ayalon [2002: 1] have put it) through which the study of gender is currently going. Articles on gender in archaeology now number into the hundreds and it would be unreasonable to expect complete homogeneity of theories and opinions by all authors.

There are many aspects of archaeology that gender has touched upon and that are worth exploring. Differences between sex and gender; gender as a significant cultural variable in society; social dynamics and the transformation of identities; issues of human origins; the diverse approaches of relating gender and power; the embodiment of gender in material culture; the role of gender in economic and social practices and in the space of the living and the dead are all issues that will be discussed throughout the following pages. To the extent that the literature allows it, the arguments will be illustrated with examples that go beyond the ghettoisation of gender (i.e. the typical treatment of gender as only related to the female gender category). Yet, despite the increase in masculinist and queer archaeologists, the bulk of the literature is still mainly centred on women.

This chapter is greatly indebted to the work of many other archaeologists who have published their work in articles and, especially, in edited volumes that echo the explosion of interest. These also demonstrate that one of the most remarkable outcomes of the interest in gender has been that archaeologists specialising in areas as diverse as the Palaeolithic and medieval studies, America and Australia have considered it worth confronting their ideas in the same forums. The capacity of gender for change has again shown its potential in practice.

## Gender as an analytical category

Gender can be defined as an individual's self-identification and the identification by others to a specific gender category on grounds of their culturally perceived sexual difference. The concept of gender is related but not equivalent to that of sex. Sex refers to the physical and genetic elements of the body related to reproduction, including genitalia, chromosomal and hormonal distinctions and reproductive organs (Voss and Schmidt 2000: 2). Understandings of the relationship between sex and gender have altered throughout the years. As opposed to previous emphasis on the biological aspects of sex (Oakley 1972: 158), stress is currently laid on the cultural perception of sexual variance. Sexuality is now seen as socially constructed and includes all kinds of sexual relations, such as sexual activities, eroticism, sexual identities, sexual meanings and sexual politics (Voss and Schmidt 2000: 2). In this new light both gender and sexual identity are connected to biological sex and sexuality. According to Voss and Schmidt sexual identities are defined by choice of sexual partner (e.g. heterosexual, homosexual, pederast). As they explain, in this definition some scholars also encompass situations usually intertwined with gender identity such as childbirth and child-rearing where sexual practices or meanings assist the construction of personal or group identity. This shows an obvious approximation of both concepts that has led some to maintain that the distinction between the two terms should be eliminated (Kessler 1998). This chapter will adhere to the so far most common view of seeing sex and gender as separate concepts.

Gender and sex categories may coincide, but by no means is this always the case. The interrelationships of sex and gender identities have the potential to create intricate social structures to an extent perhaps so far underestimated by social scientists. The complexities emerging from gender affinities, despite divergent sexual preferences, may result in a system of combined gender and sexual identities. The network of social identities created by the associations between gender and sex can yield an arrangement far removed from the simple picture currently drawn by social scientists. It would be worth exploring whether individuals have overlapping gender or sex/gender identities and how they may strategically decide to use one or the other depending on the situation they are immersed in at a particular moment (as is sometimes argued for ethnic identity). Also, it seems that gender studies would benefit from a greater consideration of the effect of age in the definition of gender categories. In most societies members of a particular gender are differently perceived depending on their age; the passage from one age group to another usually entails the acquisition of new rights and duties. Moreover, age is particularly relevant for gender categorisation displacement, because it is mostly at junctures between different age groups that some individuals may decide to shift to a different gender category. A case is found among the North American Blackfoot, among whom women, usually only after their loss of fertility, are allowed to pass to a gender with features closer to those defining the male category (Whitehead 1981).

One of the messages most often repeated by authors dealing with gender archaeology is that the (challenged) restriction to solely the male and female genders that characterises modern Western societies cannot be taken as a model for gender relations in other societies. Nor, they claim, can the sexual practices commonly associated with each gender category in Western societies be considered as the standard. Recent research in history and in anthropology has shown the variety of sexual practices linked to particular gender categories. Several scholars have shown that in some present and ancient societies, for instance, the concept of 'man' is closely linked with homosexual practices or these are sanctioned within the norm. Examples can be found among the Azande (ibid.: 81), in classical Greece (Keuls 1985; Matthews 1994; Sparkes 1998) and to a certain extent among the Mayans (Joyce 2000). Characteristics commonly used in the Western world to define or measure masculinity, such as level of direct sexual activity or paternity, economic success, body beauty or dress, might not have held any importance in other societies or in other periods. In this vein, Eleanor Scott suggests that the degree of masculinity in Roman times was not measured by such characteristics, but by public political activity, something forbidden to women (Scott 1997: 9).

Social scientists agree that, given the cultural basis of gender, there is no limit to the number of possible genders in each human group. Thus, it has been argued that the Chukchee of Siberia have two gender categories for women and three for men (Martin and Voorhies 1975). Third genders are also possible. Homosexuality has been argued as the appropriate interpretation of some of the scenes represented in late Bronze Age (*c.* 1000–500 BC) rock art carvings of Bohuslän, Sweden (Yates 1993: 46). The search for *berdaches*, members of an ethnographically well-documented third gender in North America, has been recently addressed by Hollimon (2000, 2001) and by Prine (2000). As probable evidence for their existence in past societies, these authors have pointed to particular sets of material culture that hint at their presence. Hollimon argues that the existence of pre-contact Chumash individuals belonging to this third category is indicated by specific items found in burials, which ethnographers associate with *berdaches* (see fig. 2.1). Prine sees earthlodges of an outstandingly small size and uncommon features such as double posts as signs of *berdache* dwellings in Middle Missouri. The discussion on third genders is, however, one with which archaeologists have shown some reluctance to engage, even when historical and anthropological analyses indicate their existence. This seems to be the case of the eunuchs of the Byzantine world (Ringrose 1994; Tougher 1997, 1999) and the *hirjas* of India (Nanda 1993; Suthrell 2004).

The variability in the definition of both the number of genders allowed in each society and their differing roles makes it clear that gender is not a

*Figure 2.1* Sarah Winnemucca, 1883, Northern Paiute female *berdache*. Source: Roscoe (1994: 354).

universal. It is an identity that is culturally created, historically specific and central to the social structure. The study of gender has to be guided by flexibility, as it is no longer valid to use our own ideas of gender to understand those of other societies, including those of the past. As a social construct gender needs to be continually reconfirmed and elaborated by society, and individuals must maintain an active attitude towards it; they need to demonstrate in their daily lives that they belong to their own specific gender group. In addition, because gender dynamics are included in all activities, even the most routine ones, gender constitutes an intimate element of the processes of social reproduction and not only of the formation of the social. Gender is a basic structuring principle, for it frames the primary parameters that guide our understanding of the world and creates the rules that serve as a basis for individual behaviour.

Gender archaeology represents a change in the optic of archaeological analysis. It aims to explore the importance that gender has in social dynamics, the potential number of gender categories in the construction of the social, the variations in gender relations in different periods, how they originated and how they were maintained (Sørensen 1992: 31). It also tries to enquire into how gender relations interact with other types of identities, in particular age but also ethnicity, status and religion. In the words of Margaret Conkey and Janet Spector, an archaeology of gender should examine 'the factors that seem to influence the nature of relations between men and women [and third genders?], the circumstances in which women and men exert power and influence, and the ways that gender arrangements affect or structure group responses to various conditions in their social or natural environments' (1984: 19). An archaeology of gender does not aim to add women and men to the past and stir, but to understand how gender functions in all dimensions: within the context of gender roles, gender ideology, gender relations, as a social construct, a negotiation and as an essential source of cultural meanings related to the structuration of social life (Conkey and Gero 1991: 14).

When did gender identity emerge? There is no agreement on this. Recently it has been suggested that representation of biological aspects of sexuality in the Upper Palaeolithic *c.* 30,000–50,000 years ago indicates the existence of sexuality (Voss and Schmidt 2000: 16), although not necessarily of distinct genders. One could argue that the origin of gender is probably rooted in the advent of the consciousness of the self and the symbolic perception of the world. These appeared as a result of a long process, whose first discernible results were practices such as language and artistic creation. Both are clear in *Homo sapiens*, in particular in anatomically modern humans, and claims that they emerged earlier cannot but remain open questions (Whelan 1991a: 361). Yet, language has recently been described as the prime mover in human evolution, a capability for which females are naturally gifted given the distinctive wiring of their brains (Falk 1997). Some authors propose that identities evolved as such only in the last stages of human evolution, probably during the Pleistocene (*c.* 1.6 million years), and perhaps even in the last part of the Pliocene (5.3 to 1.6 million years ago; Conroy 1993; Whelan 1991a). Others maintain that gender may not have existed as we know it today in the Upper Palaeolithic (Conkey 1991: 87n) and even that gender differentiation may be a recent phenomenon (McGuire and Hildebrandt 1994). This seems to be contested by others who have been inspired by gender analysis for these periods (Dobres 1995; Soffer *et al.* 2000) and those who even use the term with reference to apes (Roosevelt 2002)! Probably we will never know for sure, but there seems to be general agreement that gender identity has been present throughout the Holocene (11,000 years ago to the present) and most probably before.

## Hierarchies and power

Until the challenge posed by feminist scholars in the 1970s the social sciences' belief in men's superior role in human development and the organisation of society was largely seen as unproblematic. The perception then held of women as passive, as secondary members in each group, was so persuasive that it has remained powerful even despite fierce criticisms. This perception derived from the scientists' own experiences but was also theorised. In the nineteenth century the rationale behind gender imbalance had borrowed from the theoretical scheme of social evolution. This was based on belief in the progression from the simple to the complex and in its original form it was most commonly employed to elucidate the evolution from savagery, through barbarism to civilisation (Morgan 1877; for precedents see Jones 1992). Applied to gender this theory saw women as the children of society, thus accounting for the perceived lesser inclination of women to work, and their inferior intelligence. These assumptions deeply permeated the understanding of gender relations and were practically unquestioned for a century, although among the rare exceptions was the Swedish professor Oscar Montelius (Arwill-Nordbladh 1989). Later theories looked further into the roots of inequality. In the 1970s, for instance, scholars within the cultural materialist agenda contended that male supremacy and its institutionalisation 'arose as a by-product of warfare, of male monopoly over weapons, and of the use of sex for the nurturance of aggressive male personalities' (Harris 1977: 81). War and sexism would cease to be practised when their productive, reproductive and ecological functions were fulfilled by less costly alternatives (ibid.: 97). The grounding of male power in violence is also maintained by some feminist scholars today (Collier and Rosaldo 1981).

Women's social inferiority seemed to be confirmed by anthropological research. Yet, in that field recent feminist studies have also revealed the adverse effects of the androcentric bias, showing the weak basis on which the corroboration had taken place (Gilchrist 1999: 32–6; Nelson 1997: 141–7). These critical analyses showed that scholars had developed circular arguments, for they had taken gender inequality as a given in their enquiries, despite later declaring its detection as one of the results of their research. As their critics highlighted, traditional anthropologists' understanding of gender as a universal had allowed them to judge gender relations in other societies following Western schemes. Consequently, the male sphere had been assumed to be associated with responsibility and with certain activities, whereas the female one was perceived as passive and of secondary importance. Also, as anthropologists were almost exclusively men, they only had male informants. These could mainly instruct their interrogators on their gender category, and, because they talked from their own point of view, a biased account of gender relations in society was the only version they could give to the anthropologists. Finally, because of male predominance in anthropology, a whole set of concepts and fields of interest in research was developed from an exclusively male perspective. This obviously restricted and predisposed the direction of enquiry. The critique of anthropological bias evidently has implications for one of the bastions on which archaeology's belief in the universal and timeless inferior social condition for women from the earliest periods was based. Thus, if on the basis of anthropological research archaeologists could presuppose women's inferiority, for example by imagining them objectified and exchanged between prehistoric groups, we can now remark that the data in no way supported *per se* archaeologists' assumption of a particular gender group being transacted.

In recent years the search for alternatives to gender hierarchy has highlighted the importance of the use of more neutral terms such as gender inequality, asymmetry and complementarity. Janet Levy has proposed the use of the concept of heterarchy, which emphasises continually shifting standards of rank (1999: 63). Heterarchy is a system of relations

> in which each element possesses the potential of being unranked (relative to other elements) or ranked in a number of different ways, depending on systemic requirements . . . elements in a hierarchical structure are most frequently perceived as being vertical . . . whereas heterarchical structure is most easily envisioned as lateral, emphasising the number and variety of connections among elements and the varying circumstantial importance of any single element.
>
> (Crumley in Levy 1999: 73)

Of the different dimensions of power, archaeologists have mostly concentrated on one: the power that structures the overarching political economy. This type of power models the social field of action so as to render some kinds of behaviour possible, while making others less possible or impossible (Wolf 1990: 587 in Levy 1999: 72). The assumption in archaeology has been that men are the strongest element in political power. This has now been challenged by anthropological studies that demonstrate that in some societies individuals from any gender may hold power. Examples of this come from Samoa where status is not linked with gender, but with relational prestige, defined through brothers and sisters (Tcherkezoff 1993), and from the

Iñupiak in Alaska, where leadership positions are associated with skills and knowledge that are gender-neutral (Bodenhorn 1993). On the basis of Inuit myths, Barbara Crass also insists on the complementarity of men and women who, despite differences in labour, are considered equally powerful (2000). Some rock art carvings such as those from central Spain may also suggest the existence of gender complementarity rather than hierarchisation at least in mythological accounts (Díaz-Andreu 2003). This complementarity also existed in more elaborated religions such as in ancient Egypt (Roth 2000; see our fig. 2.2). In spite of research suggesting the link between state formation and gender inequality (Savage 2000; Silverblatt 1988), a revision of historical and other sources also indicates that this is not necessarily so (Jiao 2001) and even that, as opposed to what was traditionally held, written sources indicate the existence of women rulers and of very high-status women in past societies (Trocolli 1999), who also appear in the archaeological record once the androcentric bias is removed (Gräslund 2001; Nelson 1997: 139–41, 147–8; Spencer-Wood 1999: 176). In addition, it has been suggested that some biologically based characteristics of women such as their lesser tendency towards aggressive behaviour provide them with the ability to mediate, a feature favourably considered for leadership in some American societies (Trocolli 1999: 54). Likewise, it has been argued that practical arrangements may give significant control to the 'dominated' gender(s) (Gero and Scattolin 2002: 170). In some cases archaeologists have also suggested that political authority – as indeed other more subtle kinds of power (see Wilkie 2000 as an example) – may emanate from spiritual power, a type of power not uncommonly held by women (Sweely 1999a: 169).

In addition to political power, other types of power are possible. Particular

*Figure 2.2* The goddess Nut (the Sky), shown arching herself above her consort Geb (the Earth). Source: Roth (2000: fig. 15.3).

attributes of a person emphasising potency or capability can also provide authority. Power can be defined further as the ability of someone to impose their will on others in social action and interpersonal relations. In addition, there is tactical or organisational power that controls the settings in which interactions may take place (in Levy 1999: 72). Some authors have pointed to the existence of all these types of power in societies of the past, which makes the traditional monolithic relationship between men and power infeasible. Thus Aztec women, for example, despite living in a male-dominated society, had control over household production and sexual reproduction, a control associated with female deities (Tlazolteotl, Xochiquetzal, Mayahuel and Toci) representing four aspects of the Aztec mother goddess (Brumfiel 1996a: 145; McCafferty and McCafferty 1999; see our fig 2.3). It has been suggested that the misogyny expressed at the level of political power in monumental sculpture and manuscript painting was contested at another level, that of the household, through the ritual use of female figurines (Brumfiel 1996a: 157). The potential for integrating more subtle ways of analysing gender and power is further exemplified by the integration of spatial analysis. It has been argued, for example, that segregation of men and women in medieval cemeteries is not evidence of women's lesser status, but simply of difference. A detailed analysis of the circumstances by which men and women were buried separately unveils a more complex pattern. Cemeteries in lands where a particular veneration was practised only by women may have resulted in the burial of men being deemed inappropriate. In the case of the earliest town cemeteries, the lower number of female burials found can be interpreted not as an index of male power but as a reflection of the greater number of men living in the towns since these were mercantile places, an activity mostly carried out by men at this time (Gilchrist 1997: 45).

Resistance, compliance and coercion have also been a focus of research. Some archaeologists have looked at whether or not women resisted male domination and whether the dominant gender category used coercion to maintain its power. These are difficult issues to detect in the archaeological record and only sophisticated methods may reveal them. One of the authors who has attempted to study this is Elizabeth Brumfiel (1996b). On the basis of a comparison between pre-Aztec, Aztec and colonial spindle whorls measured by their weight, diameter and decoration, the author tried to analyse whether or not the quality of the cloth produced by women had improved in the colonial period, when tribute extraction had grown. She concluded that the quality had not declined and women had not resisted, but had been coerced to cooperate. As she puts it: 'Indian women did not resist tribute cloth extraction because they could not; the quality of tribute cloth was too easily monitored and the instruments of coercion too easily implemented' (ibid.: 458).

*Figure 2.3* Xochiquetzal with quetzal headdress, tin feathered plumes and jewelled face ornamentation. Source: McCafferty and McCafferty (1999: fig. 6.1).

## Material culture: the context of gender interaction

Material culture plays an essential role in structuring gender ideology. It represents the material context in which gendered individuals interact, relate to each other and negotiate their social position. Objects provide meanings that are inserted into a net of identities linked together by codes. Yet, human actions entail decisions on how to use the rules and how the messages they carry are understood. In practice, therefore, codes are constantly subjected to negotiation and, thus, exposed to endless redefinition. The capability of material culture, not only to serve as a symbol but also to have its meaning transformed, seems to be worth exploring. This may reveal how gender relations function in a social group and how gender roles can be challenged and potentially changed.

Each gender category uses material culture in distinctive ways. Archaeology has never denied this, although the understanding of how gender categories engage with material culture has traditionally been too restrictive and related more to archaeologists' own gender values than to a proper consideration of what these could have been in the past. Gender perspectives can greatly enrich archaeological investigation. This is well illustrated in the case of stone tools, a type of item many archaeologists have often declared that women did not use. This perception was partly due to archaeologists' a priori expectations regarding gender roles. Anthropological studies seemed to back up this assumption, as in ethnographic reports no information was provided about women's employment of stone tools. The accounts entirely focused on males, as only men and male tasks were systematically observed, even when, as some feminist scholars have pointed out, in some societies fieldworkers witnessed both women and men collecting and handling sharp flakes for butchering and other domestic tasks (Bird 1993; Gero 1991). Critical reviews of anthropological work have since shown that women indeed employed stone tools, albeit sometimes in distinct ways, for different tasks and consequently may have utilised tools of different typology (Bevan 1997; Gifford-Gonzalez 1993). Integrating gender difference, as well as age identity (Finlay 1997), into the research of stone tool usage in past societies has been a challenge undertaken by some archaeologists such as Joan Gero and Diane Gifford-Gonzalez. As the latter explains, the examination of stone and bones for marks other than those associated with butchering tools would reveal aspects not usually considered by archaeologists, such as cooking that the author of the analysis argues is a task most likely to have been done by women (Gifford-Gonzalez 1993). Evidence in the archaeological record such as spatial patterning, changes in technology and possible associations between stone tools and tasks may also reveal distinct gender use of stone tools (Gero 1991).

Material culture is employed to signify social identities, in terms of self-identity and membership of wider groups. Each group has rules about how material culture should be handled depending on the gender category the individual belongs to. In the case of the *hirjas* in India, for instance, their use of objects indicates their position as an alternative gender. They dress, comb their hair and are adorned as women, but they smoke hookahs or cigarettes, something women are not allowed to do (Nanda 1994: 382–3). The body can be considered as one type of material culture on which social identities are primarily portrayed through dress, painting, tattoos and decoration. Some of these media are ephemeral, but many others are not and their archaeological preservation in favourable contexts offers great potential for the archaeological study of identity. Practices like tooth evulsion in Neolithic Italy (Robb 1997) and tooth evulsion together with the practice of covering the gap left by the removed tooth by South Etruscan women (Becker 2000), contrasts in dress in Bronze Age Denmark and Germany (Sørensen 1997; see our fig. 2.4), use of particular items such as artefacts of spinning and weaving in many societies (Gilchrist 1999: 50–1; Kehoe 2000; McCafferty and McCafferty 1991) and different ways of moving around space and distinct concepts associated with the body in medieval times (Gilchrist 1994, 1997) and in Indian society (Dehejia 1997) are only some examples. Archaeology is in an ideal position to see transformations in the use of material culture by particular gender categories. Treherne's (1995) study of the appearance of toilet articles such as tweezers and razors in Bronze Age Europe, for example, indicates a change in the aesthetics of the masculine body. The author argues, perhaps influenced to a degree by current perceptions of men's role in Western societies, that during the European Bronze Age the male body became a metaphor for the emergence of the warrior elite, the advent of a masculine lifestyle based on individualism, warfare, body ornament, horses, wheeled vehicles, hunt and the ritual consumption of alcohol, which had its roots in the previous period and would survive into feudal Europe.

The ways in which material culture conveys gender identity can be manipulated through the interaction of gender identity with other types of identities. Individuals of a particular gender category may choose or be entitled to have distinctive rules regarding use of material culture. This can

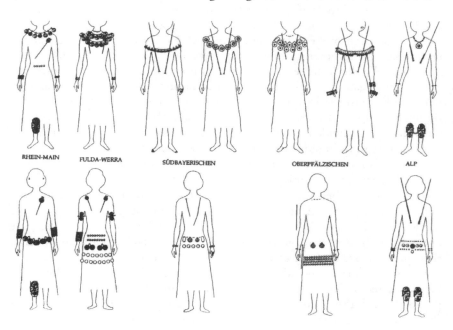

*Figure 2.4* The indication of a division into a woman's chest-costume and a waist-costume during the middle Bronze Age in Southern Germany. Source: Sørensen (1997: fig. 3).

be illustrated with the example of the figurines and statues commissioned by Iberian women in the late first millennium BC. They reveal how different groups of women followed distinct strategies to represent themselves depending on their status. Women of higher status commissioned reproductions of their own persona in order to negotiate their own position in society. They did so by selecting to be portrayed as goddesses thus defying the established representational rules and so symbolising their social position. This contrasts with the figurines ordered by women from lower social strata where this type of representation was much less common (Díaz-Andreu and Tortosa 1998). A similar case of manipulation of religious iconography by women of a particular status has been reported among women shamans of the Peruvian Moche. The sacred nature of Moche imagery allowed women shamans to improve their position through their representation as being as actively involved as men (Arsenault 1991). Different status within a particular gender category may also be reflected in spatial patterns. This can be seen among the Mende of Sierra Leone, where the higher status of senior wives entitles them to have a greater decision-making power in the organisation of the farm. This results in higher status women controlling upland farm plots whereas younger co-wives farm less desirable plots (Lane 1998: 180).

The use of material culture offers some potential to oppose established gender relations. A degree of resistance to following the rules, or a strategic change in the conditions in which material culture is employed can have a significant impact on the rules themselves and on how gender ideology is structured by the members of the group. Discordance may have notable repercussions in the whole group or may only achieve a further strengthening of the solidarity among the members of a gender category. The latter can be exemplified by the case of the silent discourse of the women's decorated calabash gourds used for feeding milk to children among the Ilchamus in Kenya (Hodder 1986). The decoration signifies and stresses the reproductive role of women in a society in which male power is based on reproduction both of children and of milking cattle (ibid.: 109). The emphasis through decoration of the objects that contain the source of women's power has been read by Ian Hodder as a strategy adopted by women to resist the pattern of male behaviour. A similar tactic to reinforce group cohesion has been argued by Rozsika Parker in her study of Victorian embroidery. The author looks at how the use of material culture by one gender category may represent a potential threat to the established gender ideology. Victorian embroidery, as well as being an enjoyable activity, is seen as a potential source of power, for, although it represented self-containment and submission, it allowed women to negotiate the constraints of femininity by spending time for their own satisfaction (Parker 1984: 11). Similarly, spinning and weaving and the symbolism associated with these two activities may have acted as an alternative, female discourse in Post-Classic Mexico, operating apart from, even in resistance to, the dominant male ideology (McCafferty and McCafferty 1988 [1991]: 214).

The symbolic power of material culture is not only employed to oppose gender inequality and subjection, but also to signify domination and submission. Aztecs, for instance, used the image of the goddess Coatlicue to symbolise the enemy's subjugation to the state, thereby also stressing that of women to men (Brumfiel 1996a: 156). Aztec artists also stressed the symbolism of *gestures* in monumental sculpture to portray inequality. Thus the kneeling position indicated the female ideal, the modest and industrious woman, common in official monumental sculpture (ibid.: 158). A further example of the correlation of a gender category to particular gestures is provided by the representation of a woman's closed legs in a Provençal medieval medical manuscript in contrast to the spread legs of the man. Michael Camille explains this as symbolising the association of open legs in women with the concupiscence of a 'sinister daughter of Eve' (1994: 83). In fourth millennium BC Mesopotamia men's power was metaphorically expressed in seals by representing women as menial labourers and not individuals of high status as some of them were (Pollock and Bernbeck 2000). Similarly in Roman Pompeii, wall paintings in houses only portrayed male control (Koloski-Ostrow 1997). As a strategy to maintain domination, material culture is also used to warn of the dangers of breaking with the established order. Thus, representations of myths such as that of Clytemnestra on Greek vases illustrated the failure of her attempt to assume a masculine role and the dangers her attitude had meant for society as a whole (Bernal 1997; see our fig. 2.5).

*Figure 2.5* Representation of Cassandra's murder by Clytemnestra, found on a red-figure cup by the Marlay Painter, Ferrara, Museo Archeologico, inv. T264. Source: Bernal (1997: fig. 11).

Material culture, as the main source for archaeological enquiry, has a great potential for the study of gender. Material culture is used in active, distinctive ways by different gender categories, and throughout its manipulation is prone to change and to be used to articulate power and control but also opposition and conflict. All these issues will be further illustrated in the remainder of the chapter, as material culture is the basis on which discussions of subsistence and production, use of space and mortuary analysis rest.

## Gender and agency in subsistence

Gender, as one of the fundamental identities in the structuration of a social group, is an essential factor to be considered when studying agency in the economic sphere. As this is an aspect of society that archaeologists have greater confidence in their ability to study, the integration of gender may yield a greater degree of sophistication in the interpretation of the data. A key aspect of the integration of gender into the study of subsistence and of production is that of the division of labour. It has been generally assumed that the division of labour is an essential element in the organisation of pre-industrial human societies. This is because the input from females may not only have been essential for reproduction but also, more importantly, for the survival of offspring during the first years of life. Yet, this important role has traditionally been assumed to have a counterpart, that of a constraint on the mobility of women and therefore the activities they were able to undertake while nursing and weaning. This view has recently been challenged by feminist scholars, who have argued that the limitations associated with mothering may actually be related to the experience of Western societies. In such societies mothers look after their own offspring on their own whereas in pre-industrial societies mothers are usually helped by other individuals in the group, including adult men (Bolen 1992; Kimmel 1987). Also, in some societies task division seems to have been far less marked than commonly assumed (Hamlin 2001).

A flexible division of labour is not contested as such by gender scholarship. Indeed the sexual specialisation of activities seems to be present in close human relatives such as chimpanzees (Boesch-Achermann and Boesch 1994). There is agreement regarding a certain division of labour already being in place in periods as early as the Upper Palaeolithic (Conkey 1991; Dobres 1995). Feminist and gender scholarship, however, has subjected to scrutiny the hierarchy of chores undertaken by each gender traditionally implied by social thinkers. This hierarchy considered men's activities essential for the survival and well-being of the group and women's activities as secondary, peripheral and unimportant. Yet, if the initial critique of androcentrism was straightforward, a more active approach has encountered difficulties, as illustrated below. This is because direct evidence relating gender categories to specific tasks is very limited. Bone malformations and pathologies may be good indicators of individuals' main activities, but more frequently than not this information is missing. The connection between particular types of material culture and specific activities is always prone to challenges.

Critical revisions of the assumptions traditionally made by archaeologists have dealt with various subsistence activities. Regarding hunting and gathering, the conventional belief is that men hunted animals, an activity that needs cooperation and specialised knowledge, whereas women undertook a supposedly much less demanding task, that of gathering. Although evidence broadly backs the association of men with hunting in many societies (Parkington 2002; Shoolongdej 2002), this is by no means a universal association, as research from regions as diverse as Japan, the Philippines, Malaysia, Zaire, Canada and Greenland has shown. In these areas, societies in which women participate in hunting expeditions in search not only of small but also big game have been reported (Bird 1993: 23; Estioko-Griffin and Griffin 1981; McBrearty and Moniz 1991: 73; McKell 1993: 116; Wadley 1998). The weight once given to hunting has also been eroded by its irrelevance in earlier hominids, leading to the rejection of theories that saw it as fundamental to the process of human evolution (Conkey and Spector 1984: 8). Moreover, from a purely economic angle, the study of particular hunter-gatherer societies such as the !Kung has indicated that the group's diet may be mainly based on products obtained by the women's gathering (ibid.: 13). Despite this, as John Parkington has shown in his study of the Kalahari hunter-gatherers and South African rock art, ideologically, hunting and the relationship of men and hunting may be dominant (Parkington 2002).

Nevertheless the inclusion of discussions on the role of gender in hunting and gathering activities may radically alter the interpretation of changes through time. This is illustrated by Thomas Jackson's (1991) study of the pre-contact Western Mono in the western Sierra Nevada of California. The author argues against other archaeologists' focus on hunting and on the transformation in lithic technology to infer social change, and in its place he points to activities such as acorn gathering and processing – which he attributes to women and male *berdaches*. Acorns were not only the main staple but were also essential for settlement location, as the alteration in vegetal processing may have been a response to environmental change. Jackson argues that archaeologists should regard this important transformation in the life of the community in the same way as shifts in hunting techniques considered vital for other groups.

Assumptions regarding fishing are similar to those for hunting, and in some societies such as the Puebloan Mimbre culture of pre-contact New Mexico there is evidence that fishing may indeed have been a male chore (Shafter *et al.* 2000). Yet, other studies reveal that this is not a universal trend. For example, the examination of the dental caries of the populations of two California Channel Island cemeteries showed that although in an earlier period men preferably consumed fish and women plants, this subsequently changed with their diets becoming more similar (Walker and Erlandson 1986). Archaeology has paid less attention to shellfishing, an activity generally related to women. Some feminist scholars have tried to remedy this by focusing their research on this activity. In the case of the American Shell Mound Archaic (5500–3000 BC) Cheryl Claassen (1991) argues that gender may be a crucial factor in understanding the economic and symbolic processes occurring in the shell mound sites as well as in the explanation of the demise of this activity. With respect to the latter, the author offers two possible scenarios. Either it occurred because, after the appearance of agriculture, women increasingly had time only for the new activity, or because men stopped using baited fishing techniques and did not need shellfish anymore (ibid.: 296). Regardless of which is more plausible, for Claassen gender had played a major role in the shift from one type of economy to another.

The bias in the way gathering has traditionally been perceived is made clear when this 'non-productive' activity is turned into a 'productive' one. Despite women's role in gathering, archaeologists have traditionally seen men as the inventors of agriculture (Watson and Kennedy 1991: 262–4). Gordon Childe may have been an exception, when he jokingly remarked that 'Probably at first cultivation was an *incidental activity* of the women while *their lords* were engaged in the *really serious business* of the chase' (Childe 1951: 71, emphasis added). Yet, the very tone chosen by him indicates that to a great extent he may have shared archaeologists' general unwillingness to accept fully women's active role in society. Being the main staple, archaeologists no longer perceive plants as secondary in agricultural societies and man is reinstated as the main actor. Women are not, however, completely banished from the researcher's imagination. Whereas archaeologists deem as male-dominated those activities thought of as 'real' work, such as sowing and threshing, other 'peripheral' activities, such as weeding, are often considered to be female (Wright 1991: 198).

As in other cases, recent research has demonstrated that in some societies not only men but also women were fully involved in agricultural activities some including food production. Patricia Bridges' (1989) study of the changes in male and female diaphyseal bone structure provided interesting conclusions. The author compared burial populations in the Archaic when people were foragers (before 1000 BC) and the Mississippian period (AD 1200–1500) in the southeast of the United States, by which time farming was well established. She found changes in the bones of both sexes, but these were more marked in women than in men. She interpreted this as due to women having been the main farmers. Similar results were obtained regarding women in the Puebloan culture area of the United States (Galle 1999; Hays-Gilpin and Whitley 1998: 140). There, 'female skeletons often have robust muscle attachment points in their necks and shoulders, together with arthritic knees, suggesting that they carried heavy loads and spent many hours daily grinding maize' (Hays Gilpin and Whitley 1998: 140). The palaeopathological data obtained from Abu Hureyra in Syria, also related to the transition from foraging to agriculture, indicates that women spent a considerable amount of their time kneeling, perhaps engaged in pounding and grinding cereal mortars. In contrast men had pathologies that may be related to the squatting position (Molleson 1994). An increase in women's workload in activities probably associated with agriculture is also seen by Peterson (2000) for the Levant area on the basis of comparative data from the Natufian to the Early Bronze Age. Finally, women ploughers are represented in the rock art of Thailand (Shoolongdej 2002), whereas seemingly only men appear in the prehistoric rock carvings of the French Alps (Barfield and Chippindale 1997). The inclusion of gender as an aspect to be considered in social change has provided challenging new insights. John Chapman (1997: 137) has proposed that the Secondary Products Revolution (SPR, an economic package composed of plough, animal traction, wool, milk and horse domestication) had the potential to change gender relations in a significant way in later Prehistoric Hungary. He argues that SPR most likely increased women's power through the control over the production of woollen textiles and the development of dairy products, activities that reinforced their hegemony in the domestic areas. At the same time, men's power presumably benefited from the rise of animal traction, horse-riding and ploughing.

In the case of trade, archaeologists have also traditionally adopted a dual attitude. As a presumed male province, items related to trade have been interpreted differently when associated with women or with men. In male burials, these objects are usually interpreted as a demonstration of some sort of involvement in trading activities or as wealth. In female tombs the same items are seen as a symbol of their husband's wealth, or perhaps something that had belonged to them, or a funerary gift from others. Only in a few cases are they interpreted as showing a *temporary* participation in trade (Conkey and Spector 1984: 11; Rega 1997: 240–41). Recent studies of this topic have proposed alternative scenarios. First, women acting as long distance traders have been documented in the Aztec *pochteca* (McCafferty and McCafferty 1988). In a very different area and period, the Viking period in Scandinavia and Old Russia, Anne Stalsberg (2001) argues that women could indeed have been actively involved in trade. She proposes that the frequency of objects related to the weighing of silver in female graves seemed to indicate that women were involved in that part of the trade. If they were not mentioned in west European and oriental written sources this was because those writing them were men of the Christian and Muslim religion, creeds that at the time maintained that the proper place of women was in the home. The references made in later Scandinavian medieval sources to women who were active in different kinds of trade (Stalsberg 1991: 81–2) could mean that women's agency was simply suppressed in earlier documents. Archaeologists' uncritical acceptance of the early sources and their biased subsequent interpretation of the archaeological record may have further served to silence women.

A very particular kind of trade is the gift-exchange of wives, in which women are supposedly regarded as the main 'object' of barter. As mentioned earlier, this type of exchange has been taken for granted in periods as early as the Upper Palaeolithic (Gilman 1984). However, whereas it has been proved that in that period certain items moved long distances from their area of origin, nothing similar has been demonstrated in the case of women. Thus, in practice, the plausible scenario proposed in these hypotheses is only at the moment a conjecture. In later periods in which the transport of women of high status for marriage is documented, archaeologists have still denied them an active role of any kind, such as building political alliances and initiating cultural and religious exchange. Thus, for instance, in the case of medieval Europe where these women had an important role in the introduction of Christianity, archaeologists have tended to deny any sort of influence exerted by them, a perspective that has now been challenged (Gilchrist 1997: 46; Gräslund 2001: 88).

## Engendering production

Archaeological studies of gender have placed a great emphasis on the analysis of the role of the different gender categories in production. It is easy to understand the origin of this interest, given the importance conferred by the archaeology of the 1950s to early 1980s on economic processes as the main agent of social and political change. Several authors have critically examined from a gender perspective the production of items such as lithics, pottery, textiles, metals and art objects. A key novel element in this critique has been to go beyond production as an important element of the economic sphere of society, in order to consider it as a social arena in which gender identities are recreated, discussed or opposed. Technology is no longer only understood as the sum of procedures to metamorphose one object into another, but as a practice in which the material and symbolic dimensions of material culture interact and are transformed through a series of gendered habits and social strategies (Dobres 1995). In the case of women's production, even in those societies where it is based in the area of habitation and combined with child-care and domestic chores, it has the potential to provide women with control over a means of production and thus provide some degree of financial or symbolic independence. In addition, technological skills probably assisted in constructing group solidarities and achieving social strategies (McCafferty and McCafferty 1998: 227). Even within apparently male-dominated societies, women's production could serve as a means to subvert social organisation (Bevan 1997: 83).

Recent analyses have demonstrated that productions traditionally associated almost exclusively with male agency, such as stone tools and metallurgy, are also connected with other gender categories. For example, the production of stone tools by women has been documented in areas like Australia and New Guinea (Bird 1993), as well as possibly in the Huaricoto site in Peru (Gero 1991). Jarvenpa and Brumbach (1995) and Spector (1991), on the basis of their studies of modern Chipewyan and Plains Indians respectively, have proved that women's toolkits may be as technologically complex as men's. Regarding metallurgy, one of the other technologies usually associated with men (Murdock and Provost 1973: 207), feminist scholars have argued against the exclusivity of male involvement and the possible role of women in its discovery. Concerning the latter, it has been pointed out that women's engagement in pottery production makes them likely discoverers of the capacity of metals to transform under high temperatures. The sole agency of men has also been challenged by studies of iron metallurgy in Africa, where it has been demonstrated that in some groups women and children have a significant input into particular stages of the process, such as preparation for a smelt, smelting and forging (Barndon 1999: 63–6; MacLean 1998: 170). Rachel MacLean (1998) proposes that there is nothing that prevents women from both smelting and smithing, and that the strict genderisation of iron production in the societies she analyses can only be explained by remarkably consistent cultural reasons. The metallurgical process is symbolised as representing the domination of male smelters over most aspects of the metaphorical female reproductive process (Schmidt 1998: 141). Ores are embryonic metals 'hidden in the "womb" of the earth. Extracted by the miner, they are matured and birthed with unnatural haste through the medium of the furnace/womb' (MacLean 1998: 170). Peter Schmidt (1998) provides an excellent account of how gender has played a central organising role in social relations of production over the last two and a half millennia of African iron smelting. MacLean (1998), Schmidt (1998) and Barndon (1999) have based their work on relatively modern societies, but as Marie Louise Sørensen (1996) has argued, genderising metallurgical processes in the prehistoric past may not be as straightforward, and this is a challenge for future gender studies.

As with stone tools and metallurgy, artistic and textile production has also been assumed to be the exclusive province of men. This supposition has been all pervading and operates for the art of all periods, from the Palaeolithic (Russell 1991) to the modern period. Early research undertaken in Australia, for example, seemed to indicate women's lack of involvement in artistic production. Yet, recent feminist studies have maintained that because anthropologists were men, they were never told about the female ritual places with paintings where only women were allowed to go (Russell 1991; Smith 1991). Theories used at the time to interpret the paintings for example as hunting magic made anthropologists reject any consideration of female authorship. This research further consolidated the belief in male authorship for European prehistoric art (Conkey 1986: 16; Díaz-Andreu 1998b). In complex societies a similar belief in male agency has also been pervasive (Dehejia 1997: 12–14). In addition, some authors dealing with art in textiles have denounced social scientists' dual system when evaluating authorship. As Rozsika Parker (1984) argues, artistic production is actually degraded to a craft when women's involvement is assumed. In the context of her work on Victorian sewing and embroidery she contends that these activities have been reduced to handiwork partly due to modern perceptions and the way constructs such as femininity have been created. She proposes that embroidery should be defined as art 'because it is, undoubtedly, a cultural practice involving iconography, style and a social function' (ibid.: 6). The link between textile production and women is made in more societies than later nineteenth-century Europe, as it has been generally confirmed by historical and ethnographic sources (fig. 2.6a). Yet, these also point to some societies in which textiles are produced by men and by third genders. Societies where men produce textiles can be found in Ecuador, where grinding, weaving and spinning activities are a male domain (Bruhns 1991). Textile production was one of the activities with which *berdaches* were associated (fig. 2.6b). A similar situation has been indicated for pre-nineteenth-century African Maraka (Stahl and Cruz 1998: 206), whereas in the Archaic period in Florida textile production seems to have been shared by both men and women (Hamlin 2001: 132). An analysis of the pelvic marks of skeletons of Pueblo men seems also to indicate that this was the case among them, as it appears that men spent many hours sitting down, perhaps because they were weaving (in Hays-Gilpin and Whitley 1998: 140). Yet, in societies where the data confirm female production the inclusion of a gendered perspective can enrich our understanding of the societies under study. An example is Maya textile production, known to have been a female task. As Rosemary Joyce has indicated, this task has to be seen not as inferior but complementary to those undertaken by men (1992). In the case of the Aztecs, Elizabeth Brumfiel has argued that production such as textiles in the household could be used by women to enhance their position in society (1991).

Women's agency is also generally accepted for the production of pottery, although it is usually assumed that it only relates to an early period when technology was simpler and the resulting pots were not sophisticated (Rice 1991; Wright 1991). The inclusion of gender in the analysis of pottery can reveal new insights into the archaeological record, as illustrated by Marshall's (1985) study of pottery production in Fiji and New Guinea. Based on ethnographic analogy that may need further testing, the author maintains that distinct gender arrangements operated in the production of pottery of different areas. In some, women predominated as producers; in others they were helped by men – except in the case of particular types of pots, such as ceremonial containers, which were an exclusive domain of men. When both men and women collaborated, women made the pots and men decorated them. Marshall (ibid.) uses these distinctions to propose a model of change in Fiji and New Guinea. Others have focused their attention not on the production of pots itself, but on the production of other goods for which pots are needed such as the cooking of food. As Brumfiel has highlighted, this activity, together with other associated ones usually assumed to be female tasks, such as processing food, has been relatively poorly studied (Brumfiel 1992: 554). This knowledge gap has been criticised as being a result of the androcentric bias of research still pervasive in archaeology. Some, like Rachel

a.

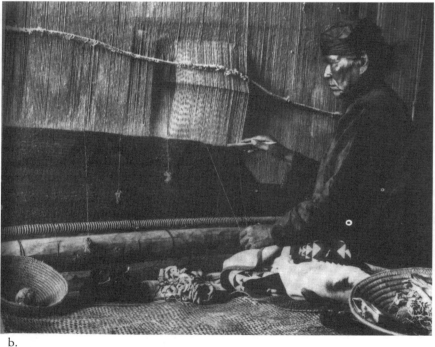

b.

*Figure 2.6* Textile production. a. Illustrations from Guaman Poma of a colonial man weaving (right) and (left) a man in a mythical past plying thread, as a woman (his wife?) spins. Source: Costin (1996: fig. 4.3); b. Hastíín Klah, a Navajo *berdache* photographed *c.* 1925. Source: Roscoe (1994: fig. 7.3).

MacLean (1998), have even argued, on the basis of her study of the Interlacustrine Early Iron Age of East Africa, that women's control over cooking may be
as important as men's control over metallurgy.

## Gender in the landscape of the living

Historical and anthropological analyses have shown that the use of space is
socially sanctioned along gender lines. Gender categories usually have distinctive norms concerning how to operate in particular areas, which may or
may not be of exclusive use (fig. 2.7). Archaeologists have long been aware of
the existence of rules, but they have always understood them as inflexible and
fixed. Moreover, their analyses have largely been prejudiced by Western
assumptions regarding space. One of these assumptions was the belief in a
dichotomy between the private and the public, which divided space into
exclusive and opposite areas thought by many to be universal and naturally
defined. Women were supposed to be associated with domestic space. In
contrast, it was taken for granted that the public areas were an exclusively
male province. Early feminist scholarship paid much attention to this duality
and finally concluded that it may be more related to a Western modern
lifestyle than to pre-industrial societies. Even in the case of Western societies
the dichotomy between the domestic and the public spheres proved less static
than it looked at first sight (Benn and Gauss 1983).

Some authors have proposed that rather than opposites it seems to be more
accurate to consider both the private and the public spheres as a continuum
(Pateman 1983), for their character changes depending on the circumstances.
When the household, the paradigmatic example of the private space, is analysed, a more mixed picture emerges. The house may indeed be the private

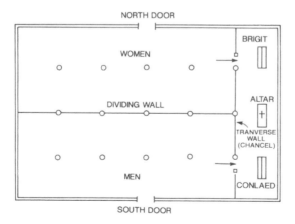

*Figure 2.7* Reconstruction of St Brigit's (Kildare, Ireland) medieval church, according to Cogitosus's *Life of Brigit* dated to the seventh century. Source:
Gilchrist (1994: 135).

place of a family, yet it may become public when visitors are accepted. Also in many societies economic activities are undertaken within the confines of the household. Some of them may be seasonal, resulting in a continual flux in the character of space. These activities may be undertaken both by men and women. Also, as Nelson argues, beyond the household in many societies women have a role in the public space 'as rulers, traders, healers and even warriors' (1997: 132) and equally men used the domestic space, either taking care of children (Bolen 1992: 49; Kimmel 1987), organising their finances, inviting their friends, or for a multitude of other activities (Yentsch 1996: 323).

Gender categories may use space in distinctive ways and particular places may convey social and symbolic meanings specific to them. It is through their actions that individuals identify, relate and may transform the meaning of a place. Absolute gender domains may be an indication of alternative ways for individuals of a gender category to live their lives – such as monasteries and nunneries (Gilchrist 1994) or the houses where *hirjas* live in groups (Nanda 1994: 409–10) – but they may also point to asymmetrical relations of dominance, coercion and subordination. Physical movement through space can be formally analysed in order to see how gender relations were spatially bounded, how regulations reinforced difference, inequality and exclusion (Gilchrist 1994: chapter 6). The engendered study of space can assist in identifying the processes by which gender hierarchisation is maintained. In societies with asymmetric power relations between genders, space may be used to reinforce the alienation of one or various gender categories restricting their social and economic mobility. This can be done by associating the gender category perceived as subordinate with locations that stand for inferiority (Lyons 1996), and by spatially symbolising pollution and taboo with women's biological events such as menstruation, through the creation of features such as huts that may be archaeologically visible (Galloway 1998; Marucci 1999). An extreme expression of this is seclusion, practised nowadays in fundamentalist Islamic societies and related to the ideal of male honour. Within an archaeological framework David Small (1991) has discussed seclusion in Ankara (Turkey) and Kayseri (Pakistan). Oppositional negotiation and symbolic emphasis are located where women come into contact with other groups inside the house, although in small communities where men do not feel their honour threatened this area can be moved to the outside due to a lessening of the restrictions placed upon women.

The maintenance of gender hierarchisation can also be analysed in a broader framework. Landscapes may be invested with specific gendered meanings as shown in the case of male monasteries and castles, which appear to be connected to the landscape as a way of signifying domination over a region (Gilchrist 1994: 63). The active role of monasteries in reshaping the landscape through their economic and political power contrasts with the marginalisation of nunneries, whose position links landscape and eremitic vocation (ibid: 91). Even at the level of the layout a consideration of gender ideology greatly helps us understand the disparities between monasteries and nunneries.

As gender studies have pointed out, space is not only used to maintain and reinforce gender ideology, but also as a medium to oppose it. Nineteenth-century women, for example, claimed their suitability to care for children and undertake tasks that needed particular care, and in this way they were able to take over traditionally male-dominated professions – and the spaces associated with them – such as selling, kindergarten teaching and work as nutritionists and secretaries (Spencer-Wood 1991: 241). In other circumstances status, and not only gender, has an influence on perceptions of where a member of a specific gender category should be placed. This is illustrated by Carmen Weber (1991) in her account of how elite women in eighteenth-century America became involved in gardening, a task/space previously only devoted to men.

## Bones, objects and graves

The study of gender in the landscape of the dead has its own problems. As in the case of the space of the living, gender has not been ignored, but rather assumed. Sex attribution has been a feature always taken into account in cemetery studies. Burials have regularly been defined as male or female, and in the case of collective burials percentages regarding the sex of the individuals buried there are usually provided. The two methods most commonly used in sexing burials are skeletal analysis and gender attribution of material culture. Both of them are extremely insightful but also potentially problematic.

The study of human bones provides invaluable insights that complement data obtained by other sources (Cohen and Bennett 1998 [1993]). Amongst the data it can supply is the sex of individuals, a process usually thought to be objective. Although this is largely the case when good samples are used (Molleson and Cox 1993: 21), a puzzling imbalance in the sex ratio in many collections all over the world, with the number of men higher than that of women, has not escaped the attention of feminist anthropologists (Donlon 1993, 1998) and archaeologists (Damm 1991: 131; Whelan 1991b). In her assessment of several studies of skeletal remains Donlon (1993) revealed several problems with the methods some physical anthropologists used to sex skeletons. She suggested that when paradigmatic bones for sexing in collections were sparse, a fairly common situation, non-diagnostic bones were often used instead. The author also argued that palaeoanthropologists seem predisposed to classify indeterminate skeletons as male, instead of categorising them as 'probably male', 'indeterminate' or 'probably female'. No similar work has been undertaken on cremated remains, where it seems easier to distinguish females than males, although both are generally overwhelmed by the 'unsexed' (J. McKinley, pers. comm.).

Despite its pitfalls the study of bones provides archaeologists with precious, otherwise unavailable data. Age determination can indicate the existence of infanticide, which has a tendency to affect girls more than boys (Scott 2001; Wicker 1998). Bone malformations and pathologies have already been mentioned earlier in the chapter as a method used to verify links between certain activities and particular gender categories. A different type of analysis is that of stable isotope ratios in bone collagen, which allows studies of diet. One such analysis was undertaken for the pre-hispanic Sausa of Peru by Christine Hastorf (1991) who verified that the comparison between pre-Inka and Inka skeletal material showed significant changes in the diet. Her analysis demonstrated that in the Inka period men consumed more meat and also more maize than women, the latter presumably in the form of *chicha*, an alcoholic ritual drink. This pattern was interpreted as a consequence of Inka dominance in gender relations. She proposed that the Inka dominance over the Sausa had led to a change that significantly wors-ened the condition of women in society. An opposite pattern was seen for the Prehistoric Northern Channel Islands, California, where the comparison of women's diet throughout time showed a better balance in fish proteins in the latter period, similar to that of men in the same time-span (Walker and Erlandson 1986).

In addition to skeletal analysis, the other procedure by which archaeolo-gists have usually inferred sex in cemetery analysis is by the attribution of material culture to a particular sex. Yet, this method contains serious pitfalls, mainly because the assignment of particular items to a specific sex/gender category is often undertaken on the basis of assumed ideas of gender, and, consequently, the results encourage the reinforcement of these assumptions. For example, a burial with weapons is almost without exception defined as masculine by archaeologists, an interpretation that unequivocally consoli-dates the stereotype of 'man the warrior'. The metaphors par excellence of 'manhood' and 'womanhood' within archaeology for more than 150 years have been weapons for men and jewellery for women (Hjørungdal 1994: 144). These stereotypes lead to *ad hoc* explanations when objects do not fit the pattern. A grinding pestle, for example, is usually taken as an indication of a female grave, because it is seen as an object associated with women's grinding activities and food elaboration. However, no such activity is inferred when the grinding pestle is found in tombs where all other indicators imply that the deceased was a man. He is now described as the manufacturer (Conkey and Spector 1984: 11). Likewise, when an imported item is found in a woman's grave it is interpreted as a present and/or taken as a sign of ownership, but never as an indication of active participation in trade, an explanation usually given when such items are found in men's burials (ibid.). Further examples have been outlined by Bevan (1997), Rega (1997) and Doucette (2001). Double standards are also found in the case of items represented in the burial, for example through engravings on burial stones. Gilchrist (1997) discusses the example of the sculpted rectangles on medieval graves. They are inter-preted as depictions of books if the deceased is thought to be a man, but when the rectangles are associated with a pair of shears the motif is interpreted as a workbox and the tomb is considered female. Gilchrist argues that there is no sound basis for this change of meaning.

The comparison of the results obtained by sexing on the basis of skeletal material and material culture may provide an illuminating insight into the complexities surrounding the engendering of burials. Sam Lucy's (1997) study of two Anglo-Saxon cemeteries is a good example of this. The classification of burials on the basis of the offerings compared with the results of the data on sex provided by physical anthropologists produced an unexpected outcome. Not all those burials that contained only jewellery were women's and not all those that contained only weapons were men's (fig. 2.8). The dichotomy of weapons and jewellery was not, after all, a metaphor for gender, but perhaps, as Lucy suggested, for other types of identities such as real or assumed lineage. The presence of weapons in female burials is not unknown in Iron Age Europe, as found in the case of the Stuttgart-Bad Cannstatt and Vix burials in Germany and France (Arnold 1991) and of the Arareva gromila grave 1 in the Central Balkans (Babić 2001: 85–7). In Spain a similar case has been seen in Baza, where archaeologists saw as unproblematic the presence of weapons in the richest tomb of the cemetery until the analysis of the cremated remains indicated that they were a woman's. It has been argued that in the male-controlled Iberian society high-status women negotiated their own ascendancy by manipulating the code structuring the gendered meaning of material culture. They metaphorically appropriated material culture usually associated with high-status men – weapons – as a means to signify their own authority (Díaz-Andreu and Tortosa 1998). Objects that do not fit into the common understanding of the use of material culture by men and women have also been interpreted as belonging to third genders. Keith Matthews (1994), for example, explained the appearance of a bracelet, a grave good usually associated with women, in inhumation 179 of the Roman cemetery of Cirencester, Gloucestershire, of an individual sexed as male, as an indication of him being gay. Yet, although this suggestion is appealing, perhaps more similar examples are needed before accepting that this interpretation sounds sufficiently reasonable.

Cemeteries are key areas of public performance. In them appropriate ways to treat the deceased are negotiated, including the definition of categories and gender roles. Changes in the way in which different categories of gender are treated give us an insight into gender relations in the society under study. Rules may apply to the location, orientation and position of the dead body. There are regulations regarding where the body of an individual belonging to a particular gender may be placed and in what position they have the right or the duty to be buried. Cases of different precepts regulating burials depending on gender are frequent in anthropological accounts (Lyons 1991). Excavations of cemeteries have been able to trace similar divisions. Burial customs in many parts of late prehistoric Europe, for example, show that the emergence of an emphasis on gender differentiation was bound up with new rules laying down the side on which men and women should be buried (Bolen

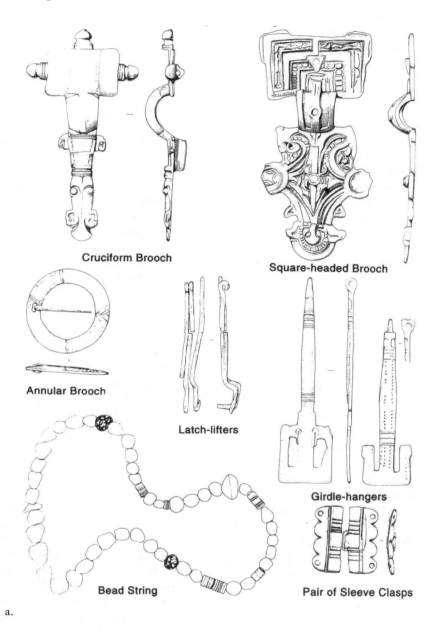

Cruciform Brooch

Square-headed Brooch

Annular Brooch

Latch-lifters

Girdle-hangers

Bead String

Pair of Sleeve Clasps

a.

*Figure 2.8* Illustration of a. Jewellery assemblage; b. Weapon assemblage from the Anglo-Saxon cemeteries of Sewerby and Heslerton (Yorkshire). Source: Lucy (1997: figs 11.3 and 11.4a).

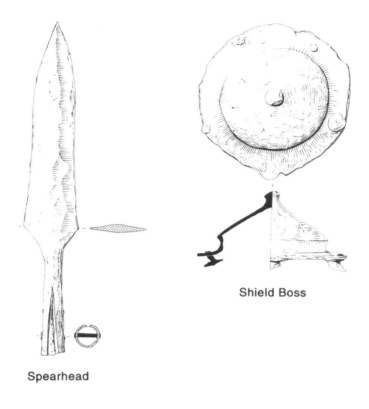

Shield Boss

Spearhead

b.

*Figure 2.8* continued

1991: 402; Chapman 1997; Damm 1991; Lucas 1996: 102, 110). The higher number of female burials in Mesolithic Sudan and adjacent areas has been interpreted as the result of the high status of women in society (Fernández 2003).

## Engendering archaeology

Including gender in archaeological interpretations is not straightforward. Although, as the literature shows, it is extremely easy to criticise male bias, to engender the past requires new working methods that allow us to analyse the symbolic nature of material culture. It is through material culture, the main evidence with which archaeologists work, that complex social messages related to gender identity are communicated and understood by those who know of the code. Dealing with gender, however, requires awareness of other identities for, as shown in this chapter, other types of identifications such as status, religion and age significantly affect the rules by which gender is understood and embodied in daily practices. Although direct evidence of gender is elusive, avoiding questioning the archaeological record about gender altogether may be irresponsible. Although, as critics of gender archaeology argue, there are obvious difficulties in trying to decode material culture even without historical or ethnographic sources, the reality is that no neutral and objective approach to the past is possible. Once objects are named and classified a decoding has taken place. This is why a gender-conscious approach is important. This does not mean that gender was always crucial in structuring social action and practice but it was certainly one of the principles that supported the social and as such, should always be taken into account by archaeologists trying to decode the past.

# 3　The archaeology of age

*Sam Lucy*

Archaeology, until remarkably recently, has paid little attention to the importance of age as one of the fundamental aspects of the organisation of past social groups. It has, furthermore, failed to see age as an extremely variable aspect. Previously, when archaeologists have written about social aspects of the past, it has been as if that past were peopled predominantly by adults, rather than also by the young (and old), who are a necessary part of any community. The nature of age groups, and the vastly differing roles they can play in the operation of different societies, has thus not been fully considered in the interpretation of archaeological material.

In other human sciences, however, age is becoming a pivotal topic. Historians such as Shulamith Shahar (1990, 1997) and Barbara Hanawalt (1993), among others, have been detailing how children, childhood and old age were viewed in the more recent, documented past. Meanwhile, both sociologists and anthropologists are currently exploring how age groups are constituted (i.e. how individuals come to be perceived, and perceive themselves, as belonging to a group of people of similar ages), and the impact this has on how societies reproduce themselves (see Amoss and Harrell 1981; James *et al*. 1998; Prout and James 1990). Moreover, researchers have demonstrated the extent to which our present ideas about childhood (and more recently old age, adolescence and adulthood) are social constructions, based partly on biological development and deterioration, but primarily on a society's views on what people of different age groups should be like, and how they should behave (Hockey and James 1993; Pilcher 1995). If the age identities in the present are social constructions, then they necessarily were in the past as well, and as archaeologists we should not assume that categories such as 'child', 'adult' or 'old person' were natural ones, with common meanings and significance attributed to them.

In the 1990s some archaeologists began research into the areas of children and childhood (see papers in Moore and Scott 1997, *Archaeological Review from Cambridge* 13[2], *World Archaeology* 31[3] and Sofaer Derevenski 2000a) but there is still very little work being done in archaeology on old age or stages of adulthood as cultural constructions (though see Gowland forthcoming; Welinder 2001). This chapter will first look at the type of work done prior to the 1990s by archaeologists, before presenting a summary of studies being carried out in other fields (which are starting to encompass wider age ranges, and different theoretical perspectives on age). It will then discuss how some current archaeologists have been dealing with issues of age, especially the role of material culture in the development and reinforcement of age categories, and how these categories cross-cut other identities such as gender, status, religion and ethnicity. Age is, of course, the one identity that is *expected* to change over an individual's lifetime, and its role in the reproduction of social norms and material culture is a fundamental one that will be explored.

## Previous archaeological work on age: children

When age groups have been looked at in archaeology, it has often been in very specific ways. Children and infants, for example, are often only discussed when their remains appear in the mortuary record, with the most discussion generated when there appears to be a possibility of infanticide (Sofaer Derevenski 1994a: 8). A curious feature of much of western European prehistory is the relatively small numbers of infant and child burials found in cemeteries and other mortuary contexts (fig. 3.1). Sometimes this would appear to be a result of preservation conditions, with small infant bones being dissolved more thoroughly by acidic soils, or small skeletons in shallow graves being more easily disturbed; sometimes it may be due to inadequate excavation – badly preserved infant bones can easily be missed, especially if grave-cuts are hard to see (Crawford 1993). It is only fairly recently that archaeologists have been comparing the treatment of younger burials with those of adults in the same cemeteries (see page 63 below). Often, numbers of children and juveniles are used to estimate population structure, which needs considerable care where the suspicion exists (as it does in most cemeteries) that not all the young deceased were being interred there. Parkin (1992: 42–3) makes the valid point that such estimates assume a static population, which rarely occurs. Thus, while the age estimation of well-preserved individuals under the age of about twenty-three is relatively straightforward, using a combination of tooth eruption, fusion of the epiphyses, and general size (see Mays 1998: 42–9), their presence within archaeological deposits, and how representative they are, is rather more problematic.

In some societies particular age groups within the population were buried apart. This is the case in infant or child cemeteries in the Roman world, the discovery of which has led to frequent assertions of infanticide (see Gowland and Chamberlain 2002 for a critique of the underlying bias in the statistical methods on which such interpretations rest). Scott (1992) and Parkin (1992) have highlighted some of the fallacies and assumptions that have contributed to the belief that infanticide was widespread. First is the common error of assuming that exposure is the same thing as infanticide. Boswell (1988) has shown how from late antiquity exposure, leaving infants in the open, was

| Age band | Number of cases in age band | % of mortuary population | % of population surviving this age group |
|----------|------------------------------|--------------------------|-------------------------------------------|
| <1 | 12 | 1.2 | 98.8 |
| 1–2 | 31 | 3.1 | 95.7 |
| 3–4 | 44 | 4.4 | 91.3 |
| 5–6 | 34 | 3.4 | 88.0 |
| 7–9 | 73 | 7.3 | 80.7 |
| 10–12 | 48 | 4.8 | 76.0 |
| 13–15 | 34 | 3.4 | 72.5 |
| 16–25 | 182 | 18.1 | 54.4 |
| 25+ | 547 | 54.4 | 0.0 |

*Figure 3.1* Table showing numbers of younger burials in a sample of Anglo-Saxon cemeteries, highlighting the paucity of neonates and infants. Source: after Crawford (1999: fig. 12).

widely used as an alternative to infanticide, and the hope was generally that a stranger would take the child in and raise them. Second, Parkin (1992: 97–8) points out that too much attention is paid to infanticide in the Roman period without looking at the wider patterns of infant death rates – the infant cemeteries that are found could easily result from a society with an infant mortality rate of around 300 per 1,000. Perhaps the most interesting aspect is not that infanticide undoubtedly occurred (as it still does today), and in certain societies was justifiable within particular religious and social contexts, but that archaeologists have discussed it with such unrelenting contempt, and lack of consideration of the contemporary situations in which it may have been socially acceptable.

Occasionally children are identified through association with particular types of material culture, such as the child's sandal from Roman London (Finlay 1997: 205). Feeding bottles also occasion mention of younger members of society (Vencl 1994: 302), for example the mammiform vessel found in what is probably a child's grave at the early Anglo-Saxon cemetery of Castledyke in South Humberside (Drinkall and Foreman 1998; see our fig 3.2). Toys (identified often by their small size and/or amusement value) have also been used to distinguish the presence of children in the past, for example those found in the medieval towns of Oslo and Bergen in the 1930s (Lillehammer 1989: 96–8), but this in itself is a problem as it serves to separate the child off from the realm of the 'serious' adult world (Sofaer Derevenski 1994a: 10). As Lillehammer (1989: 98–100) has pointed out the identification of objects by archaeologists as toys – musical objects, game-pieces, balls etc. – may be due more to the childhood memories of those archaeologists than any indications given by the context of the 'toy' itself. She highlights that small things may still be real things, designed for use by smaller people, not toys. Whether they are 'toys' or functional miniatures, these artefacts can play an invaluable role in learning about the world, and one's future social role within it (see also Sofaer Derevenski 2000b).

Sometimes children are identified through more direct traces, such as the Mesolithic piece of resin from Norway with a child's tooth impressions (Finlay 1997: 205) or the Palaeolithic footprints found on cave floors (cf. Roveland 2000: 32–5). Similarly, a recent paper (Kamp *et al.* 1999) argued through the existence of children's fingerprints on ceramic artefacts that they were manufacturers of particular Puebloan figurines. The idea that seems to characterise this approach is a telling one: before children can be considered as agents (or even present) in the past, there must be 'proof' of their existence, in concrete terms. In the same way that women had to be 'found' in archaeology in the 1970s and 1980s, the role of children cannot be considered until we 'know' that they are there (a nonsense, of course: a society without younger members is as non-viable as a society without women).

Other researchers (Bonnischen 1973; Hammond and Hammond 1981) attempted to look for traces of children's activities in the archaeological record, for example by carrying out ethnographic research looking at how children's play can affect a material assemblage. Ethnography has documented children helping in stages of activities such as pottery making (Wright 1991) and metallurgy (Barndon 1999: 63). However, given that this research mainly focused on women, these children's roles were not studied in depth (though see now Finlay 1997; Grimm 2000). Moreover, it can be argued that some of these approaches merely ended up dealing with children as randomising agents, with a destructive effect on the archaeological record, much like animal activity as a post-depositional process (Sofaer Derevenski 1994a: 8).

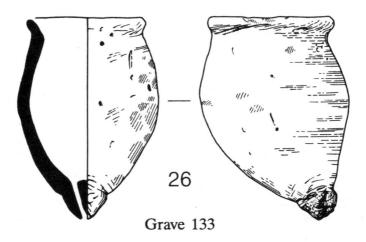

*Figure 3.2* Probable feeding bottle from an inferred infant burial at the Anglo-Saxon cemetery at Castledyke South, Humberside. Source: Drinkall and Foreman (1998, fig. 141, no. 26).

In general, though, the discussions outlined above are incidental mentions. There seems to be little consideration that young people can play an active role in society, that their presence is integral to the successful continuance of a society, both in reproductive and in cultural terms. As Claassen has pointed out, our assumptions about children's activities and the demands they make on their carers seem more dependent on the children we create today than on any past reality:

> Children are non-productive members of our imagined past societies. They distract, they demand, they serve. They do not build, destroy, achieve, share, contribute to basic survival, or environmental adaptation. Mothers must do everything for them, from feed to entertain to indulge, think archaeologists, in spite of anthropological literature to the contrary. . . . What, Lewis Binford, is the territorial knowledge of Nunimuit Eskimo children?
>
> (1992: 5–6)

This illustrates well the other main context in which children are discussed in archaeology: as the burden of motherhood, such as in the hunter-gatherer debate of the 1960s and 1970s, when it was assumed that women were more tied to the home-base because of their caring duties (Brown 1970). Anthropology and sociology can suggest alternative ways of life in which children play an active part, but as archaeologists we must be willing to countenance such possibilities, in order to give them consideration in our interpretations. For example, one of the fields that has been well studied in anthropology is that of rites of passage, with the transition from childhood to adulthood often being one of the most important in the life cycle of many groups. In many cases, rites of passage have associated structures. Thus, in the same way that Galloway (1998) asked where the menstrual huts are, we could ask where are the rites of passage huts (cf. Whitley 1992 who interpreted North American rock art in a similar way and Beausang 2000 who discusses birthing huts)?

Although adults are assumed to be the norm within archaeological inter-pretation – they are the primary actors in any archaeological reconstruction, for example – there has been virtually no work done on their adulthood as something that affects their everyday practices: it is simply assumed. It is only in the context of motherhood that women are sometimes thought of as being at a particular life-stage, but even then this is phrased (even by some feminist researchers) as a time of restriction and relative lack of freedom; Western assumptions about the demands of parenting are also evident here (Bolen 1992: 51–2; Scott 1997: 7; but see Nelson 1997). With regard to older age groups there is even less work carried out. This may, however, be a feature of the bias inherent in cemetery data, as well as our present-day assumptions about the non-productiveness of 'the elderly'.

## Understanding population statistics and age in the past

The lack of consideration of the role of older people by archaeologists may possibly be due to a generally held perception that people died young in the past; that most (if not all) would have been dead by the age of fifty. This is partly based on a common misinterpretation of a widely used statistic: the average lifespan, or life expectancy at birth. In Britain in AD1541 the average lifespan was 33.75 years, whereas in 1991 it was 70.1 years for males and 78.3 years for females (Laslett 1995: 19), making it appear as if people are now likely to live more than twice as long. In fact, the major change lies in child, rather than adult, mortality. The likelihood of a child reaching its tenth birthday in 1541 was around 61 per cent, whereas in 1991 it was about 99 per cent (ibid.: 23). The improvement has been brought about by advances in medicine, sanitation and hygiene, and while these have also decreased adult mortality, it is to a lesser extent. Those who survived their childhood in the Middle Ages were likely to reach fifty, sixty or seventy years of age, and some are documented as having lived to eighty or ninety (Shahar 1997: 32; cf. Welinder 2001 for Scandinavian data). A similar picture should be expected in prehistory (and even among Neanderthals, as the burial of the, relatively, elderly shows [Pettitt 2000]; though maximum ages are probably around fifty years).

It is perhaps worth explaining briefly some of the practical and methodological problems involved in estimating age from mature skeletal remains (see Mays 1998: 49–66). In adults over the age of about twenty-three, the skeleton has stopped maturing, and thus any estimation of age is made by assessing degenerative changes, predominantly in the teeth (Brothwell 1981; Miles 1963), and certain parts of the skeleton such as the pelvis (Katz and Suchey 1986; Lovejoy *et al.* 1985) and the rib-ends (Işcan *et al.* 1984, 1985), although cranial suture closure is still used (Meindl and Lovejoy 1985; see our fig. 3.3). Other, destructive, methods such as bone and dental microstructure are not so widely employed in the field. Obviously, use of any of these techniques is reliant on good bone preservation in the first instance, and adequate collection (and labelling of the fourth rib) during excavation. However, although these ageing methods are widely used and systematically applied, they do seem to possess some inherent biases, highlighted by the results of the Spitalfields excavations in London.

This excavation of a seventeenth- and eighteenth-century crypt under a church in London was almost unique in terms of the good bone preservation (due to the use of both lead and iron-bound coffins; fear of resurrectionists who would dig up recently buried bodies for use in medical training meant the adoption of such security measures) and also the existence of name-plates on many of the coffins. Through the name-plates (fig. 3.4) and burial registers, the sex and age of a number of excavated individuals could be known, and this was used as an independent test of the current ageing and sexing techniques. Osteologists were asked to sex and age the individuals 'blind' and

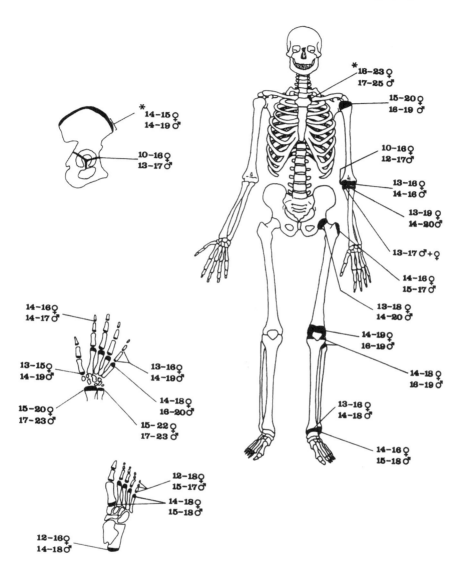

*Figure 3.3* The age range for epiphysial fusion in the human skeleton. Source: Mays (1998: fig. 3.11).

their findings were then compared with the real ages and sexes. While the sexing was quite accurate, evidence of systematic under-ageing of older individuals and over-ageing of younger individuals was found (Molleson and Cox 1993). Aykroyd *et al.* (1999) argue that this bias is due to the use of regression analysis in the ageing techniques (as these were first worked out on known age samples, the age structure of the original samples has ensured a virtual 'cut-off' point of around fifty years in the ageing of archaeological material). As none of the techniques can be used reliably to age over approximately forty-five to fifty years, the resultant age profiles of cemetery populations are skewed (see now Millard and Gowland 2002). This is highlighted by several of the Spitalfields burials who were aged up to decades younger by archaeologists than they actually were when they died. Thus, along with problems of bone preservation and collection on excavation, the very techniques that archaeologists use to age skeletal material may be producing inaccurate results, thereby making our cemetery populations seem younger than they actually were (see papers in Hoppa and Vaupel 2002 for further work on this).

Children were also present in the past, and they were there in substantial numbers. It is estimated that most prehistoric populations had childhood mortality of at least 50 per cent, which implies that in a stable or slowly growing population at least half the members in a given community would have been under eighteen years of age (Chamberlain 1997: 249).[1] The infant mortality rate in the past was much higher than now, with deaths of over 300 per 1,000 live births often historically documented. Such rates would, however, have been highly variable, depending on a variety of socio-economic practices, such as child-rearing methods, standards of hygiene, urban/rural conditions, working practices, the use of wet-nursing, the age of the mother, family size, prematurity, the mother's health (Bideau *et al.* 1997). Thus, as well as there being substantial numbers of live children in the past, there would also have been large numbers of children dying during infancy and childhood, and this can be expected to have affected the ways that societies were structured, perhaps in terms of the emotional involvement of parents with their children, and the roles surviving children would have been expected to take on.

This brief survey of past archaeological approaches to age has highlighted a number of issues. Archaeologists in the past have seemed unwilling to include certain age groups, especially younger and older age groups, in their interpretations, without direct proof that they were there. These age groups have thus only been mentioned when this evidence exists: they are not assumed to be there, and are not assumed to affect how societies would have been structured. The result is a past peopled by mature (but not old) individuals. Such stereotypical images seem tentatively supported by a relative lack of those other age groups in funerary contexts (although this would seem to be a product of faulty ageing techniques, preservation problems and differential treatment of the young in the past), and are exacerbated by misunderstandings of population statistics, such as average life expectancy. However, given the substantial numbers of both older and younger people who would have existed in any period in the past, archaeologists need to start including them in their accounts. They also need to start moving away from essentialist ideas about what children, adults or old people 'are': anthropology and sociology illuminate many possibilities of how human groups can be structured

*Figure 3.4* A coffin-plate from Spitalfields, London, showing the information present.
Source: Reeve and Adams (1993: fig. 5.7).

with relation to age, and archaeologists should not dismiss them out of hand.

The next section will draw on work in history, sociology and anthropology to argue that different age groups all have a role in the constitution and reproduction of their societies (in cultural, linguistic and socio-economic terms), and must thus be included in archaeological accounts of the past. It will also be argued that such accounts will, of necessity, have to be rooted in studies of specific societies, as culturally constituted practices cannot be generalised across time and space.

## Age, biology and culture

When humans are born, they are incapable of caring for themselves, requiring food, warmth and comfort from others. Indeed, one of the features that distinguishes humans from their closest primate relatives is the long duration of the period in which young are dependent on adults. This dependency gradually declines through the first five to ten years of life. If they survive this far, they mature, often sexually reproduce and, at some point, die. This is the biological framework on which social conceptions of age rest. In Western society, this biological framework is often divided up into phases, such as infancy, childhood, adolescence, adulthood and older ages. However, not all societies make these divisions (see Gowland forthcoming for a comparison of 'age-grade' versus 'life-course' approaches), and not all societies make all of them (adolescence, for example, has been argued to be a relatively modern conception, though see Schlegel 1995). Moreover, different societies have varying expectations about the behaviour of an age group, and where the boundaries lie between it and the previous or subsequent one. When does a child become an adolescent, for example, or an adolescent an adult?

Often, the boundaries are taken to be stages in physical development. The end of infancy, for example, can be taken as the point of weaning (in humans, the move to solid food from solely milk). In Western Europe, the start of adolescence is popularly defined by the onset of puberty, though in many other societies this can mark the onset of the transition to adulthood. Yet, these seemingly biological phenomena are culturally affected to a great extent. Aspects of childhood that seem to be 'biologically programmed', such as walking and talking, can be subject to a great deal of variation across human populations, due to parental practices (Levine 1998: 112). As a comparison of a Gusii community in rural Kenya with middle-class North Americans demonstrated, such parental practices can affect, to a surprisingly large extent, the development of primary abilities. The Gusii community was concerned with ensuring the survival of young children, and thus wanted children who were respectful, obedient and responsible. The American parents were confident of the likelihood of their children's survival, and were thus more concerned with preparing their children for educational interactions. The American children as a result were more talkative, to an extent that would have been considered inappropriate and precocious by the Gusii community (ibid.: 117–20).

Even 'natural' stages of biological growth are surprisingly variable. For example, the age of menarche (the onset of female menstruation) can vary widely between social groups and over time; in one study it can, for example, be seen to differ by up to four years between the nineteenth and twentieth centuries (Mitterauer 1992: 2–3), with an average of 17.3 years in Denmark in 1850 decreasing to 13.2 years in 1968 (ibid.: 3). Until the early twentieth century, men in Britain continued growing until their mid twenties (ibid.: 4). Today people in Western Europe tend to be 'grown up' in the biological sense many years earlier than in the past due to better nutrition and lower levels of physical labour (ibid.: 4–6). Thus, even the biological framework that is routinely used to categorise people into age groups can be seen to be affected by social factors.

## Historical constructions of age

The rise of interest in the historical construction of first childhood and then other age groups has been seen as prompted by the publication of Philippe Ariès' *Centuries of Childhood* (first published in French as *L'Enfant et la vie familiale sous l'Ancien Régime*). Ariès stated:

> In medieval society the idea of childhood did not exist; this is not to suggest that children were neglected, forsaken or despised. The idea of childhood is not to be confused with affection for children: it corresponds to an awareness of the particular nature of childhood, that particular nature which distinguishes the child from the adult, even the young adult. In medieval society, this awareness was lacking.
>
> (1962: 125)

In fact, as later historians have demonstrated, there was an awareness in the medieval period that children and infants were different, that they were not just 'small adults', but that the idea of childhood was very different from our modern one – they did not have our view of what childhood was, or should be (Wilson 1980, 1984). Ariès' work, and the subsequent reactions to it, provoked a wave of interest in the study of children, and the realisation that 'childhood' varies greatly over space and time (James 1998: 47; Stephens 1995: 5), rather than being a universal category as had previously been assumed (Prout and James 1990: 17).

Historians have now investigated ideas of childhood in depth (see Cunningham 1995; Golden 1990; Hanawalt 1993; Hendrick 1997; Heywood 2001; Hopkins 1994; Orme 2001; Pollock 1983; Schultz 1995; Shahar 1990; Sommerville 1992; Wood 1994), alongside aspects of childhood such as wet-nursing (Fildes 1988) and abandonment (Boswell 1988) and, to a lesser extent, have looked at adolescence (Mitterauer 1992) and old age (Cokayne

2003; Minois 1989; Parkin 2002; Rosenthal 1996; Shahar 1997; Sheehan 1990; Thane 2000). More recently, a 'life-course' approach has been adopted by some, looking at how the construction of different age groups articulates (cf. Harlow and Laurence 2002; Laurence 2000; Mazo Karras 2003).

Demos (1983), for example, shows how the various constructions of fatherhood and masculinity have changed in America since the seventeenth century, and emphasises that although the literary accounts may faithfully represent these constructions, the practical experience of fatherhood may have been very different from this. Indeed, this distinction between 'ideal' constructions of childhood, adolescence or adulthood is something that has recently been emphasised by Cunningham (1995: 3), who sees the historical challenge as being to tease out the relationship between ideas of childhood and the experience of being a child, and to see how they change over time. The literary and historical texts, in their representations of different age groups, may only give a picture of ideals or models of behaviour; they do, however, give access to the discursive practices that helped structure people's understanding of their world: these literary constructions will have affected the lives of real people (see Schultz 1995: 14–15).

While some of the recent historical perspectives have been challenged on the basis of essentialism, (Lesnick-Oberstein (1998: 9–19) has, for example, shown how both Shahar and Cunningham are reliant on an idea of 'the child' in an essential way, and base their arguments on a biological definition of childhood), their findings have prompted challenges to a number of disciplines, among them sociology, anthropology and developmental psychology.

## Cultural constructions of age

In development psychology, for example (see Kessel *et al.* 1991; Kessel and Siegel 1983), the traditional 'incompetence' model of child development (whereby the child has to be 'civilised' or 'socialised' into adult society) has been challenged:

> Now that 'childhood' could no longer be regarded as a universal and unvarying experience for all children and now that expectations about the abilities and competencies of 'the child' had been shown to vary cross-culturally and over time, it was suggested that biological development must be seen as contextualising, rather than unequivocally determining, children's experiences.
>
> (James *et al.* 1998: 47)

A small number of anthropologists had, in fact, from an early date demonstrated that conceptions of age and age groups could be different in non-Western societies. Benedict (1935) compared childhood among the Zuni, Kwakiutl and Dobu, and found marked differences in terms of the responsibilities that children were allowed to assume, their degree of sub-ordination to others and the way that gender characteristics were structured. Mead (1973 [1928]) looked at the experience of growing up in Samoa, high-lighting differences from contemporary Western traditions. However, both Benedict and Mead, while rejecting universality, still saw socialisation as a process of moulding by adults, something that is now being challenged (Prout and James 1990: 18).

Anthropologists had also shown that 'growing up' was not a purely bio-logical process, with Van Gennep's (1960) work on rites of passage, which were seen as marking changes in social status, rather than simply recognising physical maturity. These ritual processes can be used to magnify age differ-ences, to impose sharp discontinuities on the continuous process of ageing, thereby overawing initiates and enhancing the power of the elders (La Fon-taine 1985; Spencer 1990: 9). These are cultural processes, which are used to maintain the existing shape and operation of societies.

More recent approaches in sociology and social anthropology explore both how people's ideas about 'the child' and about the nature of 'childhood' are embedded within social structures, and how children respond to and experi-ence their categorical status as children (James *et al.* 1998: 61, see also James 1993; Jenks 1996; Levine 1998; Prout and James 1990; Stephens 1995). Others are starting to examine the cultural construction of 'old age' (Amoss and Harrell 1981; Hockey and James 1993; Pilcher 1995). The remainder of this section will outline these developments, detailing how Western concep-tions of 'age' and 'ageing' have been shown to be culturally specific. The implications of this work for archaeological research will then be explored.

Ginn and Arber (1995: 5) have usefully highlighted that there are in fact several different meanings of the term 'age'. These include chronological age (corresponding to calendar date of birth), physiological age (a medical con-struct, referring to the physical ageing of the body as seen in levels of function and impairment) and social age (the social attitudes and behaviour seen as appropriate for a particular chronological age). They argue that in all three meanings ageing is gendered and socially structured. Different societies may have varying expectations of the roles and responsibilities that an individual of a particular age (of whichever sort) may take on. Contemporary Western society sets great store by chronological age, with the life course, especially in the early years, being tightly constrained by law. Children in Britain today are legally required to attend school (or an approved equivalent) between the ages of five and sixteen, and increasing requirements are currently being laid down as to their expected academic progress with each additional year in school. Presently, they officially become adults at the ages of sixteen (hetero-sexual intercourse, marriage with parental permission and smoking), seven-teen (driving cars) and eighteen (homosexual intercourse, drinking alcohol and marriage without parental permission).

The existence of such tight control has not always been the case. In the Middle Ages, for example, although chronological age was important in some contexts, especially legal ones such as inheritance, the ability to function in a particular role (social and/or physiological age) was probably a more import-ant factor (Shahar 1997: 24). In addition, social contracts such as marriage, especially among the elite, could be contracted at a very early age, as they were linked more to dynastic interests than sexual relations. As shown above, physiological age is subject both to gender (men and women reach sexual maturity at different times) and also to social and economic factors, such as labour, health and wealth. The significance that any of these types of age takes on in a particular society is thus contingent on many other factors (ibid.: 12).

In addition to different types of age having varying significance, societies also divide up the life course in different ways, and have vastly differing expectations of the abilities of, for example, a six year old. Such expectations often contrast with Western categorisations of age and highlight that they are not natural or fixed, but are, in fact, a very particular cultural construction. The history of this construction has been detailed in several places (see, for example, Cunningham 1995; Schultz 1995 and, although heavily debated, see Wilson 1980, 1984), and has been categorically shown to be a product of the particular social and political development of Western Europe:

> The creation of a modern state and national culture is integrally related to the creation of new sorts of gendered and age-graded subjects and spaces and the establishment of institutions variously engaged in spread-ing these constructions throughout society. As conceptions of a proper modern childhood developed within the European bourgeoisie, there was also increasing concern about deviant, wayward, and dangerous classes of children and about abnormal and indigent families.
>
> (Stephens 1995: 15)

Childhood, for example, in Western societies is expected to be a time of sexual innocence and happiness, of freedom from responsibilities, accom-panied by a corresponding lack of autonomy (Ennew 1986: 18, 21). Children, up to the age of sixteen and often beyond, are seen as dependent on their parents, and incapable of caring adequately for themselves. Children in Brit-ain legally require 'babysitting' until the age of twelve: an age at which young people in other societies may be married, caring for siblings, or an important economic provider for the family (see Panter-Brick 1998: 85–9). As Hockey and James (1993: 72) have suggested, the physical dependency of a Western infant now stretches into the social dependency of childhood, with a concomitant denial of that child's personhood. Through their con-structed dependence, Western children are marginalised from society, and their activities and views are regarded as unimportant (Sofaer Derevenski 1994a: 9).

Western adulthood is viewed in contrast as such a stage of 'personhood', characterised by independence and autonomy. Because childhood is natural-ised as a stage of human development and non-self-reliance – 'we grow out of it' – proper consideration is often not given to it as a social practice (Jenks 1982: 13, 1996: 61). As children are seen as having to be socialised into adulthood (which is therefore the desired state), adults in Western society are seen as essentially morally superior, the norm to which the child is expected to conform, and the yardstick against which they can be judged more or less competent (Jenks 1982: 13). This emphasis of the differences (rather than the similarities) between adults and children is another factor that has increased children's social, political and economic dependency and marginalisation, and created the idea of the child as 'other' (Hockey and James 1993: 56).

Old age too, in modern British society, has a particular meaning, often being characterised as 'childish' dependency (Hockey and James 1993: 5). Becoming old is usually portrayed as a negative process by the media, and the language used of it – 'over the hill', 'past it', 'one foot in the grave' – reinforces these negative attitudes (ibid.: 16–17). Old people in Western society, if they become dependent on others for care, can find that they too are denied 'personhood' because others treat them like children: a process described as 'infantilisation' (ibid.). 'Caring' for others (whether they be young, old or disabled) thus becomes a relationship of power: 'care becomes part of a subtle ideology that possesses the moral high ground, defies opposition and exercises a continual control over the other in the name of "what is best for them"' (Jenks 1996: 42). Thus the modern British experience of dependency has come about as the result of particular ideas about individualism and childhood (Hockey and James 1993: 45).

Such characterisations of age are not inevitable, however. In a renowned study of urban Hausa society in Nigeria, Schildkrout (1978) demonstrated that children there had freedom like no other group. Due to the women of the society living in purdah, the carrying out of much domestic and economic activity was dependent on the ability of young children to wander freely in and out of other people's houses. Even strangers could approach children to make purchases for them, offer sales or take messages to others. These children, from the age of nine or ten also played a significant role in the care of younger children. Although not playing a major role in basic subsistence, they were crucial in the social, economic and political definitions of adult roles. Also different from Western norms was the characterisation of old people. In urban Hausa society, wisdom was felt to come from experience, and thus older people received respect, deference and obedience from the young. It would be a mistake, however, to assume that in all, or most, non- or pre-industrial societies the old were universally respected and cared for (contra Holy 1990: 167). As Spencer (1990: 8–10) points out, not all those who reach old age are respected: knowledge and ritual actions have to be manipulated in order to overawe from a superior age. We should beware of looking back to any 'golden age', whether of idyllic childhood or peaceful and powerful old age: each society will be different and should be examined on its own terms, rather than assumptions made about its essential nature. Even 'adulthood' can be constructed differently: among the Chewong of the Malay peninsular, social personhood as an adult must be achieved by the birth of a child, rather than simply reached (Howell 1987 cited by James *et al*. 1998: 63). In contemporary British society there are categories of people who, although of adult age, are not treated as social persons in their own right; among these can be those suffering from mental illness or with learning impairments (Jenkins 1990).

Our terms 'children', 'adults' and the 'elderly' are therefore culturally loaded, replete with particular assumptions and expectations about how people so categorised should behave. Such categories serve to gloss over the diversity of social experience of the members of these groups (Hockey and James 1993: 47). How, then, should age be thought about, so that its role in the constitution of society and the reproduction of culture can be investigated?

A prominent view in recent sociological work is that the experience of being a child cannot be regarded simply as a universal condition of immaturity (James *et al*. 1998: 63; Stephens 1995: 5–6). Similarly, assumptions cannot be made about what it is to be an adult, or an old person. Rather, it is the meanings and significances that are given to age differences within particular cultural settings that must be examined, in other words the social constructions that are made of age (Jenks 1982: 12; Prout and James 1990: 8). From this perspective, the experience of being young, middle-aged or old will vary from society to society, depending on the socio-cultural and historical setting, and other variables, such as rates of mortality and life expectancy, familial organisation, kinship patterns, and different ideologies of care and philosophies of dependency (Jenks 1996: 41, 69).

## Age and other identities

As age is not a 'natural' category, but a constructed one, it cannot be studied in isolation from other aspects of identity, such as gender, status and ethnicity (Prout and James 1990: 8). As James (1998: 59) has pointed out, 'children are not just children; they are boys and girls, members of different social classes and diverse ethnic groups. Thus, any similarities or differences between their lives must, in part, be a function of their different membership of such groups'. Similarly, when talking about older people, age and sex differences, among others, need to be taken into account (Amoss and Harrell 1981: 6). Examining these interrelationships is important, because identities are often seen to change with age. Gender especially, with its link to sexuality and reproduction, is integrally bound up with age classifications. Thus 'gender and age are intertwined throughout the life-course of the individual as gendered expectations, ideologies, self-perceptions and perceptions by others change, both from biological and social points of view' (Sofaer Derevenski 1997a: 876).

Gender is not, however, something individuals automatically acquire: it has to be learnt. Children are gradually engendered as they develop an awareness of gender identity, gender roles and gender ideology, and their gender changes as they absorb, learn and comply with culturally defined gender rules, which often vary with age (Sofaer Derevenski 1997b: 194). An early study by Oakley (1972: 173–88) illustrated how activities and behaviour can become engendered at a surprisingly early age. In various studies of Western mothers' interactions with their children, she showed that even responses to newborn infants (verbal, physical and through material culture) were gendered, with mothers holding male infants for longer, and using more visual stimulation with them too. While parents had very little awareness of their role in this, through the use of dress, praise, particular toys and exposure to activities, the children studied already had a firm knowledge of sex identity by the age of four, and could perceive distinctions of gender role.

An ethnic identity, similarly, has to be learnt (whether in childhood or later), alongside everyday cultural and social practices. Similarly, religious identities and expectations of behaviour according to family or group status have to be acquired through observation and practice. Through learning these cultural practices and identities, children are often in a position to transform them (Sillar 1994: 49). They may try modifications in play, and can potentially generate new cultural and material forms (ibid.). Indeed, in certain areas, such as intra- and inter-generational linguistic change, they may become prime movers (Scott 1997: 7). Children, therefore, are necessarily the main vehicles of culture into succeeding generations (James *et al.* 1998: 82), for it is through their learning (and manipulation) that culture is transmitted (and transformed). Children's worlds let us see those processes of cultural reproduction taking place, such that we must see 'children as active contributors to, rather than simply spectators of, the complex processes of cultural continuity and change within which they learn to live out their present and future lives' (ibid.: 83; see also Sofaer Derevenski 1997b).

## Age and agency

Studies of the appropriation and transformation of culture by young people (see, for example, the study by Hebdige 1979 on punk culture) have given prominence to ideas of agency, and suggest that through learning about the world, children and young people often transform it through engagement with its social and institutional structures (James *et al.* 1998: 89).

Edelstein (1983) has suggested that the transmission of such cultural practices may be considerably slowed if more than one generation is involved. In traditional societies in Iceland, most often comprising three-generational farms, the care of children is undertaken by both parents and grandparents, allowing for only very slow change in beliefs and practices between generations. With the onset of industrialisation, however, both the father then the mother leave the home to go to work, the children go to school and cultural change can occur a great deal more quickly, with the children exposed to a wider range of influences, which cannot be controlled so much by the immediate family. The socio-economic environment may thus have a large impact on the speed at which cultural innovations are adopted (see also Greenfield 2004).

Poole (1994: 837) has argued that even the youngest children are active, creative participants and agents in the processes of socialisation and enculturation; that we need further examination of how children shape the course of their own development by affecting the character of the interactions in which they are engaged; and that interaction with their peers may be fundamental in this (ibid.: 839). This can be seen as a microcosm of one of the central issues relating to the study of age, due to its dynamic nature: as people age in their successive cohorts or generations, there are concomitant changes in society as people of different ages pass through social institutions organised by age (Riley 1987: 2). As each age group lives through a unique segment of historical time it confronts its own sequence of change (ibid.: 4); this is what makes age so difficult to generalise about.

A necessary corollary of this argument that identities and cultures are learnt, and can be transformed in the process, is that individuals of all ages have to be regarded as social agents in their own right: even children and the dependent elderly are active in the construction and determination of their own social lives and the lives of others (Prout and James 1990: 8). 'The "childhood" which they enact is, then, quite literally one which children themselves help to socially construct through their everyday actions' (James *et al.* 1998: 60). The aged – like everyone else – can manipulate their own environments, and shape circumstances to their advantage (Amoss and Harrell 1981: 24). The elderly may also play an important role in the transmission of cultural norms and practices through their traditional roles as keepers of oral traditions (and, in some societies, frequent role in childcare). It is not the case, however, that any individual is an entirely free agent in the construction of their social world: the agency of children (and, one could also argue, other age groups) exists in the context of the constraints and potentialities of nature and the actions of others (Wartofsky 1983: 188). Such constraints may include school architecture, playgrounds, child labour laws, family living spaces (ibid.: 198): all help to determine what a child may or may not do; where he or she may have access to and where not. All these factors will influence a child's view of his or her position in the world.

Young people can, in addition, be regarded as an economic force. Our perception of children as necessarily dependent can blind us to the work that they carry out in present society, and also to the work they perform in other societies (fig. 3.5). We tend to overemphasise children's reliance on adults and thereby underplay the dependence of adults on children (Sillar 1994: 49). Even children as young as three years old can make genuine economic contributions to their society (see Hockey and James 1993: 90). Similarly the work of older people is important (although in our own society it is often disregarded), even if with age the nature of that work has to change to, for

*Figure 3.5* Three-year-old Maya girl learning to weave, Nabenchauk, 1991. Source: Greenfield (2004: fig. 2.21; copyright Lauren Greenfield).

example, taking care of young children, thus freeing others to leave the home (Hockey and James 1993: 144). In other societies, however, the inability to do traditional work is not necessarily accompanied by a loss of status as it often is in the West, with its strict divide between work and leisure (ibid.: 148–9). It is therefore necessary to examine carefully in particular societies the structural contexts that both constrain and enable action (James *et al.* 1998: 83).

Age is thus a cultural construction resting on biological foundations. There are different types of age, and those types can take on different meanings and significances within specific societies. Both children and the elderly should be seen as active agents within their societies, creating their own realities (not having them forced upon them), although the existing social structures will necessarily determine expectations of different age groups in terms of roles, behaviour and responsibilities. In learning those roles, children can often transform them. Similarly, older people can negotiate and transform what is expected of them by their societies. This is the conception of age with which archaeologists must work. What is rarely mentioned by the sociologists of age, however, is the role of material culture in the transmission of social roles and norms.

## Constructions of age and material culture

Archaeologists, on the other hand, are starting to explore the subtle ways in which both gender and age can be constructed through interaction with material culture (cf. Sofaer Derevenski 2000b; Sørensen 2000). Especial focus has been placed on the way that children, as both producers and consumers of material culture, are inducted into gender roles, and have the potential to transform those roles in the process (Sofaer Derevenski 1994b: 3). As objects construct the physical world of a person, they act as the conduit for the communication and maintenance of symbolic and social values. As children are active in their own development, for they master skills and gather large and complex bodies of knowledge throughout their childhood, they learn the symbolic values of objects through observation and interaction (Sofaer Derevenski 1994a: 14). As Sofaer Derevenski has stated: 'since material culture is an important repository of cultural values, this raises interesting issues of social and cultural reproduction crucial to archaeology' (ibid.). This includes the reproduction of gender roles and relations.

Material culture can also create and reinforce conceptions of age. Although individuals may share the same cultural milieu, as some become able, or are allowed, to engage in particular activities, the items of material culture used on a daily basis change with age (Sofaer Derevenski 1997c: 488). Thus, for example, being allowed to practice with a bow and arrow in a hunting society may signal the beginnings of the transition to an adult role, and will affect both self-perception and other people's perceptions of an individual's roles and abilities. In archaeological terms, this focus on the cultural specificities of the use of material culture means that cross-cultural generalisations about the number, timing or social importance of stages in the gendering of individuals cannot be made, and that attention should rather be paid to how gender and age are constructed in specific contexts (Sofaer Derevenski 1997a: 877).

Some archaeologists have recently started to explore such issues. A study of material culture from both ethnographic and archaeological contexts in Inuit societies (Park 1998) has produced some interesting findings. Examining ethnographic data first, he concluded that evidence for everyday children's activities was associated with an extensive miniature material culture. While miniature types were also found archaeologically, they could not automatically be assumed to relate to children, as these objects were also used as grave offerings or in shamanistic rituals. However, by examining the archaeological contexts in which miniatures were found, it was possible to identify some objects from the winter settlement sites as 'toys'. Park then looked at the relative numbers of those items, and their relationships with adult activities, and found similar percentages of miniature and full-size items, enabling him to argue that this was completely consistent with children playing at their future adult roles (ibid.: 279). This 'playing' did not, however, appear to be engendered until the age of nine or ten years, with young boys and girls playing with both male- and female-related adult artefacts (ibid.).

Similarly, a study of children in a sample of cemetery populations from Sweden dating from 3500 BC to AD 1000 (Welinder 1998) has identified patterning in associated material culture. The main findings were that, although it was not until the Viking Age that objects unique to children's graves were found (these being jingle-bells and mirrors), before this many children seemed to have been buried in special dress, rather than everyday clothing. Children's graves were present in this particular archaeological sample, and were generally numerous, though different proportions of children (under fifteen years old) were found in different periods, ranging from 15–20 per cent in Neolithic cemeteries to between 1–62 per cent in those of the Iron Age. As the author states: 'it is a paradox that childhood in prehistory has to be studied through populations of dead children. Thus, what we observe is not childhood but burial rituals for children' (ibid.: 188). It is, however, hoped that these correspond to various views of adult–child relations, while recognising that these might have been abstract and idealised relations (ibid.). Differences through childhood can thus be observed in individual populations, which correspond to the different ways in which children become adults: 'children did not simply grow into adults as time went on. They had to learn how to behave as an adult according to the traditional norms of their society, and they had to learn to conform to accepted female and male norms, that is they had to adapt to a gender' (ibid.: 194).

Detailed examination of mortuary contexts can thus help shed light on the ideological roles that different age groups may have played within a society. One such mortuary context is the *tophet*, the sacred enclosure characteristically lying on the edge of Phoenician colonial centres in the central Mediterranean in which child sacrifice was practised (Aubet 1993: 207–17; Lee 1994). The *tophet* at Carthage, for example, was in use from *c.* 750 BC until the destruction of the city by the Romans in 146 BC and its analysis offers a chronological perspective on mortuary practices in this social context between the eighth and second centuries BC. Only children under the age of four are found, cremated and placed in urns, although an animal was sometimes substituted. Over time, burial of premature infants and substitution by animals decreased, while the age range of the cremations increased, suggesting a greater degree of sacrifice of viable infants and older children (fig. 3.6). This evidence is interpreted, not as showing an inherently 'cruel' society, but as attempts to control the social and individual conditions of existence, within a culturally accepted religious framework (see Houby-Nielsen 2000 for contemporary practices from Athens).

Differential funerary treatment according to age can be seen in other spheres. In Iron Age Iberia, for example, foetuses and infants are often found buried beneath house walls, while other very young children are usually inhumed in the same cemeteries where adults are cremated (Chapa 2003: 119–21). This could indicate that certain age groupings were viewed as possessing different degrees of humanness (see also Finlay 2000 for an Irish tradition of separate burial grounds for children in the post-medieval period with potentially early roots).

In a similar attempt to discern social attitudes from mortuary treatment, Lucy (1994) looked at the differential treatment of children in pre-Christian and Christian cemeteries in Yorkshire between the fifth and twelfth centuries AD. Pre-Christian cemeteries, although having relatively smaller numbers of children, tended to distinguish them from adults in terms of the goods with which they were furnished, spatial location and burial position, with a greater number of younger burials being flexed or crouched. In contrast, in the

*Figure 3.6* The *tophet* at Sulcis. Source: Aubet (1993: fig. 43).

Christian cemeteries, adult/child distinctions were made solely by spatial position, in terms of location around the church. Much more inter-cemetery variability was seen in the pre-Christian cemeteries, which was argued to represent a far more flexible notion of what constituted an adult and a child (with more weight perhaps being placed on aspects such as personality and ability, rather than skeletally determined chronological age). The rigidity seen in the Christian cemeteries was, in contrast, argued to represent a more fixed notion of what a child was, certainly in chronological terms, and it was suggested that this might correspond with contemporary legal documents that suggest an age of majority of ten or twelve, which perhaps encoded Christian expectations of age groups. Although this analysis could not shed light on the actual experience of being a child in these two periods, it does give an idea of the ideological milieu within which childhoods would have been enacted.

One problem that plagues attempts to interrelate sex, gender and age in mortuary data is our current inability (in the absence of cheap DNA analysis) to judge skeletal sex from immature remains. Sofaer Derevenski (1997a) has, however, suggested an interesting way to distinguish between sex- and gender-linked variables when looking at the age construction of cemetery material. Using the example of the Tiszapolgár-Basatanya Copper Age cemetery in Hungary, she demonstrated that some variables, such as burial on the left hand side as opposed to the right, and the presence or absence of some artefacts, were linked to sex (i.e. they were found with all age groups of one sex), whereas others had differing age-related distributions and could thus be linked to the social constructions of age and gender. She further suggested that sudden changes associated with age (such as an object that was only found with a defined, gendered age group) may be related to some kind of stage achievement, such as a *rite de passage*. What is not being suggested here is some kind of direct 'reading off' of the evidence that is assumed to represent sex, gender or age. Rather, this is a study that takes the context of burial into account, looking at how people of different sexes and ages are buried, and what this may mean in terms of the ideological representations of sex, gender and life-stage (see also Sofaer Derevenski 2000c for the role of metal objects in configuring age and gender relations in the Copper Age Carpathian Basin).

Others have started to explore social reproduction through architectural analysis. Brück (1999), for example, linked the life cycle of Bronze Age settlements in Britain to those of their inhabitants, seeing changing site morphology as reflecting the expansion and contraction of settlements through birth, marriage and death. Ware (2003) has put forward similar arguments for early medieval settlements and house-use in Britain (see also Boivin 2000). Harlow and Laurence (2002) similarly draw on archaeological domestic and architectural evidence in their account of the life course in ancient Rome.

These are just a few examples of the types of approaches that can be taken to the study of age within archaeology, which recognise the limitations of the evidence, and seek to interpret it in its own terms. An interesting feature of these studies is the predominance of cemetery examination; further studies of settlement data will provide a broader base of comparative material. It is also notable how focused many studies still are on children and infants. Still largely lacking in the archaeological literature is any substantial work done on aspects of adulthood and old age; motherhood, fatherhood and grandparenthood would all have been significant in the structuring of family and social relations in the past, and need to be taken into account. Also interesting would be studies of non-viable communities, such as the medieval monasteries and nunneries, which explore them in terms of age relationships, alongside those of gender, status and religion. Archaeological science, with the development of more reliable ageing techniques, alongside, for example, methods for analysing past diet and nutrition (cf. Humphrey 2000), can add another dimension to such studies (Polet and Katzenberg 2003; Privat *et al.* 2002). Further studies of architecture too, looking at how physical space in settlements and the wider landscape was structured, and how that affected the movement and access of different groups of people within it, can help shed light on such issues. The important thing, though, is not to assume that we know what age was and how people of different ages behaved in the past. They were different from people now, and they would have behaved in different ways, at various times and places. Archaeology has to learn how to interpret the evidence that does exist, rather than assuming they were 'like us'.

## Conclusions

Age groups are contingent and constructed, lacking fixed parameters, roles and meanings. Being four years old and female in Britain in 3000 BC would have been an entirely different experience from being ten years old and male in Rome in AD 200. Those societies would have had different expectations of how a person of a certain age should behave, dress and function as a member of that society, and this would also have been intersected by their gender, status, religion and ethnicity. What is certain is that conceptions of different age identities in the past, and the experience of being an individual of a certain age, would have been radically different from those of modern Western society. We have an image of childhood as an age of innocence, which needs protection from the dangers and responsibilities of the adult world. This particular image can be argued to be a product of industrialisation and educational and welfare reform, and especially the introduction of compulsory schooling that prohibits the early entry of children into the workforce of modern Western Europe, thus ensuring prolonged dependence on their elders (Hockey and James 1993: 51–4).

Thus, many archaeologists, when they have used terms such as 'child' and 'youth' have used them in such a normative way, drawing on their own assumptions about what those terms mean. 'Our notion of "child" . . . marginalises the economic and social importance of children and is culturally specific in regarding children as passive and unproductive. Yet this attitude to children has heavily influenced attitudes to the past, leading to backwards inferences about the activities of children' (Sofaer Derevenski 1994a: 9). This leads to the assumption that it is adults (sexually mature people) who have political and social control in past societies (Sofaer Derevenski 1997b: 193). In addition, the use of such terminology lumps together individuals at different stages of development and with widely differing levels of dependence and independence (ibid.). Similarly, we often view old people as needing care in their 'childish dependency', and archaeologists have failed to take them into account at all.

Other human sciences offer a wealth of contrasting evidence, showing that the Western construction of age is by no means inevitable, but just one possibility, which has arisen out of specific political and social trajectories. It would be wrong to impose such limited possibilities on the past. Archaeological evidence can be interpreted in alternative ways, if those studying past societies have the willingness and imagination to do so.

## Note

1 Although an apparent paradox, this is because higher infant and childhood death rates result in a smaller proportion of the population reaching adulthood; thus a greater proportion of the population's total person-years are lived in childhood (Chamberlain 2000: 207).

# 4    Status identity and archaeology

*Staša Babić*

Relative status is a major factor determining the behaviour of people towards one another, and success in this game seems to be the prime pursuit in our social lives. Consequently, one of the basic issues in the study of human affairs is the variability in access to the relatively restricted number of highly esteemed social positions. Throughout its history, archaeology has not been the exception, and the appeal of archaeological research has often lain in the discoveries of material testimonies to the sometimes high social statuses achieved in the past. The hunt for splendid objects or impressive masonry forms a substantial element of the public image of archaeologists, and archaeologists themselves have not been disinclined to produce such evidence. However, the golden jewellery on the covers of archaeological publications has not always been accompanied by investigation into the factors determining the status of groups and individuals. A more or less implicit assumption has prevailed instead that inequality of status is exclusively the consequence of power obtained through and expressed in economic prerogatives. An attempt to move forward and incorporate current ideas into the studies of archaeology and status must therefore begin by briefly considering the history of ideas concerning inequality.

## Inequality

The unequal distribution of wealth and power has been the subject of scrutiny over centuries, in forms ranging from myths, religious and literary texts, to philosophical and political discussions. Although exciting in its own right, a detailed treatise on this enormous body of evidence is well beyond the scope of this chapter. The debate pertinent here may be traced back to the Enlightenment. Its proponents spoke in favour of rationalism and advocated new forms of non-theological learning as a means to improve humanity. The Divine Right of the European monarchs was challenged and the grounds of their power to rule were questioned. Questions were asked in the works of Smith, Hobbes and Rousseau, for example, about how actual societies of the time might be improved, but also how present societies diverged from the natural – the original human condition. Answers were sought by investigating the European past and the exotic present of contemporaneous non-European cultures, thus giving rise to the first steps of the disciplines of anthropology and archaeology (Layton 1997: 3–6). In the process, the powerful yet abstract concepts of *reason* and *progress* marched onto the historical stage, bringing with them the potential to break the limits of political domination by the autonomous use of reason (Wolf 1999: 25).

The concepts of the Enlightenment were further developed into nineteenth-century ideas about inequality. Karl Marx shared the conviction that reason can unmask the sources of human misery and that a greater realm of freedom may be reached by our own efforts, including the use of reason, without invoking the consolations of religion. In his work, the category of *practical reason* was introduced to account not only for observing the world, but also for altering it and evaluating the results of the actions. Social relations change through time, taking up particular forms of inequality and domination, broadly defined by Marx as the control by one group over the production and reproduction of another, occurring within and being decisively shaped by specific forms of property (Layton 1997: 8–18; Miller *et al.* 1989: 4–5; Miller and Tilley 1984: 5; Wilk 1996: 83–90; Wolf 1999: 30–35). Inequality and power thus came to be explicitly formulated as a function of economic relations. This legacy of Marx had a deep and long-lasting impact in the decades to come.

Another strain of thought concerning society was put forward by Emile Durkheim who investigated the instruments of social control over individuals. He developed the idea of *collective consciousness* to describe the shared feelings and beliefs giving order to the world, best expressed in rituals as conscious expressions of togetherness, authority and power rooted in the collective. Disobedience is controlled by a set of sanctions and punishments put into motion in the case of actions countering the collectively upheld social order (Durkheim 1947 [1912]; Layton 1997: 22–3; Wilk 1996: 77–8).

The work of Max Weber elaborated the issue of obedience to social rules – *voluntary submission* not entailing force – by investigating forms of legitimacy resulting in the right to command and the duty to obey. He also introduced the principle of *exclusionary closure*: the attempt of a group to secure its privileges, through tactics giving rise to the category of ineligibles or outsiders. Weber's concept of social relations denied universal and dominant power to economic factors, stressing that they would always co-occur with multiple other social and ideational factors. The ideas and values shaping people's social lives, relations of inequality and legitimacy of such relations are all generated by particular historical circumstances, and even the form of rationality shared within a group is a social product of a particular time and setting (Weber 1958; Wilk 1996: 108–11; Wolf 1999: 40–42).

The opposition drawn by Marx and Weber in their understanding of social life may best be summarised by saying that in Weber's logic, economic behaviour is deeply embedded in culture and beliefs, whereas Marx saw things very much in reverse. This difference has generated an enduring polarity that still structures the contemporary debate (Miller *et al.* 1989: 17; Wilk 1996: 110; Wolf 1999: 42). On the other hand, some possibilities of reconciliation have been pointed out, and a number of more recent authors have drawn on both Marx and Weber, extending and combining their arguments in very dynamic ways (cf. Miller *et al.* 1989: 6; Wolf 1999: 42). The inferences of Maurice Godelier (1982), based upon his ethnographic work among the Baruya in New Guinea, are thoroughly informed by the Marxist notions of *economic base* and *exploitation*. At the same time he investigates the importance of control over ritual and position in the kinship system as the vital parameters of one's social status, ultimately stressing that economic power may not invariably be translated into political power. Godelier (1988: 3; Wilk 1996: 92–4) thus explores 'the relations between thought, the economy and society', and analyses 'the respective weight of the mental and the material in the production of social relations, in the motion of societies, in history at large'. This line of enquiry will be returned to later, but first, archaeological work on status from the inception of the discipline will be briefly investigated.

## Rich, splendid, powerful

The culture-historical approach, especially characteristic of the first half of the twentieth century, but also very much present in the practice of archaeologists up to the present days (cf. Biehl *et al.* 2002), is often identified by its rather implicit nature, operating without explicit theoretical formulations (Jones 1997: 24). The emphasis is laid upon the collection of finds, their description and typological–chronological seriation, the ultimate product embodied in chronological charts and maps of distribution. The objects described and classified often develop a life of their own, divorced from the human beings who produced and used them, in their turn almost deprived of active intelligence (Miller and Tilley 1984). In such a framework, special attention is paid to exceptional finds, standing out by their perceived aesthetic qualities and/or the value ascribed to the raw material for their production. If recovered from a context exceptional in its own right and/or in a substantial quantity, these finds easily assume the label of 'treasures' (such as Fol *et al.* 1986; Mohen *et al.* 1987). The search for the people behind these splendid, beautiful and luxurious objects often runs along the lines of the following statement (fig. 4.1):

> The Rogozen treasure is likely to have belonged to a *wealthy* Thracian *ruling* family. . . . Their splendor and magnificence accords with the *idea* of a Thracian aristocracy aspiring to manifest both *power and authority through wealth and opulence*.
>
> (Fol *et al.* 1986: 15, our emphasis)

The concept of the economic basis of social domination certainly lies behind

*Figure 4.1* Silver vessels from the Rogozen treasure (Bulgaria). Source: Fol *et al.* (1986: front page).

the automatic correlation between *authority* and *wealth*. This powerful idea, formulated during the nineteenth century in the works of Marx, and elaborated later on many occasions, imposed a strong common-sense image of the rich and powerful possessing splendid objects along with the right to be obeyed. At the same time, an equally distant echo of Weber's work may be seen in the above quote, in ascribing to the Thracian aristocracy a certain *idea*, to which the material assemblage before us is supposed to neatly correspond. Neither of the concepts is elaborated. More generalised statements may run as follows:

> During the course of the Bronze Age a number of important changes took place . . . [among them] the rise of the privileged. In most parts of Bronze Age Europe one finds – in distinction to Neolithic practice – 'rich' graves and 'poor' graves side by side. . . . It is hard to think of this process in terms other than those of aggrandisement of the few, the rise of the elite, and the start of social stratification.
>
> (Coles and Harding 1979: 535)

Although admittedly more cautious, this statement in its essence also stems from the well-rooted assumption that 'rich' finds indicate social stratification in a universal and straightforward manner. The disinclination of the culture-historical method to 'deviate' from purely archaeological procedures and tools of investigation – description, typology, chronology – ultimately leads to the uncritical application of uninvestigated concepts, taken as general truths of human social life.

## Measurable status

The dramatic shift in the archaeological theory that came about in the 1960s and early 1970s was targeted towards these very inadequacies of the discipline. A more *scientific* and more *anthropological* procedure was to be formulated in order to account for the past and to produce generalised laws on human behaviour. The new approach emphasised *systems thinking*, based upon a notion of culture as a set of interdependent subsystems, the social subsystem being one of the main constituent components (Clarke 1968: 42–72; Johnson 1999: 64–75). Consequently, the development of cross-cultural methodology for social inference became one of the primary goals of archaeological investigation. The necessary prerequisites of such an endeavour have been listed as follows: 'Archaeological inference of social organization requires a model of society, archaeological data, and a reliable connection between them' (Wason 1994: 3; also cf. Brown 1981: 26). The model of society corresponding to the archaeologically recovered material was supposed to account for various possible forms of social organisation over time. To meet this need, a generalised pattern of development of human society leading from egalitarian to stratified forms was borrowed from neo-evolutionary anthropology (Service 1975), and soon became a standard item in the archaeological toolkit (cf. Bintliff 1984; Renfrew 1973; Wenke 1981). The reliable connection between the thus acquired model and archaeological data was secured by *middle range theory* (Wason 1994: 4, fig. 1.1, 12), the typical route of processual archaeology for bridging the gap between the statics of the material record and the dynamics of the past (Binford 1983).

Quite rapidly the new perspective was gaining ground, and during the 1970s and 1980s a substantial number of archaeologists, especially in the Anglo-American world, were adhering to the neo-evolutionary sequence of stages of social development. The material correlates of these stages of cultural evolution came to be explicitly formulated (cf. Burnham and Kingsbury 1979; Gibson and Geselowitz 1988; Peebles and Kus 1977), and burial practices soon received special attention (cf. Chapman *et al.* 1981; Wason 1994: 67–102). On the basis of a large sample of archaeological and ethnographic material a model was created that met the request for cross-cultural generalised inference, carrying the processual credo to its limits by expressing the causal relationship between data and interpretation in a quantitative manner (Binford 1972: 208–43; Saxe 1970; Tainter 1978). According to this model, which was to become very influential in the years to come, the rank of the deceased is precisely reflected in the measurable communal effort and *energy expenditure* invested in the funerary rite and erection of the monument:

> In any system of hierarchical ranking, increased relative ranking of status positions will positively covary with increased numbers of persons recognizing duty-status relationships with individuals holding such status positions. [This] entitles the deceased to a larger amount of corporate involvement in the act of interment, and to a larger degree of disruption of normal community activities for the mortuary ritual.
>
> (Tainter 1977: 332)

Compared to the implicit and vague assumptions typical of the culture-historical procedure, this explicit, positive causation was certainly a major breakthrough, and many archaeologists dealing with funerary data have been enthusiastic to embrace the model (cf. Babić 2002: 79).

In the early 1980s, 'the ecological contexts of social hierarchy' (Brown 1981: 28) were actively sought, and the volume explicitly linking ranking with control over resources (Renfrew and Shennan 1982) is another important reference point in the archaeological search for status. The collection of essays based on data sets from various periods and places focused on the cross-cultural regularities linking social ranking to the resources at the disposal of a community. Along this line of argument, monumental funerary constructions were defined as territorial claims of a community over resources – 'social statements about control of and access to land' (Renfrew 1982: 4). The control over resources was further coupled with the mode of exchange to determine decisively the social order of a community. Following the work of Karl Polanyi, certain modes of economic exchange came to be associated with social evolutionary stages (Humphreys 1978), also implying the predominant manner of movement and distribution of goods, which is expected to be reflected in the archaeological record. A classical integrated example linking control over exchange and resources in a reconstruction of a social system is the model proposed by Frankenstein and Rowlands (1978). In its foundation lay the notions of *chiefdom* as a stage in social evolution, and *redistribution* – 'the fundamentally important process in ranked societies' (Renfrew 1982: 5). The emergence of the elite in Iron Age society is explained by its role in external exchange, the control over production of the goods to be exchanged and the exclusive possession of the ones received. Along with evidence from funerary contexts, settlement patterns were included, establishing 'a very general and strong positive correlation between size and centrality of a settlement' (ibid.: 3), and further implying the equation between a central place and a central person. These *central places* were seen as the major sites of production, craft specialisation and commercial activities – the processes controlled by an individual or a group in power, presiding therein. The relation of a settlement to its environment and exploitation of resources, as well as the relationship with other settlements in the vicinity, was established on the basis of a number of quantified models, such as catchment analysis or Thiessen polygons (cf. Burnham and Kingsbury 1979; Flannery 1976; Hodder and Orton 1976). However, the potential of settlement analysis for the investigation of social patterns seems not to have been extensively elaborated, even in the volumes expressly suggesting this line of enquiry (cf. Champion and Megaw 1985: 5).

For over two decades the processual framework of inference has remained almost exclusively limited to the archaeologists dealing with prehistory. However, a number of scholars working at the chronological margins of classical archaeology brought an interesting perspective to the analysis of funerary remains based upon the model proposed by Binford, Saxe and Tainter. Ian Morris (1987) aimed to investigate the social structure of the early Greek city states by studying the burials in Attika from the eleventh to fifth centuries BC, introducing into the analysis the notion of burial as a reflection of *social structure* – an idealised project, a kind of 'mental template' of society, to be distinguished from *social organisation* – the actual state of affairs. The difference between structure, enacted in ritual, and organisation is, for Morris, the manifestation of ideology. Therefore, 'the roles and relationships enacted in the rituals and detected by the archaeologists may not so much mirror real life relationships as distort them' (ibid.: 39), since 'roles and social personae are attached to all the participants and are given symbolic recognition' through tripartite *rites of passage* (ibid.: 42–3). Introducing into the archaeological inference the concepts of M. Bloch, R. Hertz and A. Van Gennep on ritual actions (Morris 1992: 8–10), Morris coupled them with the New Archaeology's approaches to burial that 'may seem very abstract and systematised to ancient historians, but they contain valuable ideas and methods which can be deployed in more "humanist" ways' (ibid.: 210).

The processual approach seemed 'very abstract' not only to ancient historians, but also to a number of archaeologists. By the beginning of the 1980s a critical reaction to the project of New Archaeology emerged, voicing the dissatisfaction with the uncritical acceptance of a positivist epistemology, the tendency towards mathematisation as the goal of archaeology and the resultant reduction of past social systems to equations, in which the external factors, especially the environmental ones, play the decisive role (Miller and Tilley 1984: 2, 3). The presumed neutrality of the concept of stages of social evolution was demonstrated to be value laden, judgemental and essentialist, resulting from the dominant Western discourse of modernity (Miller and Tilley 1984: 2; Rowlands 1989: 32; Thomas 2000b: 143) and reducing the dynamics of the past societies to adaptations to externally induced socio-environmental stresses or internal pathologies. However, the neo-evolutionary sequence seemed not to lose its appeal and volumes elaborating on the idea were published well into the 1990s (e.g. Earle 1991; Hedeager 1992; Wason 1994), along with some noteworthy attempts to account for and remedy its shortcomings (e.g. Earle 1997; Yoffee 1993).

## 'Inequality reexamined'

Let us now return to the discussions on inequality taking place outside archaeology. In the years prior to the Second World War the work of Antonio Gramsci introduced the concept of *hegemony*. He argued that class domination does not merely rest on the formal political system and apparatus of coercion, but that it spreads well beyond, into the social and cultural arrangements of everyday life. He sought to identify the social groups producing and disseminating the *hegemonic* forms, and discussed the role of power in producing and distributing cultural norms and practices, favouring some and disfavouring others. Although based upon the Marxist notion of *false consciousness* – a state in which people do not clearly see the relations of domination in which they are bound, Gramsci's idea of hegemony may not be reduced to economic forces. Instead, it introduces the possibility of analysing the role of various cultural forms in establishing and maintaining the relations of inequality (Gramsci 1971; Miller *et al*. 1989: 11, 12; Wilk 1996: 87; Wolf 1999: 44–7).

Louis Althusser provided a vital element to the study of inequality by linking Marxist ideas to structuralist thought, and further exploring the role of ideological strategies in reproducing systems of social domination. Not denying the importance of economic factors, Althusser maintained at the same time that economic relations themselves may be structured politically and ideologically, especially in pre-capitalist societies. Althusser thus emphasises ideological legitimation as playing a key role in the maintenance of relations of dominance (Althusser 1984; Miller *et al*. 1989: 7–10; Thomas 2000a: 11–12).

Michel Foucault's work on disciplinary technologies conceptualised the ideas of surveillance techniques constraining human actions, including bodily behaviour. In such a framework, topics such as sexuality or madness are seen as discourses structured in the realm of power, and imposed through a variety of institutional forms, such as schooling, working environment, military or medical establishments. Power, then, is produced in every relation, in the domain of everyday activities and every individual, as a series of 'micropowers' permeating every aspect of life (Buchli 1999: 11–22; Foucault 1977; Miller *et al*. 1989: 14, 15; Miller and Tilley 1984).

The works of Gramsci, Althusser and Foucault underlie most of the recent studies that stress the structural heterogeneity of power. The concepts of wealth, status and class are seen as mutually translatable, but not entirely reducible to one another. Furthermore, the influx of ideas originally developed in the domain of linguistics gave rise to investigation into the relation between power and the signs that humans use in their communication, be it verbal or non-verbal. Starting with Ferdinand de Saussure and Charles Peirce in the second half of the nineteenth century, semiotics – the study of signs – developed into a vital component of general study into human affairs (cf. Thomas 2000a; Tilley 1999). Basic notions are that signs depend, for their formulation and function, upon the network of practices we call culture, and that the capacity to assign cultural significance to signs constitutes an important aspect of domination (Eco 1962; Miller 1989: 65; Thomas 2000b: 154; Wolf 1999: 49–54).

Pierre Bourdieu developed the concept of *habitus* to explain a body of implicit knowledge, or a set of assumptions people share as deeply embedded common and agreed-upon truths. However, although everyone knows the rules for proper behaviour, these rules are broken or manipulated all the time, by using *strategy* to pursue individual interests. Control is often provided by using what Bourdieu calls *symbolic violence* to force individuals into line. Akin to Foucault, he sees power as diffuse, penetrating everyday social encounters, with the very language and forms through which people express themselves providing the instruments for their own oppression: the language becomes not only an instrument of communication or of knowledge, but also an instrument of power, the language of authority (Bourdieu 1977; Layton 1997: 200–204; Miller 1989: 65; Miller *et al*. 1989: 15; Wilk 1996: 142–5; Wolf 1999: 55).

Bourdieu is therefore very much concerned with *fields of social and cultural production* and their role in the reproduction of social relations. His *Distinction: A Social Critique of the Judgement of Taste* demonstrates that the distinctions in people's consumption preferences reflect their key social distinctions: 'art and cultural consumption are predisposed, consciously and deliberately or not, to fulfill a social function of legitimating social differences' (Bourdieu 1984: 7). On these grounds Bourdieu argued that 'the structure of consumption is the key to the reproduction of class relations, but also that it thereby provides a novel mechanism by which analysts could study social relations in some objectified form – here as a pattern of taste' (Miller 1995: 267).

We have now moved a long way from the assumption, so present in archaeological writing, that social status is decisively if not exclusively defined by economic factors. In the works of Foucault and Bourdieu social relations and the resulting inequality of status are inextricably linked with values other than economic. Status is thus conceptualised as *socially constructed* in constant negotiation and interaction by individuals and groups, taking up *culturally specific* forms dependent upon the particular historical and geographical setting.

Furthermore, economic phenomena have undergone a reconsideration along similar lines, which has undermined the idea of economic value itself as an intrinsic and permanent quality of an object. An assumption is put forward that it is generated by a judgement made about it, the politics of value in many contexts being the politics of knowledge. Commodity as an object of economic transaction is not one kind of thing rather than another, but one phase in the life of some things. The very process of exchange bears the economic value of an object, the production of commodities being a cultural and cognitive process. Finally, power relations are reflected in the right to exclude or withdraw an object from exchange, therefore cancelling its economic value altogether and ascribing a symbolic one instead (Appadurai

1986; Kopytoff 1986). Exclusionary practices may be justified by patterns of consumption and lifestyle rather than economic prerogatives, and even the apparently purely economic factors determining people's social status may be demonstrated to depend ultimately upon culturally ascribed criteria, such as gender (Miller et al. 1989: 7; Wilk 1996: 15–17).

Finally, the perpetual human concern with inequality initiates various responses to it, theoretical as well as practical, ranging from religious to rebellious and back. The common thread is the demand for equality, but not always defined according to the same criteria. Current political and economic theory offers a variety of answers, such as equal income, welfare levels, rights and liberties. However, the demand for equality in terms of one variable may be contradictory in terms of another, thus raising the issue of the priority and validity of criteria. This question – 'equality of what?' – ultimately derives from the actual diversity of human beings in terms of their internal character-istics (age, gender, talents, abilities), as well as external circumstances (Sen 1992). There is no reason whatsoever to doubt that an equally diverse humankind existed in the past and that the resulting inequality may have been perceived, articulated, expressed and contested in a variety of ways, giving rise to a wide variety of status identities. One of the goals set before archaeologists may therefore be the identification of those ways, thereby transcending the equation linking social prestige directly to possession (cf. Thomas 2000b).

## Archaeology re-examined

Attempts to identify the stimuli behind the latest shift in archaeological theory during the 1980s list a very diverse set of ideas, from structuralism and post-structuralism, neo-Marxism and critical theory, to feminist thinking (Bapty and Yates 1990; Chapman 2002; Johnson 1999: 98; Thomas 2000a). However, one of the recurrent topics linking this variety of viewpoints is the concern for active strategies of individuals in their social lives, present as well as past.[1] The majority of archaeological writings raising the issue more or less explicitly state their theoretical foundations in the works of Foucault, Bourdieu and Anthony Giddens (for example Barrett 2000; Johnson 1989).

Among the early volumes indicating this paradigm shift were the ones dealing with ideology, power and prehistory (Miller and Tilley 1984), and domination and resistance (Miller et al. 1989). These collections of papers, especially in their introductory essays, raised the issues of archaeological approaches to distribution of power. The starting point in this endeavour is to ascribe an active intelligence to past peoples, as opposed to a passive stimu-lus-response conception (Miller and Tilley 1984: 2). This leads to the state-ment that 'inequality therefore, if perceived superficially as the conditions of rank or status ordering, or as the relative distribution of power in society, is too unsubtle a concept to encompass this diversity of heterogeneity in social forms that might need to be addressed as being "complex"' (Miller et al.

1989: 2). The approach is advocated emphasising 'understanding [of] the nature of societal differences and the conditions that promote societal change and continuity while eschewing objectivist tendencies to work solely towards the production of high-level cross-cultural generalizations' (ibid.: 1). The path is set by a thorough introductory theoretical investigation and a number of case studies collected in these two volumes.

However, perhaps due to the fact that the same mighty wave of reconstruction brought into the discipline topics that had previously been virtually non-existent, such as gender relations, or notoriously laden with problems, such as the concept of ethnic affiliation of past groups, the direction set by Miller, Rowlands and Tilley was not immediately followed by a proliferation of contributions. The newly acquired theoretical tools to deal with power relations have been harnessed mainly to discuss the decisive influence of the *present* power relations on the archaeological study (cf. Layton 1989a, 1989b; Tilley 1989), and the possibilities of exploring the past in the same way have been more hinted at than pursued. Archaeologists interested in discussing past social relations have mainly remained devoted to the neo-evolutionary pattern and its derivatives, very much maintaining and occasionally refreshing the processual approach (e.g. Earle 1991, 1997; Hedeager 1992; Richards and Van Buren 2000; Wason 1994; Yoffee 1993).

At the end of the 1990s a welcome explicit integration of the topics of age, sex and class occurred on the archaeological agenda, in 'an attempt to link large-scale social process with individual variation and choice' (Meskell 1999: 6). Referring back to 'the most influential social theorists of the twentieth century' (ibid.: 24), such as Ricoeur, Bourdieu, Derrida, Foucault and third-wave feminist authors, the volume explores issues of social status in the context of everyday life, incorporating the topics of age and gender, in an attempt to overcome the divide between the two levels of investigation, namely those of individuals and of their social relations. Somewhat surprisingly, though, the chapter discussing status and class on the grounds of funerary data (ibid.: 140), although starting by addressing in a critical tone the 'usual suspects' from the processual camp (such as Binford 1972; Chapman *et al.* 1981; Wason 1994), ends up in the spatial analysis of tombs and the hierarchic scaling of tomb construction and expenditure (Meskell 1999: 143), relying on the works of Brown (1981) and Tainter (1978). Meskell offers exciting and individualised social histories of actual people, including their personal names, stories of 'social mobility through merit, favouritism, bribery, crime, or adoption' (Meskell 1999: 21), but these accounts are based upon detailed written evidence. Unfortunately, from the archaeological point of view, this does not offer much hope to researchers eager to investigate individual social biographies without the benefit of inscriptions. Material culture, the specific source of information with which archaeologists deal, determines the course of action by its own limitations and specific difficulties, but at the same time opens up a whole set of promising and exciting possibilities for approaching the human past.

## Material culture

Over the past decades the structuralist strain of influence in archaeological theory has given rise to the perception of the communicative qualities of material culture, leading to the idea of things being regarded as texts – *structured sign systems*, posing archaeologists the task of decoding their relationships with each other and with the social world. Inspired by the post-structuralist reconsideration of the generative principles of systems of meaning, a number of archaeologists during the 1980s explored the issues of polysemy, biographical, historical and cultural shifts of meanings of things, as well as the active role of material culture in constituting, rather than merely reflecting, social realities (Buchli 1995; Tilley 1990, 1999, 2002). This active discursive nature of material culture is coupled with its physicality and durability, vital to the way in which it transgresses, interconnects and symbolises social practices, enabling us to speak about *intertextuality of objects* (Sørensen 2000: 76–82). Consequently, in the process of interpretation one should bear in mind that the *meaning of things* changes depending upon the context, as well as upon the observer. Critically exploring archaeologists' understanding of both the social and the material, a recent account summarises the role played by objects in the eternal social competition for status in the following way: 'Occupying different positions in the network of power, people will interpret their material surroundings in different ways. . . . These differences in understanding will tend to give rise to hegemonic struggles over the definition of reality' (Thomas 2000: 154–5).

This multiple interplay of material culture and social ordering is apparent in the study of architecture. Built forms not only constitute the backdrop for the majority of human actions and consequently the context in which other material objects are produced, used and understood, but they are also themselves susceptible to the same structuring practices (Buchli 2002: 207). An inspiring example is provided by McGuire (1991) in his analysis of 'building power' founded upon an example peculiar to the majority of European archaeologists – that of the late nineteenth-century industrial context. Analysing the residential architecture, built working environments and funerary monuments, the author reaches the conclusion that 'the elites . . . consciously used the landscape to reinforce their view of the world and to give reality to that view. . . . However, it affected the day-to-day experience and consciousness of the working class in ways never intended by its creators: in ways of resistance' (ibid.: 109). The complexity of status negotiations is well illustrated in this passage, and testifies that alternative, competing and inverted ideologies constitute a staple ingredient of our social lives (cf. Miller 1989).

The point is elaborated in Buchli's study of a housing complex designed and erected with the express intention of making material and bringing into domestic life the values and goals of Soviet social reform (Buchli 1999, 2002). Along with the extension of state power into the most private domain, the reform aimed at the generation of new forms of kinship, gender, individuation and public/private interfaces, in order to meet the new ideological demands and to facilitate state legitimacy. However, active individual strategies and subtle forms of resistance may be 'read' in the ways in which the inhabitants of the housing bloc manipulated their living space in order to accommodate it to their social aspirations.

These two case studies open up the possibility of moving away from the usual object of archaeological scrutiny when searching for status – namely the funerary record. Owing much to Foucault and Bourdieu, they explore the possibilities of enquiry into social negotiations of power and inequality far removed from the binary scheme of the traditional approach. The focus is on the more subtle close-up examination of strategies of wo/men in their social lives in the course of their daily routine.

On the other hand, the chronological location of the works of McGuire and Buchli raises the issue of the limits of archaeology as a research strategy. In the course of the 1980s, the constant demands for a meaningful inter-disciplinary exchange have led a number of archaeologists into areas of mutual interest with a number of other disciplines, ranging from anthropology to museum studies, and resulting in the joint project of *material culture studies*, which aims at exploring the active role of material culture in our social lives, regardless of time and space (Buchli 2002). The framework of this welcome synergy gave rise to *consumption studies* (Miller 2002). The central theoretical point of reference is provided by the work of Pierre Bourdieu, especially his study of consumption preferences linking them to the social reproduction of distinctions (Miller 1995: 275, 276; 2002). Although primarily focused upon the study of postcolonial settings (cf. Miller 1994), this approach opens up a broader range of possibilities for transforming the humanities in a challenging manner (Miller 1995). This vein of enquiry has already led to a number of significant contributions in the domains of history, sociology and media studies (Miller 1987, 2002), but it seems that the potential of the strategy is not yet fully appreciated in the field of archaeology.

## A proposal

One of the recurrent objections made against archaeological theory over the last couple of decades is that there has been little or no work on its method-ological implications (cf. Chapman 2002: 226) – or, in other words, that all the fashionable buzzwords borrowed from the vocabulary of anthropology, philosophy and sociology have been imported into the debate, without touch-ing upon the *real* archaeological experience of dealing with actual objects. Perhaps it is therefore not only appropriate, but also necessary to test the applicability of some theoretical assumptions discussed above on an actual practical problem.

The starting point is provided by a series of funerary assemblages dated to the early Iron Age of temperate Europe (seventh to fifth centuries BC), which have been interpreted as *graves of community leaders* due to their elaborate architectural traits and opulence of the offerings. Objects of Greek manufacture feature prominently, ranging from bronze vessels and pottery, to jewellery and parts of armoury (Frankenstein and Rowlands 1978; Mohen *et al.* 1987). Recent analysis of this type of tomb from the region of the Central Balkans (Babić 2002) pointed to the importance of symbolic manipulation of certain objects in maintaining and communicating the leading role in the community. Position in the kinship system and lines of descent is identified as the crucial principle in ascribing social status. Some ritual elements indicate that ideological apparatus was in place, legitimising the hereditary power of the community leaders. Finally, the *insignia* are regularly chosen among the objects obtained through the network of external ritual exchange, emphasising the exclusive right of the group in power to possess and display exotic and rare goods.

However, by the end of the period the pattern is broken by the appearance of several bronze helmets of Greek origin (fig. 4.2) retrieved from graves lacking other crucial characteristics of the type (masonry, offerings), and therefore not ascribed to the members of the group in power (Babić 2001). Several points are worth stressing in this respect: first, these 'secondary' owners of the Greek products appear on the stage at the moment when a number of other factors indicate the disintegration of the social and symbolic pattern ordering the elite tombs; second, the exotic goods in their possession are limited to the pieces of bronze headgear, all identical in type; finally, the inventory of these graves strongly indicates male individuals,[2] emphatically identified by their warrior role (cf. Treherne 1995). The transfer of these originally exclusive belongings outside the social group with supreme power raises the question of the status of the new owners, which enabled them to share some of the prerogatives of the paramount elite, yet not belong to it.

Let us now reiterate some of the theoretical concepts and explore their interpretative potential in this particular case. Bourdieu's work on consumption preferences, based upon the ethnographic studies both in capitalist and pre-capitalist settings, may be a potentially very rewarding path to follow for material culture researchers, as already stressed by Miller (1995: 275). Bourdieu asserts that distinction in consumption patterns reflects the key forms of social inequalities, while at the same time providing the foundations for the reproduction of these inequalities. In the particular case of early Iron Age temperate Europe, the pattern is established that elite social status is signalled by the possession and over/consumption of exceptional goods of Greek origin. However, the irregularity in this respect appears concerning one particular kind of Greek product – bronze helmets buried with a number of individuals of 'lesser' status. Explanation is called for, to account for the change in the consumption pattern, which allowed access to the exclusive domain of material status symbols by individuals outside of the legitimate group in power. Investigating the limits of dominance, Miller brings in the observation that legitimatory claims include structural opposites and

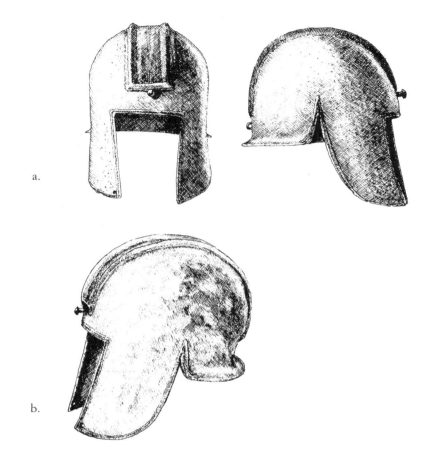

a.

b.

*Figure 4.2* Bronze helmets from the Central Balkans early Iron Age warrior graves.
a. Ražana; b. Pilatovići. (Drawing by D. Jovanović.)

contradictions, giving rise to competing strategies (Miller 1989). Returning
to the Iron Age case, it is tempting to interpret the contradiction of the Greek
headgear along these very lines, and to suggest that the helmets may have
been manipulated in terms of emulation of taste of the elite, in order to
mimic and to claim prerogatives. It seems plausible to infer that by the
beginning of the fifth century, position in the kinship system, previously the
key criterion in ascribing status, started losing ground. The new ideological
ordering is reflected in the new consumption practices. The seemingly irregu-
lar patterning of material culture at this moment reflects the emergence of
a subversive strategy undermining the status of the hereditary elite. The
choice of the objects employed in this strategy may have been guided by the
identifying component of the claimant group: the Greek helmets not only

presented the desired consumption pattern of the hereditary elite but, at the same time, their martial character corresponded to the lifestyle of those challenging the supremacy. Their practical protective purpose was supplemented by the message they conveyed concerning the status identity of the owners. The exotic bronze headgear would certainly have added to the splendid appearance of a warrior, both during his lifetime and at the moment of his burial, underlining his prowess in combat – the essence of his social status, and the newly acquired right to participate in the elite consumption pattern. As stressed by Treherne (1995: 127), 'socio-culturally organised regimes of self-adornment not only physically protect the individual, but symbolically express narratives of self-identity'. These regimes of self-adornment often extend from parts of costume to the human body itself.

## The body

The universal human experience of corporeality as the means of perceiving, understanding and ultimately ordering the social world has been one of the recurrent topics in humanities over the past decades. The cornerstone is laid by the seminal work of Marcel Mauss (1979 [1950]) on *techniques of the body*, thus introducing the concept that modes of socially accepted behaviour are often learned and reproduced through everyday bodily actions. Mary Douglas (1966, 1970) extended the argument, stating that a society constrains the way in which an individual physical body is perceived. Even before birth, the human body ceases to be merely a biological given, and is transformed into a *cultural artefact* through a series of culturally specific ideological and symbolic mechanisms (Godelier and Panoff 1998). In turn, the body system provides a set of analogies and metaphors for understanding the social system, and the natural symbols and images of the body encode social and cultural norms (Douglas 1970; Hamilakis *et al.* 2002a: 11; Tilley 1999: 37–40). The visual representations of the human body may thus be harnessed to construct narratives – public statements relating to social categories and relations, as demonstrated by Tilley (1999: 133–73) in his study of the Scandinavian rock carvings of the late Bronze Age.

On the other hand, actual human bodies, both living and dead, are also employed in communicating messages concerning people's social standing. Pierre Bourdieu (1977, 1984) elaborated upon the ideas of Mauss (1979 [1950]) by introducing the concept of the bodily *hexis* to describe the ways in which cultural norms are appropriated, experienced and made durable by the actions of a human body. Consequently, the principles of social differentiation may be both read and enacted through bodily posture and gestures. Furthermore, various interventions and transformations, bodily decoration, adornment and clothing also express an individual's relation to society and the self (also Tilley 1999: 38; Treherne 1995).

The emerging archaeological interest in the human body, primarily associated with the exploration of gender issues (chapter 2 of this volume), has recently brought other aspects of human corporeality into the research agenda, such as food consumption, which leads to the concept of the 'consuming body', or spatial orientation, which raises the concern of bodily engagement with landscapes (Hamilakis *et al.* 2002a). The everlasting archaeological interest in grave offerings as signals of social status has also been reconsidered from the point of view of socio-culturally constructed bodies. Paul Treherne (1995) explicitly applied some of Bourdieu's concepts exploring the self-identity of the Bronze Age warriors, which was very much dependent upon their attitude towards masculine bodies. The group *lifestyle* included certain *aesthetics* – requirements and attitudes towards bodily appearance considered appropriate. The toilet articles recovered from the warriors' graves are therefore interpreted not only as props aimed at demonstrating to onlookers the importance of the owners, but also and perhaps primarily as the instruments of self-identification and subjectification. The interventions in human bodies achieved by those implements actively participated in the status identity of the warriors. The lifestyle then is transformed in the corresponding *deathstyle* befitting the social status.

The processual model proposed by Binford, Saxe and Tainter, discussed above, established an explicit causal relationship between the social status achieved and the ways in which a human body is treated after death. However, this expenditure model measures and equates the quantity of communal work invested into structure and of offerings laid into the grave with the position of the deceased on the social ladder, without touching upon the reasons for specific choices of objects or the treatment of the body. On the other hand, as proposed by Treherne, these choices are intimately related to the ways in which people themselves understand their social status and actively communicate it to the community. Consequently, dead bodies often retain and encapsulate some elements of the lived social identity of the deceased. Susan Kus (1992) addressed some of the issues of the sensual and emotional responses to death, as an event acutely stressing the corporeality of human existence. Aside from intimate personal bereavement, the sense of physical perishing may extend to people socially relevant to the whole community. Referring back to Weber, Kus (1992: 171) states that 'the logic of the legitimacy of charismatic leadership is undermined by the physical decline of a leader'. From the visual representations of the first Roman emperor, Augustus, never reaching the age of thirty, to the actual embalmed bodies of the Egyptian pharaohs, there is a marked tendency to counteract the biological limitations of a leader and to preserve his/her body. Religious ideas of afterlife often play a role in this process, but even in ideological settings emphatically rejecting religious explanations, dead leaders' bodies continued their political lives. The burial of Lenin's and Stalin's embalmed bodies in the Kremlin, and the subsequent removal of the latter as a consequence of the political shift in the Soviet Union in the early 1960s (Verdery 1999), serves well to illustrate that the body of a deceased leader may continue his political destiny after his death (fig. 4.3).

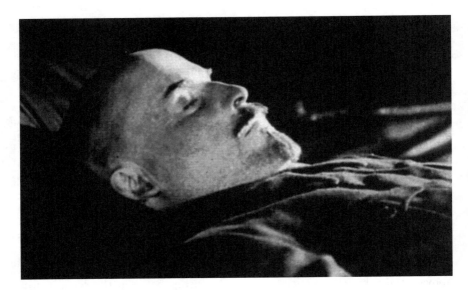

*Figure 4.3* The embalmed body of Lenin, exposed in his mausoleum. Source: Zbarsky and Hutchinson (1997: 84).

Current archaeological theory has already introduced the issues of sensuous human activity and the experiencing human body as a rewarding path to follow (Hamilakis *et al.* 2002b: 13; Kus 1992: 173; Thomas 2000b: 155). The concept of the *human body as a cultural artefact*, shaped and perceived according to the social context, changes our approach to staple archaeological data, such as funerary remains. The premise that 'the physical experience of the body, always modified by the social categories through which it is known, sustains a particular view of a society' (Douglas 1970: 93) may be further explored in order to contribute to our investigation of status identities in the past.

## Summing up

Archaeological enquiry into human affairs of the past owes a substantial part of its appeal, both for professionals and the general public, to the potential of the discipline to speak about eternal human concerns, such as the ways in which societies are shaped, kept together and changed over time. The quest for the individuals considered exceptionally successful in social competition, such as Schliemann's search for the material traces of Homeric heroes, has very much shaped the public image of archaeology and the expectations put before researchers. On the other hand, the theoretical assumptions of archaeological research into social status have mainly been tacit, implicit or simplified, especially in the framework of the culture-historical approach. The processual shift of the 1960s brought in an explicit theoretical tool in the shape of a quantified model, which did indeed signify an important advance in the archaeological approach to social status. However, the processual approach has been criticised for its virtual neglect of consideration for the particular, the individual, the acting human.

When dealing with the issues of social status, the current context of the humanities obliges us to consider the importance of individuals as self-aware authors of their own social conduct and of the social forms in which they participate (Cohen 1994). This is the challenge archaeology faces today, and it seems that, a couple of decades after the last massive shift in archaeological theory, the 'long term project in the remaking of the discipline' (Barrett 2000: 68) is far from complete. Surely one of the objectives in this project remains the ability to incorporate interdisciplinary experiences into archaeo- logical investigation in an informed and meaningful manner. On the other hand, the potential of the discipline to contribute its specific insight into human affairs is not fully realised among archaeologists themselves, nor among colleagues from adjacent areas of research. When dealing with topics pervasive throughout all humanities and social sciences, as certainly is the case with social status, the sheer chronological span offered by archaeology renders it a vital partner in the project. Since 'wherever possible we should try to identify the social agents who install and defend institutions and who organize coherence, for whom and against whom' (Wolf 1999: 67), it is certainly true that investigation into various historical settings brings us closer to understanding 'forms of social closure, exclusion and differentiation common to all social systems' (Miller *et al.* 1989: 2).

## Notes

1  'A fundamental change in archaeological perspectives occurs when we think about archaeologically recovered material as having once ordered a world in which differ- ent kinds of human agency could find their place' (Barrett 2000: 66).
2  For a number of practical reasons, the analysis of human bones from these graves never took place.

# 5 Ethnic and cultural identities

*Sam Lucy*

## Introduction

From its very start, archaeology has had as one of its central projects the identification of 'peoples' (now often termed 'ethnic groups') in the past. Such identification has traditionally been made through the study of distributions of material culture, with the geographical spread of characteristic artefacts being seen as marking the territory of a particular group. For many years there was also a widely held assumption that such groups were 'racially' linked, sharing a language and a whole suite of cultural practices. In this way, the past was envisaged as occupied by bounded, homogeneous groupings, whose histories, expansions and movements could be traced through looking at their material remains. Indeed, it meant that when changes were seen in the distributions of that material culture, this could *only* be explained through expansion or movement of that group.

In recent years, however, these long-held views about the nature, composition and behaviour of ethnic groups have been challenged, as have ideas about what 'ethnicity' (the quality these groups are assumed to share) actually is. Characteristic artefacts, languages and 'cultures' have frequently been noted not to coincide.

Contemporary observations made by sociologists and anthropologists have suggested that ethnic groups are more of an idea than a thing; if 'they' are characterised by anything, it is that their members choose to do (some) things in similar ways to each other, and in different ways from other people. These similarities and differences are then articulated as 'ethnic' ones (often framed in terms of members of the group having shared 'origins' or descent). Similarly, rather than view 'ethnicity' as something with which people are born, as some inherent characteristic, researchers are now starting to see it as an aspect of social relationships, again, more as a way of behaving than a thing, as an identity that can work on a number of different levels, and which cross-cuts other aspects of social identity such as gender, religion and age. It is something that has to be learnt, and it may well be fluid, both over an individual's lifetime, and depending on the contexts in which people interact.

These emerging ideas have some serious consequences for the way that archaeologists deal with their material. They mean that there is no longer a clear and direct link between the artefacts that people use, the way they dress, the houses they live in, and their 'ethnic identity'; such an identity is a much more complex phenomenon, and has to be studied with greater subtlety and a greater regard for issues of action, interaction and practice. In order to study aspects of ethnicity, which we choose to define, after Levine (1999: 168) as 'that method of classifying people (both self and other) that uses origin (socially constructed) as its primary reference', and other forms of communal cultural identity (such as local identity, territoriality or much wider group-ings), archaeologists need to pay more attention to the contexts in which things are used, and the ways in which people use them. It is these differences in practice that may serve as the locus for emphasising ethnic or communal distinctions, and it is these differences (fortunately) that are accessible to archaeologists.

These developments in how ethnicity is thought about also have implica-tions for the ways in which the wider world makes use of archaeology. In popular understandings of the past, national and regional groups are often 'traced back' in time, through such distributions of archaeological material, and these created histories are often used to justify political or nationalistic claims. The presence of a 'people' in a certain area in the past is used as justification for the control of that land by the present-day 'people' of the same name. These manipulations of archaeology are obviously abuses of the past, but countering such attitudes depends greatly on the ability of archae-ologists to challenge dubious methodologies. In order to start to do this, we must first examine how such methodologies came to be developed and used.

## Previous understandings of ethnicity and culture in archaeology

By the late nineteenth century there were classifications developing of archae-ology, linguistics and physical anthropology, and the 'culture concept' was being developed by German anthropologists and archaeologists (Mirza and Dungworth 1995: 350). In 1895, Kossinna propounded the idea that archae-ology was capable of isolating cultural areas (*Kulturprovinzen* or *Kulturkreis*), which could be identified with specific ethnic or national units and traced back into prehistory (Malina and Vasícek 1990: 62; cf. Meinander 1981: 101; see our fig. 5.1). The correlation of these three kinds of classification, and the combination of them with the method of *Kulturkreislehre* soon led to a para-digm that saw a direct relationship between language, material culture and people (Kossinna 1911: 3; Meinander 1981: 107; Jones 1997: 16; Olsen and Kobylínski 1991: 9 cited in Díaz-Andreu 2001b; Veit 1989: 37). Kossinna thus believed that 'sharply delineated archaeological culture areas coincide with clearly recognizable peoples or tribes', and it was assumed that cultural continuity indicated ethnic continuity (Jones 1997: 16). This, then, is the start of the 'billiard ball' school of history (Wolf 1982: 6): the notion that the past was populated by distinct bounded entities, characterised by anthropology, language and culture; the true subjects of history, whose destinies could be traced through millennia, spinning off each other in a global pool hall.

Kossinna's work had an impact on the archaeologist V. Gordon Childe (Díaz-Andreu 1996: 48), although Childe rejected Kossinna's Indo-Germanic interpretation of European prehistory (with European innovations deriving from the activities and expansions of a superior 'Aryan' race), and to a large extent its racist assumptions (Hides 1996: 26; Jones 1997: 16). Childe (1929: v–vi) stated that a culture was 'certain types of remains – pots, implements, ornaments, burial rites, house forms – constantly recurring together' and he assumed that such a complex was the material expression of a 'people' (ibid.). This observation was based on fieldwork: 'specific types of tools, weapons, and ornaments repeatedly associated together in graves and settlements' (Childe 1935: 2). In later years, however, these observations were qualified, when he stated that not all traits of an archaeological assemblage were likely to be found together, and that the archaeological picture of a culture was built up out of many fragments, seen at various times in different places, but always associated with one or more of 'the symbolic traits found to be distinctive of that assemblage' (Childe 1951: 30–31). At no time, however, did Childe ever suggest that cultures corresponded to 'races'. Cultures defined peoples, but there were no grounds for assuming that a people as a whole spoke a single language, acted as a political unit, or that its members were related physiologically or belonged to one zoological race (Childe 1951: 40, see also 1929: vi; 1933: 197–200; 1935: 3–4).

Through his use of archaeological distributions Childe did, though, contribute to the picture of prehistory as occupied by distinct 'peoples', which could be mapped on the ground; those mappings were often based, not on a complete assemblage, but on a limited number of 'diagnostic' types (Jones 1997: 18). Thus, bronze cruciform brooches of the fifth and sixth centuries AD in Britain have been termed 'Anglo-Saxon' (fig. 5.2) and certain styles of Iron Age metalwork 'Celtic'. These names tend to be those (or versions of them) mentioned in early documentary sources, and it was assumed that archaeological material and such historical references could simply be equated. For the truly prehistoric period, however, there are no such records, and so from the turn of the twentieth century archaeologists have talked of 'cultures', such as the 'Beaker culture' of the Bronze Age in western Europe (named after a characteristic pottery style). Given the common equations often made between artefact distributions and group identity, these have tended to be reified as ethnic groups (or using the Greek term, as *ethnoi*), such that 'the Beaker folk' became an acceptable archaeological label. This approach to the archaeological past has been termed 'culture-history', and has been the main archaeological paradigm this century, carrying with it a whole range of implicit assumptions and values about the nature of human groups in the past (Jones 1997: 12; see chapter 1 of this volume for more detail).

From the 1950s to the early 1980s, the study of ethnicity became

*Figure 5.1* Map showing supposed 'Germanic' territorial expansion (pale grey = core Germanic area; black = area of expansion by 1600 BC; dark grey = area of expansion by 800 BC) during the Bronze Age, produced in 1945 by German archaeologist Hans Reinerth for the AMT Rosenberg. Source: Jones (1997: fig. 1.1).

*Figure* 5.2 Map showing E.T. Leeds' interpretation of early medieval political and cultural divisions in Britain. Source: Leeds (1913: fig. 4).

increasingly unfashionable in most countries of Western Europe and the United States, with the rise of positivist and scientific approaches to the past. With their emphasis on socio-economics and systems theory, the cultural approach became of less importance, denoting a lack of interest in ethnic questions (Demoule 1999: 194–5). One notable exception to this was the so-called 'style' debate, which pondered the reasons for the typological and decorative differences between certain classes of artefacts. For example, the well-known debate on the Mousterian period between Binford (1973) and Bordes (1973) centred around this very issue. Bordes identified several Mousterian 'facies' (stylistic groups) and interpreted them as representative of different human groups, and then as different cultures or ethnic groups; Binford, however, saw them as representing functionally different occupations of the same group (cf. Demoule 1999: 196). Sackett (1977) thought that stylistic variation could be 'read off' as social variation, more specifically as representing ethnic differences between groups (see also Sackett 1990). Primarily though, the emphasis was more on socio-economic factors, such as subsistence strategies, than the more 'ideational systems' involved in ethnicity.

Despite these developments, many processual and post-processual accounts still assume the existence of homogeneous bounded societies in the past, which can be categorised in terms of one-dimensional distributions of material culture (Díaz-Andreu 1996: 56; Jones 1997: 137). Although post-processual archaeology, in particular, has emphasised the active use of material culture, there has been little reconsideration of the nature of the communities within which people are being active (see Jones 1997 for a detailed treatment of the history of archaeological conceptions of ethnic groups).

## Rethinking culture; rethinking ethnicity

Attempts to trace ethnic groups in prehistoric archaeology were based on the assumption that certain ethnic groups were characterised by a stable repertoire of cultural traits, such as language, typical artefacts and architectural forms, which could be objectively identified. This meant that any sudden emergence or disappearance of a distinct material culture could only be explained by migration, colonisation, conquest or assimilation (Olsen and Kobylínski 1991: 9). Recently, however, several archaeologists and ethno-archaeologists have challenged the idea that language, artefacts and culture coincide neatly to delimit an ethnic group.

First, correlations between material culture distributions and population groups have been questioned (Håland 1977; Zvelebil 1995: 40–42). DeCorse (1989) in studying the Limba, Yalunka and Kuranko groups of northeastern Sierra Leone concluded that material culture distributions provided only a limited indication of the divisions between them. Thus, different social groups may share a relatively homogeneous material culture, while still maintaining 'ethnic' orientation or identity (DeCorse 1989: 125–40; cf. also Hill 1989: 24). Hodder (1982b) in his ethnoarchaeological studies around Lake Baringo in Kenya demonstrated that while some aspects of material culture related to ethnic (actually tribal) boundaries, others cross-cut them. The boundaries between these groups had, however, been maintained for several generations, despite a great deal of interaction between the groups, and even the movement of whole families from one tribe to another (ibid.: 24). This boundary maintenance had to be seen within the context of social strategies within and between the groups, for example in the negotiations between age and sex groups (ibid.: 75–86).

Similarly, the correlations between specific languages and groups of people have been called into doubt, on both theoretical and empirical grounds. Robb (1993) and Moore (1994) have both criticised the 'cladistic' approach towards language history, which attributes similarities between contemporary languages to a hypothetical ancestor (cf. Sims-Williams 1998 for detailed argument on this). This results in scenarios of original unity leading to diversity, like a branching tree, but these are misleading in the extreme. The processes of language development have been shown to be extremely complex, and not well accounted for by this analogy (Pluciennik 1996b: 43): at any time populations speaking different languages can decrease or intensify their contact, the acceptable language can change, words can be borrowed or become obsolete, people can move. Language change can be a strategic choice in response to political, economic and cultural factors, and the possible role of specialist languages (trade, prestige, gender-associated) should be considered (Robb 1993: 748, 754–5). The tree analogy encourages seeing languages as things, whereas languages exist only insofar as people speak to each other (again, an alien thought in these days of national educational systems and dictionaries, which serve to codify and attempt to fossilise languages). In empirical terms, there are many anthropological case studies of ethnic groups that lack a common language (Elwert 1997: 266) and separate groups that share a language (Olsen and Kobylínski 1991: 15), while people living in border zones can exhibit incredible abilities to learn foreign languages (ibid.: 15). With regard to this last instance, Zvelebil (1995: 46) refers to Thomason and Kaufman's (1988) model for contact-induced language change, which sees the degree of change depending on the relative number of speakers from each community, the intensity of contact, the duration of contact and the social context of interactions. Indeed, Sims-Williams (1998: 517) argues that 70–80 per cent of the world's population can be said to be bilingual. Language distribution and language shift are therefore not easily explainable phenomena, and cannot be simply equated with specific groups, either in the present or in the past.

The increasing use of genetic data to identify population groups has also been subject to critique. There have been some recent attempts to map population distributions and movements using genetic data. Sokal *et al.* (1993), for example, aimed to test whether modern European allele frequencies reflect prehistoric and historic population movements of 'ethnic' units into and across Europe. They used their own 'European ethnohistory database', said to document the known locations and movements of 891 ethnic units in Europe over the last 4,000 years (!). In fact, each record in this database 'lists the name of a "gens" or tribe (or that of an archaeological horizon in the case of prehistoric records, or of a modern historical nation in the case of more recent ones' (ibid.: 57). There are obvious problems with such studies. First, they rely on an unfounded assumption of a link between 'ethnic' or 'racial' groups and genetic variation (Mirza and Dungworth 1995), and, second, they generally try to use modern data (i.e. the genome distributions of modern-day populations) as indicators of past populations (cf. Evison 2000). Such techniques, however, can have no time depth: if parallels are found between eastern England and Germany, we can have no way of knowing whether a group of people moved from Germany to Britain (or vice versa) 100, 1,000, or even 10,000 years ago, especially given that all are ultimately derived from the same parent population (Pluciennik 1996a; Sykes 2001; see also discussion in Hills 2003: 65–71). Palaeogenetic studies (using DNA derived from archaeological deposits such as burials) may give greater time resolution, but still cannot answer questions as to the (constructed and imagined) social or ethnic identities of those people (Hills 2003; Shennan 1991: 33; see also Tyrrell 2000, who deals with issues of 'body idiom', whereby physical similarities – natural or created – can become identifiers of ethnic identity in certain situations, and who also provides a useful critique of the use of skeletal non-metric traits in reconstructing ethnicity). One can also raise doubts as to the uses to which such research might be put. There are strongly voiced concerns that archaeological studies along these lines could be used to justify the exclusion of those whose 'ethnicity' is not 'European', that is whose DNA cannot be traced back to an arbitrary point in history (Mirza and Dungworth 1995: 352).

In addition, the nature of material culture distributions is being discussed more intensively. Although this discussion started over thirty years ago, with Clarke (1968) defining 'cultures' as polythetic entities, and pointing out that the distributions of archaeological types seen as representing a culture do not exactly coincide with each other (Shennan 1978: 113; see also Hodder 1978: 12–13; 1982: 6–8; and Childe 1951: 38, who also noted that the boundaries of the several fields of culture do not necessarily coincide), very little attention has been given to this issue until recently. Archaeological distributions, though, comprise an enormous variety of cross-cutting patterns, produced by different factors (Shennan 1989b: 13), and this 'untidiness' should be recognised as the essence of the situation, rather than squeezed (as Childe and others tried to do) into convenient packages of 'culture' (ibid.; see our fig. 5.3). Thus, the historical basis for the identification of 'peoples' in the past, distinguished by language, culture and 'race', is gradually being dismantled and shown to be far more fragmentary and inconclusive than was thought to be the case; and a small number of archaeologists are questioning the very

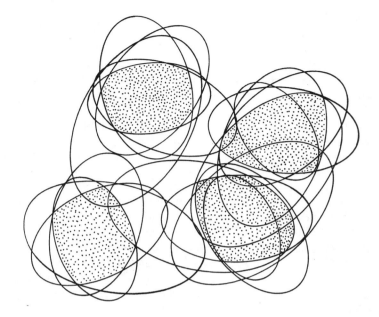

*Figure 5.3* Clarke's schematic model expressing the relationship between the distributional boundaries of the sets of cultural assemblage artefact types (enclosed areas) and (shaded) the boundaries of four cultures within a culture group. Source: Clarke (1968: fig. 72).

existence of ethnic groups as fixed, bounded entities in the past (Jones 1997: 109; Shennan 1989b: 11–14).

   This questioning of the nature of ethnic groups in the past within archaeology is rooted within a wider debate in the social sciences, especially within sociology and anthropology. These perspectives can offer a new way in which to look at ethnicity in the past. In 1969, Frederik Barth published an influential collection of papers, entitled *Ethnic Groups and Boundaries*. The essays in this volume, rather than paying attention to the differences between ethnic groups, were attempts to explore the different processes that seemed to be involved in generating and maintaining those groups (Barth 1969: 9–10). For the first time, the focus was on the ethnic group as a created idea, rather than as a natural entity. Barth (ibid.: 11) challenged the idea that ethnic groups have natural and fixed boundaries between them, generated by the isolation that ethnic characteristics (such as racial difference, cultural difference, language barriers and enmity) should entail. Whereas previous studies of ethnicity had assumed that ethnic identities were maintained as long as little or no contact existed between the groups, Barth's fieldwork indicated that, even when ethnic boundaries had people continually moving across them (people marrying into, or trading with, neighbouring groups, for example), people within the groups still maintained their ethnic identities. It also suggested that people choose ethnic markers that are relevant to them; one could not assume, for example, that linguistic or cultural differences would equate to ethnic differences. The publication of this work prompted interest in examination of the nature of the boundaries between groups and the social relations across them, and stressed that ethnic groups had to be maintained by continual expression and validation of those boundaries: if the boundaries were no longer held to be significant, the ethnic groups would cease to exist in those forms (Barth 1969: 10, 15; Olsen and Kobylínski 1991: 6). It was also significant in that it emphasised people's actions as important, rather than seeing individuals as repositories of ethnicity, which they would involuntarily express (Jenkins 1994: 197).

While Barth focused attention on the importance of the boundary with others for the identity of the group, others were prompted to ask how ethnic identities are generated, and how they are transmitted to others and maintained over time (Epstein 1978: 96). These developments matched changes in the nature of anthropological enquiry itself; rather than seeing 'societies' or 'cultures' as static, isolated and homogeneous, interest was growing in showing the flux and development, ambiguity and complexity in analyses of social worlds (Eriksen 1993: 9). In recent years, following a lengthy debate about the role of ethnicity, and whether it should be seen as an inherent 'primordial' quality, or as something designed to maximise self-interest (see Jones 1997: 56–79 for a detailed account) a partial consensus on the nature of ethnicity seems to have developed within sociology and anthropology. It is now seen primarily as a subjective phenomenon, with how you identify yourself being important, rather than how you are classified by supposedly 'objective' observers: the ethnic group is seen as a 'self-defining system', and ethnicity as a 'situational construct' (Barth 1969; Epstein 1978; Geary 1983; Jones 1997: 60). There are, however, some problems with this approach.

First, it runs the risk of reifying the ethnic group. Although we talk of an individual's ethnicity, or of an ethnic group (i.e. seeing the ethnicity as the property of the person or group, as characterising them), ethnicity makes more sense when thought of as being an aspect of a relationship (Eriksen 1993: 12). It has long been recognised that ethnic identities are created in opposition to other ethnic identities, as part of an ongoing historical process. When groups of 'us' start to identify 'them' in terms of cultural differences (often based ultimately on socially constructed notions of 'origins'), then ethnic relations are being established (Ramstad 1998: 355). Indeed, it is only when such cultural differences are perceived as important that social relationships can be said to have an ethnic element to them (Eriksen 1993: 12). These cannot be static identifications, however, as in defining oneself in relation to others, a stereotype of 'them' is being created that may well have an impact on how 'they' define themselves. If a person or group is categorised by others in the same way for long enough, they are likely to adjust their self-image in accordance (Jenkins 1994: 206). Alternatively, being categorised may serve to strengthen existing group identities through a process of resistance and reaction (ibid.: 203). This process should be seen as a dialectic, a continuing communication, rather than a simple binary opposition between two 'ethnic groups'. Seeing ethnic groups as 'self-defining systems' fails to account for the complexity of the processes of definition. A detailed example of this can be seen in Linda Colley's book *Britons* (1992), in which she argues that Protestant British identity was forged in opposition to the qualities perceived in the Catholic French during the eighteenth and nineteenth centuries, and vice versa (even today we still recognise the stereotypes of the British 'stiff upper lip' as opposed to the 'emotional' French).

Second, such a 'self-defining' perspective fails to take account of the limitations that can exist within those processes of definition. In present-day situations, ethnicity, while flexible, is not infinitely malleable. There are constraints, as well as choices, in terms of how ethnicity can be constructed (Eriksen 1993: 57). Present-day conceptions of ethnic identity, while often phrased in terms of from whom one is descended, cannot be entirely arbitrary (Bentley 1987: 36), for, in order for them to have any currency, they have to make genuine contact with people's actual experience (Eriksen 1993: 94). Ethnic names, cultural aspects, norms and many other features can be seen as an inventory on which a group may draw in order to designate its limits, but those symbols of 'identity' must be plausible to their intended audience (Elwert 1997: 256). There must also be mechanisms whereby new 'traditions' can be generated in response to changing circumstances (ibid.: 261–2; cf. Hobsbawm 1983). In addition, given the role that external definition and categorisation may play in this process, attention has to be paid to structures of power and authority and how they impact on the social construction of ethnic (and other) identities (Jenkins 1994: 219). Jenkins, for example (ibid.: 207, 217–18), has looked at how the Mapuche, an indigenous Chilean people, were affected by their categorisation by first the Spanish and then the Chileans, and how this categorisation, in turn, influenced the construction of Chilean ethnicity. Through their monopolisation of violence and resources the white Chileans were able to make their categorisation of the Mapuche count far more in the social construction of Mapuche life than would have been the case otherwise (see also Vail 1989 and Comaroff and Comaroff 1992 for examples of the potential impact of colonialism and ethnography).

Within this view of ethnicity (and other communal-type identities) as an aspect of relationships, it is the idea of the group that has to be constantly maintained (in the same way as Barth's boundaries). In its maintenance over time, it will be subject to small changes, which will lead to its gradual transformation. The interest lies, then, in how that reproduction of ethnic feelings (and thus ethnic relationships) happens in a society. One of the most powerful ways to reproduce feelings of ethnic belonging is to make use of symbolic resources, especially material culture and everyday practices. The role of dress and bodily adornment is a good example. While rarely consciously articulated, the ways in which people dress are subject to a whole range of culturally informed ideas and expectations. Cultural differences in dress are one resource that can be seized on in the articulation of ethnic difference, as can be seen with national or regional costumes, or differences in military dress between countries. The symbolic resources drawn on in the construction of ethnicity are not arbitrary. The cultural practices and representations that become objectified as symbols of ethnicity have to resonate with people's usual practices and experiences (Jones 1997: 90). Again, it is pre-existing differences that are drawn upon in the creation of ethnic feelings; it is interaction with others of a different cultural tradition (as perceived from the outside, at least) that makes people think about the observed differences in a conscious way (Eriksen 1993: 34; Jenkins 1997: 76–7; Jones 1997: 95).

In addition, obvious cultural differences and similarities may not be the only ones chosen for the articulation of ethnicity. It has been recognised that humans are adept at subtle categorisation (although it may not always conform to Western norms of classification), including the categorisation of others, and the most mundane features can be seized upon as the locus of difference. The use of different methods of washing-up, for example, is one of the ways in which Danes have been said to distinguish themselves discursively from Swedes (Linde-Laursen 1993). This example highlights the role of everyday practices and habitual aspects of behaviour in the creation of identities, to which modern anthropologists and sociologists are now paying far more attention (Jenkins 1997: 76–7; McGuire 1982: 160–61). The Danish way of washing-up is not different *in order* to distinguish it from the Swedish – they *are* different due to historically generated attitudes to hygiene, and this fact is seized on as important. Similarly, the British do not drive on the left because they are British, but it is something that marks out their everyday practice as different: someone driving off a cross-channel ferry is immediately aware of being in another country, where things are done differently (see Graves-Brown 1996: 90).

Ethnic groups do not, then, constitute a 'natural' order. They are more an idea, which is dependent on constant reiteration through both everyday actions and discursive practice, rather than a solid thing. They are dependent on social relationships that have to be continually recreated, and the boundaries of those groups thereby redefined. People can leave ethnic groups and join others, and they can hold a range of different ethnic, local or other communal identities, without the idea of the ethnic group being challenged, if enough people believe in it. Hodder's (1982) studies in the Baringo area of Kenya showed how the different tribal groups were characterised by distinctive styles of dress, especially ear decoration. People moving to different areas could, however, change their ethnic affiliation by changing their appearance (ibid.: 21). A striking example of boundary redefinition comes from Nazi Germany, where the *Volksdeutsche*, the ethnic Germans, were taken to include the Austrian *Sudeten-Deutsche* and the Mennonites of Dutch origin in Russia and the Ukraine, but to exclude the Jewish population of eastern Europe, which had been the main organiser of German schools and institutions in those areas, and whose German ethnicity had been hailed by Germany's High

Command in the First World War (Elwert 1997: 252–3). In this light, ethnic groupings, as continually imagined (though not imaginary) groupings (Jenkins 1997: 77), can have no fixed boundaries. They are not things, in the sense of solid, bounded categorisations, but are rather 'ideational beings' (Olsen and Kobylínski 1991: 12), and are a reflection of the fluid and situational aspects of individual and group identities (Jones 1997: 75). Like a reflection in water, if one delves too deeply, the image of solidity disappears (cf. Sahlins 2000: 161).

Why, then, do humans often have strong ties to groups that can be termed 'ethnic'? Ethnic attachments obviously do not have the same relevance and emotional force in all societies at all times (Jenkins 1997: 77), yet, in certain circumstances, they can be very real, and very important. Part of the explanation may be that ethnic classifications are convenient ways of ordering our world. Being able to group others through the use of stereotypes (in the sense of the application of standardised notions of the cultural distinctiveness of a group) helps to create order, and enables people to know how to behave towards those others (Eriksen 1993: 23, 60). This is in spite of the fact that actual inter-ethnic relations may well diverge dramatically from those stereotypes (ibid.: 24). Such categorisations may be especially useful in urban multi-ethnic settings (where, incidentally, most anthropological fieldwork on ethnicity takes place), where people tend to become more self-conscious with regard to their origins, and where ethnic identities acquire an everyday relevance (ibid.: 80–81).

Another partial explanation is that the roots of ethnic identity are often laid down during childhood, and this is how it can acquire its potent emotional charge (Epstein 1978: xiv). Ethnicity is something that often gets learnt from an early age, when through primary socialisation a child learns who they are and what this means in terms of behaviour and self-esteem (Jenkins 1994: 204). It is thus something that can be called upon in interactive situations to defend the individual or social group against outsiders, albeit in a symbolic way. Yet, we must beware of mistaking description for explanation. Seeing ethnic groups in the present does not mean that the existence of those ethnic groups is the cause of, or reason for, conflict or difference. Although previous conflicts in Bosnia or Somalia, for example, may look as if they were due to 'natural' hatred between groups, the violence is organised, requires logistics and planning, and would seem to have more to do with the role of warlords or political entrepreneurs than vague historical traditions (Elwert 1997: 251).

The role of history, and interpretation of the past does, however, seem fundamental to the creation and maintenance of ethnic feelings and identities, for a number of reasons. Notions of shared origins are usually very important for ethnic identities. This may be partly related to modern nationalist constructions of ethnicity, which stress the importance of blood relations. This means that interpretations of history become important to ideologies that are trying to justify, maintain and strengthen particular ethnic boundaries (Eriksen 1993: 59): 'Mass-produced accounts of "our people" and "our culture" are important tools in the fashioning of an ethnic identity with a presumed cultural continuity in time' (ibid.: 91).

Indeed, the writing or narrating of history has a particular importance for the creation of ethnic identities. By selectively stressing certain values, they enable people to identify positively with those they see as their forebears (Epstein 1978: xiii–xiv). However, given the potential number of ancestors that any given person has, this is necessarily a very partial selection. Eriksen (1993: 71) has pointed out that while North Americans often trace their ancestry back to the European aristocracy, they make little mention of the manual workers, thieves or prostitutes who would also have inhabited their family trees. This, essentially, is ethnic history writ small: in writing the history of a 'people' a selection is made of innumerable historical facts or myths, and these are rearranged into a narrative structure in order to legitim-ate the current supposed existence of that 'people'. Through literacy people can create 'authorised' versions of history (Eriksen 1993; cf. Collins and Blot 2003). As Smith (1984: 119) has noted: 'since myths and memories are capable of infinite reinterpretation and multiform dissemination, the educa-tor-intellectuals, especially historians and linguists, help to "recreate" a sense of ethnicity out of the chronicles, traditions, memories and artefacts at their disposal' (cf. Amory 1994; Geary 1983; Gutiérrez 1997: 170; James 1989: 47; Jones 1998; Lucy 2000a; Moreland 2000). This emphasis on blood ties and ancestry has sometimes been assumed to be an inherent facet of human nature (cf. Smith 1986), but the possibility must be entertained that it is something that first arose with literacy, and was elaborated through the nationalistic uses of the past in the nineteenth and twentieth centuries. As Banks has noted, 'the manifestations of ethnicity we study today contain within them the ghosts of previous academic formulations. In the modern world ethnicity is indissolubly linked to nationalism and race, to ideas about normative political situations and relations, and to ideas about descent and blood' (Banks 1996: 189; see also Curta 2001; Díaz-Andreu 1998a; Geary 2002). For example, Rowlands (1998: 262), commenting on Hodder's work in the Baringo district, which showed that ethnic boundaries need not corres-pond to cultural similarities and differences, argues that this may be due to the ethnic/tribal divisions in East Africa mostly being colonial inventions. He thus suggests that there is no reason to suppose that these boundaries would correspond with more long-term cultural and linguistic continuities.

We also need to think about the scale at which identities are now created. Increasingly, global transport, media and maps have revolutionised ways that communities can be recognised. Similarly, uniform educational and adminis-trative systems covering large areas serve to facilitate the development of abstract identification with people one will never meet (Eriksen 1993: 91, 106). These modern factors have also affected how both nationalism and ethnicity are constructed (a point that the NATO bombing of Serbian broad-casting centres in 1999 makes all too clearly). Thus, we may have to allow for the possibility that ethnicity as we understand it today may be very different from how it may have operated in the past: the emphasis on ancestry and blood relations may be a new one. We should also be aware that such communal identities can operate on many different levels. Present-day ethnic groups can encompass many hundreds of thousands of people who, through education and communication, all feel themselves to be members, yet will always remain strangers. In the past, especially the prehistoric past, groups of such size seem highly unlikely, and we should probably be looking for groupings on a much smaller scale. The nature of contact between groups in the past would also seem to be important: we might well suspect different feelings of 'belongingness' expressed towards those one lives with, works with and sees everyday, as opposed to those one may only meet once a month or once a year. The definitions of those groups will also be important; the extended family will experience contact with other groups in a different way from those who define themselves by their occupation or exploitation of a limited territory. Perhaps we can start to explore different sorts of communal identities in the past: territorial aspects, based on where people lived, and social aspects, based on where they came from (or at least imagined they did).

Ethnicity, of course, cannot be teased out from the other strands that interact to form social identities. Members of 'ethnic' groups, depending on age, sex, class etc., experience ethnicity differently, leading to a diverse range that casts doubt on any uniform 'ethnicity', and which thus cannot be studied in isolation from other aspects of identity or social belonging (Mirza and Dungworth 1995: 349). Eriksen (1991: 139) has shown in his studies on Mauritius and Trinidad how 'one is never simply "male" or "middle-class": one is *Indian* male or *Coloured* middle-class'. Larick (1986) has demonstrated how information about age is transmitted alongside ethnic traits in the spear style of the Liokup of northern Kenya, and how such material culture is used in an active way: a young male may manipulate his position amongst his peers by owning a specific form of spear. New spear styles are often borrowed from neighbouring, more successful ethnic groups (ibid.: 276–8). This serves to make the point that ethnicity is often interwoven with questions of dominance, hierarchy and social stratification (Epstein 1978: xiii; Jenkins 1997: 73; Jones 1997: 96), and that gender divisions are also enmeshed in the creation of ethnic groups (Jones 1997: 85). Similarly O'Brien (1994) has shown, through the study of a village in French Catalonia, how gender can influence ethnic identity, with male identities staying more or less constant, while females shift between French and Catalan identities (and languages) as they go through life, and how, through their raising of children and grandchildren, they help to perpetuate this difference.

To summarise, ethnicity should not be seen either as a primordial and inherent aspect of humanity, or as instrumental and infinitely malleable. It is an aspect of social relationships, whereby cultural differences can be identified (and therefore propagated) at a discursive level as indications of ethnic divisions. Ethnic feelings are always generated in opposition to others, and the use of stereotypes plays a strong role in this. The idea that people belong to 'an ethnic group' is thus something that must be constantly maintained through the articulation of both difference and similarity. Present-day constructions of ethnicity have also been strongly affected by the role that nationalism has played in the construction of national and sub-national communities, with the expectation that everyone has an ethnicity, that a person's ethnicity corresponds largely to the nation-state in which they were raised, and that it should be objectively identifiable, through appearance, language, habits, etc. This will not have been true for the majority of human history. Rather, when we think about ethnicity (or more likely, communal identities) in the past, we should envisage a range of different identities, from kin-based ties to large communal groupings, from weakly felt identities to those that people are willing to kill or die for. We can expect that individuals would have had a range of such identities, and that these would have been emphasised differently depending on the situation. As an aspect of social identity, ethnicity would have been expressed through social interactions, and articulated through such things as behaviour, everyday practice, use of space, architecture and landscape, and personal appearance. However, before such interactions can start to be investigated by archaeologists, an adequate consideration of material culture, which sees it as both actively used by people and capable of taking on diverse meanings and significances, needs to be in place.

## Ethnicity as cultural identity: archaeology and material culture

Ethnicity (feelings of social belonging based on culturally constructed notions of shared origins) and other types of communal identities (those based on territory, for example) are aspects of social practice, which have to be continually constructed and generated, and are most effective when this is done through the use of shared ways of doing things. Studying those identities, therefore, involves paying attention to the uses of material culture in social interactions. Anthropological examples can suggest how material culture may become influential in the articulation of modern-day ethnicities. This has been demonstrated by work in Papua New Guinea by Mackenzie (1991: 136–41) who has studied the ways in which *bilums*, the ubiquitous string bags, are used in structuring social relations. The Telefol women acknowledge their cultural affinity with other Mountain Ok women, by saying they all make 'one kind' of *bilum*. However, the different groups elaborate their bags with distinctive stylistic features, thereby exaggerating the uniqueness of the product, and confirming the sense of belonging to one's own group. These identifications are not static, however. The opening up of the region with the building of airstrips has led to an accelerated diffusion of *bilum* styles, and increased blurring in the indication of tribal distinctions. This, in turn, is reflecting in part wider political processes that are pressing for the recognition of a united Min identity. It should be remembered, though, that as well as expressing ethnic relations, the *bilum* also has the potential to evoke culturally and contextually appropriate aspects of woman-ness (ibid.: 145).

Archaeologists too have started to investigate the role of material culture in these interactional spheres. This approach has its origins in the afore-mentioned 'style debate', in which several (mainly North American) archae-ologists argued over the communicative role of material culture. One of the main participants in this debate was Sackett, who in 1977 (and still in 1990), argued that style (i.e. the form and decorative aspects of material culture) was a passive aspect of artefacts, intended to communicate group identity or relations to others (see also Wobst 1977). The idea lying behind this view obviously relates to the 'material culture as text' perspective, as if it were a language just needing decoding, which can directly reflect various social or cultural phenomena, such as the 'ethnic group' (Conkey 1990: 9). The main problem with this argument was that it saw style first as an end-product – there was little attention paid to the processes of production or manufacture of material culture – but also that style came to be seen as possessed by the object itself; there was little consideration of the role of living human beings in the interactions made possible by those artefacts (Boast 1997: 181–2). As Conkey (1990: 10) has said, 'we too easily overlooked the contexts within which the variation arose, how the artifacts in question were used, and that they were a part of the production of meaning to prehistoric peoples just as much as being a part of the way we produce meanings about the past'.

We see more potential in approaches that take account of all the stages of production (sometimes termed 'chaîne opératoire'), including usage, rather than just looking at static aspects of, for example, decoration (cf. Edmonds 1990, drawing on Conkey 1990: 12–13; Dietler and Herbich 1998; Lemon-nier 1993: 2–3; Mauss 1979 [1950]). Within this perspective, the know-ledge drawn on in the creation and use of artefacts (and ways of doing things, such as food preparation) is constituted in social and historical worlds, and this knowledge is generally context specific, and not necessarily explicitly discussed (Edmonds 1990). These ideas have major implications for discus-sions of ethnicity in archaeology. Previously, it was thought that ethnicity could be inferred from artefacts by looking at those very static, decorative features (those features that, for example, distinguish a Beaker from an early medieval cremation urn). Within this perspective however: 'not only decora-tive patterns or secondary aspects of shape are used to define one's status or ethnic identity, but also the use of given artefacts or entire processes of production' (Lemonnier 1993: 20). Material culture is thus actively involved in social practice (and, indeed, social practice cannot exist without material culture). Social practice involving material culture is how the idea of the group (whether that be social, familial, ethnic or other) becomes articulated: it is not something that can be 'read off' from the artefactual evidence, without regard for its contexts of use and production.

From this perspective, it is thus important to employ subtle analyses of material culture. Díaz-Andreu (1998a), for example, argues against the use of Llíria pottery as a diagnostic type for defining Iron Age Edetanian territory and ethnicity (inferred mainly from classical sources) in eastern Iberia (fig. 5.4). She points out that when the context of use of this pottery is examined, it appears to have a largely aristocratic character, a highly limited span of use, and is associated particularly with male spheres. She also notes a double standard in its interpretation: when found within the supposed Edetanian territory it is used as a diagnostic type for ethnic definition, but when found outside, it is explained as the result of elite exchange. This pottery type should, instead, be viewed as a resource that is drawn on in the daily recreation of identities, rather than a simplistic 'ethnic' indicator. Conversely, Frankel (2000) demonstrates different social practices (reflecting distinct *habitus*) employed in Bronze Age, as opposed to Chalcolithic, societies in Cyprus, and argues that, given the chronological overlap in evidence, they represent different ethnicities, contact between which eventually resulted in acculturation of the indigenous community, without any obvious conflict.

Re-examinations of late Iron Age and Roman material in Britain have come to similar conclusions regarding the active use of material culture in the creation of cultural identities. Willis (1994) argues against the assumptions often made about the significance of Roman imports found on native Iron Age sites, urging that the contexts of use and re-use have to be examined in a subtle manner before conclusions can be drawn about the social impact of this material. Hill (1995) highlights that the traditional picture of Iron Age 'tribes' in Britain in fact masks a range of regional variations, with some areas such as Dorset, Norfolk and Cambridgeshire developing and then maintaining strong 'regional identities' for many generations. This should not be perceived as 'backwardness' in the context of adoption of Roman or Gallic material culture in other areas, but rather as a deliberate creation of strong local identities because of, and through, regular inter-regional contacts (cf. Collis 2003 and James 1999 for critiques of the identities traditionally termed 'Celtic' in these British Iron Age societies).

Lucy (2000a) demonstrated that the material culture previously identified as 'Anglian', 'Saxon' and 'Jutish' in fifth- and sixth-century eastern England did not correspond in its geographical distribution to the later kingdoms of those names; it is argued that these 'Anglo-Saxon' identities were in fact a later creation (see also Hills 2003). Moreland (2000), arguing along similar lines, demonstrates how this created ethnicity was in fact one that was restricted to an elite: it was a status distinction, allied to an ethnic (but not a racial) one. Yorke (2000) also argued for the importance of political allegiance in the creation of ethnic identities at this time. Similar arguments are now being advanced regarding the 'Viking' settlement of England (cf. papers in Hadley 1999 and for supposed Irish migrations into northern and western Britain, Campbell 2001). Even the cultural construction of the 'British' is

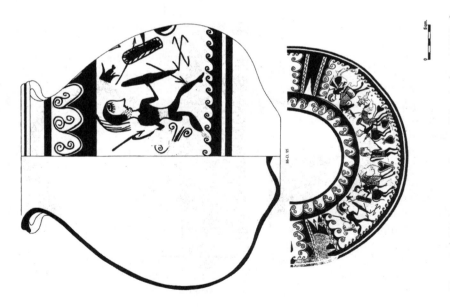

*Figure 5.4* Llíria pottery. Source: Díaz-Andreu (1998: figs 2 and 3).

0 5cm.

now being studied from a more critical archaeological perspective (cf. papers in Lawrence 2003).

Another aspect to the analyses of the contexts of use and production of material culture is the way in which textiles and artefacts can be combined to produce costumes. For example, the early Bronze Age burials of the north German plain give evidence for great similarities in regional traditions, dress and appearance. By the middle Bronze Age, however, despite evidence of increased contact between groups and of a growth in trade and movement between areas, costume shows much clearer distinctions and the development of regional divergence (Rowlands 1998: 263), suggesting perhaps that these regional identities are the product of contact, rather than isolation.

Local and regional variations of mortuary ritual also suggest the active uses that can be made both of artefacts and of 'ways of doing'. Lucy (1998) demonstrated that what had previously been assumed to be a fairly homogeneous cultural distribution, the use of the 'Anglian' burial rite in East Yorkshire in the fifth to seventh centuries AD, was in fact much more complex. Variations were evident, even between neighbouring cemeteries, in the ways that people were treated in death. Age and sex were demonstrated to play a strong role in the structuring of the burial rite, and it was argued that a deliberate selection was being made from available material culture in order to facilitate the marking out of differences between social groups within communities. The suggestion was made that this evidence represented not an 'invasion' from the continent (as previously assumed on the basis of the introduction of new material culture types), but a continuing recreation and rearticulation of identities through the burial rite that fed back into the structuring of those societies.

Consumption of various foods, and different ways of preparing them can be one of the factors that emphasise communal similarity and difference. Hastorf (1998a) cites ethnographic evidence that in Peru, specific varieties of peppers are associated with certain female lineages (cf. Shipek 1989: 163 who cites evidence that some tree species can be used to identify the territory of indigenous south Californian residents). Hastorf (1998b: 779–80) has intriguingly suggested a major role for plants in the early development of notions of territoriality. By nurturing plants in a specific locale, that area could become associated with certain people and groups, thereby creating some of the conditions for the development of named territories. Food and its associated activities (processing, consumption) could thus become social markers used in group affiliation. She uses the example of the Inka state's use of maize and its preparations as the 'symbolic food of the empire', with those products being used at every political and religious gathering. Others have also explored the potential of food preparation and consumption in the creation and maintenance of political and ethnic (as well as other) identities (cf. Hamilakis 1999). This area would seem ripe for further study, particularly in combination with new scientific techniques, such as trace element and stable isotope analyses of human bone, which can reveal dietary patterns, and thus contribute to this detailed, contextual approach.

The bone-chemistry analysis of African-American adults from a slave cemetery at the former Remley Plantation near Charleston, South Carolina by Crist (Crist 1995), for example, suggested significant differences in the nature of the diet of slaves on this plantation than suggested by contemporary documentary evidence. Documents of the period suggest that slaves would have eaten a homogeneous diet, provided by a centralised kitchen. The bone-analysis, however, suggested that diet differed between age and sex groups, suggesting variation in the diet, with some exploitation of vegetable and marine resources. In another study Schurr (1992) analysed a sample of burials from a Middle Mississippian civic-ceremonial centre in southwestern Indiana (c. AD 1200–1450), both in terms of bone chemistry, and in terms of mortuary ritual. Several individuals were found not to exhibit traces of the usual maize diet at the Angel site, and it was noted that they were all found to have differential treatment in death. Interestingly, they were all female, and the author suggests that the Angel population was augmented by females from another population (i.e. non-maize agriculturalists) who, in turn, had their foreign origins recognised in their mortuary treatment. Such rich analyses can only serve to better inform our interpretations of the intersection of ethnic and communal identities with age, gender and status. More recently, Barrett *et al.* (2001) have demonstrated how a more maritime-oriented subsistence strategy was introduced to Viking Age northern Scotland, presumably by Norse colonists.

A key recent development in these scientific approaches is the ability to identify place of childhood residence through the analysis of oxygen and strontium stable isotope ratios. Price *et al.* (2001) and Bentley *et al.* (2003) have used strontium isotopes to demonstrate a complex interrelationship between migration and acculturation in the spread of *Linearbandkeramik* farming in Neolithic central Europe; similar debates are now dominating discussions of the Mesolithic–Neolithic transition in northern Europe (cf. Milner *et al.* 2004; Richards *et al.* 2003) and are even creeping into the earlier Mesolithic and Palaeolithic (cf. Bergsvik 2003). This technique would seem to be of particular value in those areas of archaeology where the material culture can be dated closely enough to allow potential identification of those who would traditionally be thought of as first-generation immigrants into a new area. Initial explorations of early Anglo-Saxon cemeteries in this light (cf. Budd *et al.* 2004) are already suggesting that although this period appears to see a high degree of population mobility, those who can be identified skeletally as immigrants from across the English Channel are not those who are being interred with stereotypical 'Anglo-Saxon' assemblages (fig. 5.5).

Architecture, and the structuring of space can also be used to emphasise communal similarity and difference, at both conscious and unconscious levels. Blake (1999) focuses on the *nuraghi* (conical or sub-rectangular stone towers) of the Sardinian Bronze Age as meaningful spaces that would have helped affirm a 'Nuragic' way of life. In the late Bronze Age and early Iron Age, divergence in the constructional styles of the *nuraghi* are argued to be

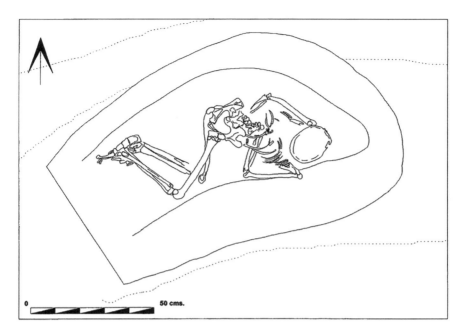

*Figure 5.5* Unfurnished grave 166 from West Heslerton (Yorkshire), identified as an immigrant from Scandinavia through analysis of stable isotopes. Source: Haughton and Powlesland (1999: 216).

evidence for social hierarchies, while a more diverse ceramic repertoire is interpreted as signifying that internal social identities had become more influential than cultural identity in determining action; in other words, that as that cultural identity had become more secure it had slipped into the background of social interactions (see also Bukach 2003 on passage-graves in the British Channel Islands and Robb 2001 on Malta's Neolithic 'temples').

In a similar vein, Donley-Reid (1990) looked at the origins of Swahili settlements in East Africa, arguing that there can be no simplistic correlation between ethnic identity and architectural styles, but that the contexts of the building and its uses must be taken into account. She argues that Swahili settlements were originally founded in the eighth and ninth centuries AD by foreign traders, who drew on aspects of Islamic culture in a deliberate attempt to create power for themselves. Over time, inter-marriage created a new ethnic identity, based on a combination (or recreation) of Arab, Persian, Indian and African elements. While the study is rooted in the debate over the 'African' versus the 'Arab' origins for the houses and settlements, the answers are not so simple or clear-cut.

Garman (1998) hypothesises about the architectural proximity of slaves and their owners in southern New England in the seventeenth and eighteenth centuries. He shows how specific social relations and the owners' dependence on slaves for certain forms of economic production would have affected their interactions, and he argues that neither the concepts of 'acculturation' nor 'domination/resistance' are adequate to explain these. Rather he uses the term 'resistant accommodation', showing through the use of probate inventories how semi-private space was ceded to African-American slaves as part of this interaction.

Several archaeologists have focused on 'social boundaries' in their attempts to understand the role of material culture in both creating and transforming social relations. For example, Wells (1992) in a study of relations across the Roman-'Germanic' border during the Roman Empire stresses the importance of examining how those Roman goods that crossed the border were used by the native communities (whereas previous studies had assumed that Rome was the dominant power in the relations, and that therefore the native communities would wish to emulate them). Using four small case studies, he demonstrates how Roman objects can become appropriated into different social practices; some of them of an everyday nature, and some of them involved in overt demonstrations of status. He argues that these native elites were not trying to 'become Roman', as previously has been argued, but that they were using those imports to assert their status (perhaps contested) and express new identities connected with Rome, for their own advantage in their local communities. Along similar lines, Hunter (2001) re-examined Roman material found on native settlement sites in Scotland, and demonstrated how its use was incorporated into local practices, rather than it representing cultural domination, as previously assumed. Wells (2001) has since developed this argument for continental Europe, showing how the 'German' created the 'Roman', as much as vice versa.

Indeed, sophisticated understandings of Romanisation, and of the creation of new late Roman and antique cultural identities, are now emerging, both for Britain and the Continent (cf. Hill 2001; Woolf 1998; papers in Gardner 1999; Laurence and Berry 1998; Pohl 1998; Wells 1999; and Lyons and Papadopoulos 2002 for a broad range of case studies), and we can expect to see further developments of these arguments as the results from the sophisticated studies of material culture and skeletal analysis described above become more widely disseminated.

## Conclusions

The studies briefly mentioned above serve to emphasise the point that archaeology needs to start approaching ethnicity from a different direction. In the past we have assumed we knew how it worked; because we have ideas about how our present ethnic identities are constituted, these have been projected into the past. Instead, archaeology needs to start by identifying people who chose to act or look the same. It can then start to explore the contexts in which they did so, and whether these changed through time. It also needs to explore similarities and differences in more depth: are all cultural practices the same, or just some? We need to start exploring the construction of communal identities in the past, rather than just observing cultural differences and assuming we know what they represent. New scientific approaches offer the possibility of identifying migrants through analysis of their skeletal remains: these results can be employed in contextual analyses that can examine the contribution of incoming people and ideas to the transformation of current identities.

The solution must lie in revising the scales at which archaeologists work. Given that from a 'bird's eye view' the construction of ethnicity is likely to be manifested as multiple overlapping boundaries made up by various representations of cultural difference (Jones 1996: 70–71), it is little use having such an elevated viewpoint that none of the patterning can be observed at all (i.e. by trying to trace distributions of artefacts over whole continents). By working at a local level, employing detailed analyses of data in order to tease out the complex interrelationships of artefacts and the minutiae of spatial patterning, archaeologists can at least start to identify the contexts in which social identities would have been recreated through everyday practices. Thus we would agree with Pluciennik (1996b: 43): 'we do not have to subsume variability of material culture, regional histories, languages and economies into one grand narrative. . . . I would find complexity more convincing than simplicity'. So would we. Perhaps when we start to examine the detailed local contexts of use and deposition of artefacts that previously would have been interpreted as evidence for 'migration' or 'invasion' we will start to identify subtle local variations pointing to the appropriation of items of material culture for particular purposes (Niles 1997). It is at that scale that we may be able to identify certain patterns of use that point to the deliberate articulation of cultural differences, but it cannot be achieved at a coarser level of resolution. It is also in the historical depth that archaeology provides that we may be able to trace the formation of new types of identities, through the use of material culture. We must always remember, however, as Maceachern (1998) has reminded us, that ethnicity may not have been as relevant to people in the past as it seems to be in the present, and that any patterning at this detailed level that we do discern may be due to other types of communal identities, such as familial lineages or territorial groupings, rather than to anything we, from our modern perspective, might recognise as ethnically based.

# 6   The archaeology of religion

*David N. Edwards*

In the early years of the twenty-first century religion is again commonly a basis for intense solidarities, interwoven with, and often fundamental to, national and ethnic identities. If the role of religion in the West may have appeared to be of declining importance during the twentieth century (Towler 1974: vii), we now have plentiful reminders that such secularisation was by no means universal; multi-religious ethnic groups appear to be rare (Enloe 1980). On the other hand, in twentieth-century Japan, in some ways a byword for secular modernity, we encounter the paradox where the sum total of Japanese adherents to the main religions of Shinto, Buddhism and Christianity reputedly exceeds 200 per cent of the current population. Individuals are active in more than one religious tradition, while several traditions may be combined in one religious activity; funerals are commonly Buddhist while births and marriages are Shinto. We find a 'secular' country that is also home to many tens of thousands of shrines.

While religion is now so familiar as an essential element in the construction of social identities, archaeology has tended to be uncertain about how it may be approached (Renfrew 1994; Whitley and Keyser 2003). An interest in 'primitive religion' was, however, an integral part of philosophy and the developing social sciences of the nineteenth century. For Durkheim, Weber, Spencer and even Marx, the religious ideologies and institutions of both present and more ancient peoples were an integral part of their investigations. For Feuerbach, 'religion is man's earliest and also indirect form of self-knowledge' (1957: 13). Despite this common perception that religion was indeed of central importance in defining humanity and human history as a whole, archaeology is a discipline that rarely claims to 'study religion', leaving that to anthropology, sociology, psychology, comparative religion, history of religion, and, of course, theology. Archaeology itself has no theory of religion and when theoretical stances are taken, these look to other areas of the social sciences.

Other disciplines have taken their own lines of development, for archaeology to follow. Sociology has perhaps seen religion relegated to a rather peripheral position although maintaining an interest in what may be seen as peculiarly Western concerns with Christianity and secularism. Anthropology has looked further afield, but often with an emphasis on the more exotic manifestations of what may be seen as religious behaviour, in 'magic' and 'witchcraft' for example. Tensions between different approaches have exposed a plethora of issues that are relevant to archaeology, although all too often not adequately confronted. How may we conceive of, and define 'religion' itself. To what extent can it meaningfully be classified as a separate field of human activity? We are also drawn towards the ideas and practical attitudes by which people made sense of their societies and of their world as they experienced it, forcing us to confront views of the world that may be fundamentally foreign to us. This chapter will explore some of the broader issues that arise when we consider ancient religion and religious identities, with brief references to studies in other fields of research that may challenge and inspire, with a deliberate emphasis on material from outside the Western experience of religion, which tends to dominate archaeological discourse.

## Archaeology and religion

Fragmentation and uncertainty are key features of archaeologies of religion. Archaeologists, potentially well placed to contemplate the long-term, have been reluctant to create their own master narratives concerning the development of religion (but see Parker Pearson 1999, 2001). There has also been a widespread scepticism about the possibilities of studying ancient religion, at least where conceived of as reconstructing ancient belief-systems, apparent for example, within British archaeology in Grahame Clarke's early (Clarke 1939) work and more famously expressed in Christopher Hawkes' 'ladder of inference' (Hawkes 1954). Perceived problems in recognising or explaining 'irrational' religious behaviour on the basis of material remains may also be linked to intellectual traditions of nineteenth-century scepticism and secularism, and in many cases overt antipathy to religion; essentially unsympathetic to the wide range of the human religious experience through time and space. Intellectual currents in the later twentieth century were commonly more interested in Marxist concepts of ideology and their relation to power structures (e.g. Miller and Tilley 1984; Parker Pearson 1984).

Elsewhere in the social sciences, important conceptual divisions have arisen, for example, between the 'tribal religions', studied by anthropologists, and the 'historical religions' studied by others, often with very different theoretical treatments. Very similar divisions have arisen within archaeology. Archaeologists are most confident in dealing with historical religions. There are strong biases in the West towards the archaeology of Christianity (e.g. Blair and Pyrah 1996; Frend 1996; Platt 1987), as well as important specialist literatures devoted mainly to the 'World Religions' of Islam, Judaism, Buddhism and Hinduism (e.g. Barnes 1995; Chakrabarti 2001; Hachlili 2001; Insoll 1999, 2001a, 2004). These may in turn coincide with divisions within the discipline along the lines of area studies (e.g. south Asian studies), as well as other specific fields of research concerned with the religions of, for example, pre-colonial Meso- and South American societies, the classical world, the ancient Near East or ancient Egypt, all areas with a strong textual/historical component.

The major World Religions may lay claim to an ancestry of perhaps 3,000 years or so. Some might claim an even more ancient and prehistoric ancestry for Hinduism, as indeed for a non-World Religion such as Shinto (Smart 1998). However, attempts to bridge the divide between the historical and World Religions and what went before, or to contextualise them within wider streams of religious experience, have been limited. Compared with its profile in historical times, religion appears to be a more limited resource in earlier periods. The archaeology of the preliterate and the 'tribal' is commonly the preserve of a different set of practitioners ('prehistorians'). The potentially 'religious' tends to be approached rather differently, while theoretical bases often also appear uncertain. 'That the advent of literacy and state systems has had important implications with respect to the nature and organization of religious systems no one would deny; that it merits a different theoretical approach is questionable. But this is what has occurred' (B. Morris 1987: 2).

In such contexts we are concerned much more with something apparently different: 'ritual' practice, and its identification in the archaeological record (e.g. Garwood *et al.* 1991; Gibson and Simpson 1998, and in some circumstances, the archaeology of cult, see Renfrew 1985; *Journal of Prehistoric Religion passim*). Outside the cult monuments and shrines (fig. 6.1), religion becomes more obscure and gives rise to speculation on the possible religious significance of wider cultural phenomena (e.g. Alexander 1979). There are also more specific contributions concerning more 'primitive' forms of belief, such as shamanism (e.g. Price 2001) while the 'sacred' may be invoked in exploring ancient landscapes (e.g. Ashmore and Knapp 1999; Bauer 1998; Carmichael *et al.* 1994).

A more reflexive relationship between religion and archaeology has also emerged in recent decades, both in religious claims of 'indigenous' peoples within archaeological arenas, and as part of changing social and political agendas within the wider world, thus raising new ethical issues (Bergquist 2001). The religious claims of indigenous peoples have redefined the bounds of archaeology in many parts of the world. In North America this has been especially evident in terms of the 'repatriation' of Native American remains (Bray 2001; Fforde *et al.* 2002). Archaeology may be finding new ways of operating that move beyond conventional oppositions of secular and sacred, science and religion (e.g. Dowdall and Parrish 2003). Archaeology has also become directly implicated in political controversies, notably the Ayodhya confrontation in India between Muslim and Hindu claims on the sacred space occupied by the Babri Masjid (Rao 1999). There are also new relationships emerging between a wide spectrum of 'New Age' (or indeed 'Old'?) religions and the practice of archaeology, seen both in the changing ways in which archaeological objects, as well as sites and monuments are treated. What is thought to be a Bronze Age religious structure – 'Sea Henge' – may be

*Figure 6.1* Hindu shrine at Tilaurakot (Nepal), reputedly the Buddha's childhood
home. (Photo courtesy of Ruth Young.)

claimed as a site of religious significance by modern 'pagans', amongst others
(Pryor 2002).

Both within historic and prehistoric contexts, issues of religion tend to be
approached in relatively restricted ways. The particularist nature of much of
what passes as an archaeology of religion – 'excavation reports of sanctuaries
or descriptions of specific groups of votive offerings' (Derks 1998: 11) – tends
to have limited points of contact with research that may be concerned with
the 'social' and especially with the role of religion in the construction of social
identities, or its relationship with power. Its material manifestations may be
described and analysed, but more searching questions are less commonly
asked. An enduring visibility of the temples and sacred writing of ancient
Egypt might make us suppose, like Herodotus (II.37), that the ancient Egyptians were 'religious to excess, beyond any other nation in the world'. However, the abundant studies of temple reliefs and texts are rarely complemented
by the question 'how religious were the Ancient Egyptians?' (Kemp 1995).

## Confronting religion

Before further exploring some archaeological treatments of religion, some
relatively fundamental issues need to be addressed. How indeed may we
define the religious, an issue commonly avoided by archaeologists (e.g. Insoll
2001b)? Was ancient religion and religious experience necessarily different

from that of more modern times? How might this relate to notions of the 'sacred' and 'profane' and how may these be distinguished?

That religion might not be such an unproblematic concept, as early social scientists may have supposed, has become more evident with their wider experience of the world, through time and space. To what extent is religion a distinctive arena of human practice and analytically separable from other forms of activity? To what extent does it, and has it existed as a transcultural and transhistorical phenomenon? Anthropologists would suggest not. As Talal Asad has argued, religion is very much a cultural construction: 'there cannot be a universal definition of religion not only because its constituent elements and relationships are culturally specific, but because that definition itself is the historical product of discursive processes' (1993: 29). This is also the case with other related categories. What distinctions may be made between religion and magic, or between witchcraft and sorcery? What do we mean by 'pilgrimage'? Most can only be understood within their own terms of reference. In studying African religions, for example, the common cross-cultural use of terms such as 'magic' or 'witchcraft' often conceals the fact that the concepts to which they are applied actually have nothing in common (MacGaffey 1980).

Can Confucianism or Taoism, for example, be considered 'religions'? In the late nineteenth century, when the future of religion and moral education was being debated in Japan, Confucianism was generally excluded from debates concerned with religious direction (Luhmer 1990). However, with their specific use of symbols, special loci of activity and the existence of specialised personnel, they certainly have many of the characteristics of what is commonly considered religion. It would also be manifest archaeologically. How may African magico-religious practices be classified when encountered in the archaeology of African and Afro-American slaves in the Americas? How may they relate to the construction of new identities constrained by slavery (Russell 1997; Singleton 1995; Wilkie 1997)?

Was prehistoric religion different (fig. 6.2)? Early archaeologies of prehistoric religion followed nineteenth-century evolutionist speculations on 'primitive religion'. The primitive might be found in many guises, for example in Hegel's 'religions of nature', or in 'fetishism' and 'animism' or 'totemism', following a gradual progress from primitive to complex (see Parker Pearson 2001 for a useful review), although with the possibility that within the world of 'primitive' cultures then being discovered by the West 'survivals' of earlier stages of human history might be found. Notable amongst theorists were Tylor (1871), who emphasised animism as the basis of religion, and Herbert Spencer who identified ancestor worship as 'the root of every religion' (Spencer 1876: 411). The complex was commonly taken to lie in Judaeo-Christian beliefs, and strong notions of progress may be seen for example in Otto's 'Idea of the Holy' (or 'Sacred'), moving towards Christianity that 'stands out in complete superiority over all sister religions' (Otto 1950: 142). Similar approaches have remained prominent until relatively

*Figure 6.2* Places of power? Bronze Age rock drawings on the Nile (Third Cataract, northern Sudan). (Photo by David N. Edwards.)

recently; Wallace's (1966) schema identified four stages of religious activity from Individual, Shamanistic, Communal and Ecclesiastical.

The separation of the sacred from the profane, which lay at the heart of Durkheim's definition of religion, has proved to be of considerable analytical value, and much used by later writers (e.g. Eliade 1958). Reappearing in other guises, as in distinctions between the 'mystical' and the 'empirical', this remains very familiar to archaeologists, if now being subjected to some critical examination. Emanating from many of these early speculations are also currents of thought that would like to see a deep religious and symbolic content of the 'primitive world view', maintaining the 'myth of the pious primitive' (Douglas 1975: 81). Durkheim, a militant atheist, observed that 'originally . . . everything social is religious; the two worlds are synonymous. Then, little by little, political, economic, scientific functions free themselves from the religious function. . . . God who was at first present in all human relations, progressively withdraws from them' (Durkheim 1912 [1947]: 169); a view that must strike a chord with many post-processualist archaeologists. Ethnographic experiences warn us that familiar oppositions between the 'sacred' and 'profane' may not always be altogether satisfactory as a universal (e.g. Holy 1991). One way forward may be to question the usefulness of the boundaries that we erect between sacred, ritual and secular practices in archaeological arenas (e.g. Brück 1999). How certain types of practices are defined is ultimately less important than what they may tell us about how people relate to the world and to each other.

To what extent should we be concerned with 'systems of ideas', which might be equated with, for example, a theology (MacGaffey 1972)? In an African context, Vansina (1973) was very sceptical about maintaining the notion of religious 'systems', finding considerable problems in defining non-literate religions as a system of ideas, as opposed to defining them as systems of behaviour and practice.

If we are concerned more with practice, we need to consider further the relationship between religion and ritual. 'The Tio had no sacred books, no dogma, no catechism, no compulsion to believe the same things as long as they participated fully in the same rituals' (ibid.: 227). A concern with practice should be especially helpful and useful for archaeologists, even more so for those concerned with prehistory where, while we may be able to identify *orthopraxy* (right behaviour), it is rather more difficult to claim to identify *orthodoxy* (right belief) in the archaeological record. Performance of the appropriate rituals may be both necessary and sufficient to maintain a community identity: 'the neighbourhood is described by the Majangir as a group of people who share "the same coffee", the settlement as persons who share "the same fields", and the community as persons who share "the same beer" (Karp 1980: 115); for 'beer' read a shared ritual and ceremonial life, which, as in many African communities, is framed around beer consumption (Edwards 1996).

While we may be confronted by many different and often competing definitions of ritual (e.g. Durkheim 1947 [1912]; Tambiah 1979; Turner 1977), the great importance of ritual in the creation and maintenance of forms of communal and personal identities has been widely recognised. A key issue remains the definition of ritual and how it may be distinguished from everyday life, echoing the problems encountered in maintaining distinctions between the sacred and the profane. Understanding ritualisation, rather than ritual, in the abstract, is probably of particular importance, and a contextual approach is required as ritual can only be understood in relation to other areas of practice: 'ritualization is a matter of various culturally specific strategies for setting some activities apart from others, for creating and privileging a qualitative distinction between sacred and profane, and for ascribing such distinctions to realities thought to transcend the powers of human actors' (Bell 1992: 74).

## Historical constructions of religion and religious identities

Here, we argue for the social construction of religious identities, and the importance of religion in the definition of boundaries between different social groups. Past approaches can de defined as primordial, with a concern for religious essences, and more fluid and instrumental approaches; these are exactly the same issues that emerge in relation to other forms of identity, such as ethnicity.

Recent debates concerning the origins and development of Hinduism may be instructive. Studies of its origins commonly see its religious forms taking shape in the texts of the early Puranas, themselves displaying some continuities with earlier Vedic religious traditions, whose textual roots may date back to the second half of the second millennium BC. Recent archaeological contributions have remained cautious on tracing the roots of Hinduism although it has been suggested that an organised Brahmanical framework may be traced back to the later first millennium BC (Chakrabarti 2001). However, a considerable body of research would argue that Hinduism was essentially constructed or invented during the nineteenth century, and did not exist in any meaningful way before then. This invention has been attributed to varying combinations and alliances of European (especially British) colonial administrators, Orientalist scholars, missionaries and indeed indigenous nationalists (Lorenzen 1999). According to such arguments, self-perceptions among Hindus that they all belonged to a single religious community followed the development of this concept of Hinduism by these Europeans.

Such arguments have by no means been universally accepted and the debates continue (e.g. Dube 1998; Talbot 1995), and can be countered on a number of levels. There seems good evidence that sets of beliefs and practices that have since come to be known as Hinduism are recorded many centuries before, in some of the earliest European accounts of south Asia. Other lines of research argue that a Hindu religion with a self-conscious identity really emerged between about 1200 and 1500, being constructed in opposition to, and rivalry with, the growing Muslim presence in the subcontinent (Lorenzen 1999).

Such interest in the 'invention' of religions may not be just a matter of postmodern fashion, but is also a recognition of problems inherent in the sheer complexity of what we may call Hindu religious practice. As W.C. Smith observed, presaging these postmodern arguments: 'What obstructs a definition of Hinduism . . . is the richness of what exists, in all its extravagant variety from century to century and from village to village. . . . As an ideal "Hinduism" might conceivably be defined (though only by a Hindu), but not as a historical reality' (Smith 1962: 144–5). Similarly, in a critique of Gellner's *Muslim Society* (1981), and its assumed existence of an essential Islamic social structure, Asad points out that 'Islam is neither a distinctive social structure nor a heterogeneous collection of artefacts, customs, and morals. It is a tradition' (1986: 14; see our fig. 6.3).

Such problems are of course not restricted to Hinduism or Islam. Notions of 'orthodoxy', 'deviance', 'true belief' and 'superstition' are not simply descriptive or evaluative terms but are also themselves concepts that are part of cultural discourse (Holy 1991: 8). In terms of 'practical religion', questions of true belief or erroneous belief are contested issues. They may also be intimately connected with the exercise of power (Asad 1986, 1993). Diversity and contradictions may equally be encountered within the many

*Figure 6.3* Creating new identities. The Khatmiyya centre (Kassala, eastern Sudan), an important centre of Islam and new Islamic identities in Sudan since the early nineteenth century. (Photograph by David N. Edwards.)

manifestations of what all their adherents profess to be Christianity, Islam or indeed most other religions.

At the beginning of the twenty-first century, Orthodox monks may be expelled from their monasteries on Mount Athos for heterodox opinions while radical 'fundamentalist' Islamic currents of thought may be particularly vocal, intent on reforming and purifying religious practice, as well as political practice. Historical dimensions of similar tensions are not difficult to identify. Medieval 'heresy' in the Christian world was a widespread phenomenon, part of movements of people who saw themselves as authentic Christians, reclaiming the true teaching of the gospels. Reaction to it took a very particular form due to the distinctive disciplinary practices developed by the Church, as an institution, to protect and enforce its monopoly of Truth (Asad 1986).

Heterodoxy can of course be found within many religions, even if their structures of discipline may be very variable. Medieval Islamic jurists such as Ibn Taimiyya were actively fighting manifestations of 'corrupt' popular religion in the thirteenth and fourteenth centuries (Memon 1976). They in turn have come to represent 'authentic' Sunnah for more recent groups such as the Salafi/Wahhabi. As Abu Lughod has argued, an emphasis needs to be placed on the existence of a multiplicity of traditions, discursive traditions, both oral and literate, historically situated (1989: 297). At the heart of the issue is the divide between literate orthodoxy – the orthodoxy of the urban *ulama* (Muslim clerics) – and the practice of the illiterate rural population, exactly the distinctions between the 'Great' and 'Little Traditions' popularised by Redfield (1956). Ioan Lewis (1983) has drawn attention to some of the problems encountered when following more traditional approaches to 'orthodoxy' and 'deviance', with a particular focus on marginal and potentially heretical beliefs and practices commonly represented as superstitions and 'pre-Islamic survival'. Many communities of Muslims may regard other Muslims' beliefs and practices to be un-Islamic, just as many Christian communities and institutions have challenged the veracity of others' beliefs.

## Religious change

The potential significance of religious change in more than matters of belief is also a fertile area, and one which is much discussed in European contexts, for example, in relation to processes of 'Christianisation' during the late Roman and early medieval periods (Fletcher 1997). Considerable uncertainty remains, however, about what this process actually involved, how it may have been manifested (for a recent discussion see Schülke 1999) and how it might be related to the abundant evidence for the survival of 'pagan' beliefs and practices for many centuries, and indeed their assimilation by the Church (Dowden 2000; Jones and Pennick 1995). Many issues are raised, not least regarding the way Christianisation is so often assumed to be a process developing towards an approved end – an 'authentic' Christianity. Issues surrounding the development of syncretic practices, a term commonly having pejorative connotations, are also important, not least in drawing attention to the creation of new cultural forms, in this case religious, as part of the creation of new identities.

This may be seen in the role of religion in many colonial encounters where, as part of the process, Christian missionaries were trying not only to spread their theological message through 'conversion', but also to reconstruct the everyday worlds of the colonised. Conversion is not simply a matter of ideological arguments, of images and messages, but of a re-formation of the colonised heathen. One influential contribution in relation to relatively recent colonial history may be found in Jean and John Comaroff's (1986, 1989, 1991) exploration of encounters between British missionaries and the Southern Tswana peoples in nineteenth-century South Africa. Confronting issues of power and resistance, agency and intention, they suggest the evangelists' efforts produced new forms of consciousness in not only the colonised but also the colonisers. It is also clear that while some cultural forms were incorporated into the everyday world of the colonised, others were contested or rejected (Lane 1999; Reid *et al.* 1997).

The Protestant missions shared a broadly similar set of symbols of modernity with which they wished to transform the 'native' populations. This control and manipulation of symbols lay at the heart of the colonial relationship.

It took its own particular form with the Tswana, peoples whose symbolic and ceremonial practice was parsimonious and unelaborated. Instead

> it saturated the ground of everyday activity, breathing life into habitual forms of social existence. It was on this terrain that the missions had to battle for control over the salient signs of the world they wanted to conquer . . . a battle not for sacred sites but, for mastery of the mundane.
> (Comaroff and Comaroff 1989: 272)

In the interests of moral rectitude, great emphasis was commonly placed on introducing Western styles of dress. The promiscuous and potentially immoral mixing of the sexes could be avoided by changing the shape and spatial organisation of domestic buildings. New gender roles were to be promoted, both at home and at work, in irrigating and cultivating the land (usurping the roles of rainmaker and chiefs), in commerce and in worthy and improving industry. In short, 'the ideology of Christian evangelism in south-ern Africa . . . demanded a radical transformation of bodily practices and the material fabric of society' (Lane 1999: 155).

Agriculture was certainly a core part of the project, part of the civilising role of cultivation carried to many parts of the world by European colonisers. The irrigated garden became an icon of the civilising mission – to bring a 'rich harvest of souls'. Men would be brought to 'honest labour' in the fields, replacing their womenfolk who, as another part of civilising reform, would be confined to the house, in domestic work. Adopting the plough would also redefine the division of labour along the lines of the bourgeois family. In the event, 'the first reaction of the Tswana to the fertile mission garden was to steal its fruit' (Comaroff and Comaroff 1989: 278–9), while the women found the irrigating of the gardens in such an arid environment quite unreasonable.

Religious change may also fundamentally alter peoples' relationships with their past. In the Sudanese Nile Valley, once the home of both Christian medieval kingdoms and an earlier 'pagan' state sharing many elements with the ancient Egyptian religion, subsequent Islamicisation has fundamentally changed perceptions of that past and its relation to the modern Sudanese. While many features of medieval Nubian culture persist, at various levels 'the political associations of Christianity rule out for modern Sudanese . . . any overt recognition of this religion as a historical antecedent and cultural source' (James and Johnson 1988: 7). As the adoption of Islam has also been intimately connected with the adoption of new Arab identities, and geneal-ogies, the inhabitants of the Middle Nile embraced 'not only a new destiny but a new history' (Adams 1977: 563). It may be added that where some identification with a Nubian heritage is maintained, this may be as an act of resistance to current political regime with its particular Islamic agendas, whether amongst ethnic Nubians, marginalised by the current government, or others, often in exile (e.g. Boddy 1995).

## Religion and other identities

As religion cannot easily be distinguished as a discrete sphere of activity it can rarely be separated from other forms of social identities. The melding of new identities in which religion is strongly implicated may be seen in many contexts of cultural contact, including colonial and 'Mission' encounters (Graham 1998). With the spread of Christianity, developments such as the use of vernacular languages, as well as more general accommodations with existing indigenous practice, have given rise to a vast array of what may be seen as syncretic religions, or, alternatively, simply new forms of Christianity. Such processes of change have now gained acceptance in the fashionable missionary notion of 'inculturation', which allows the creation of 'authentic' Latin American, Indian or African forms of Christianity. One potential outcome of such developments may of course be the end of Western hegemony in determining Christian identity. That this is of course not something new within the Christian experience is evident in the myriad earlier forms of Christianity that emerged during the medieval period, from 'Celtic' traditions on the western margins of Europe, to the Nestorians, Syriacs, Nubians and Ethiopian traditions of the East and northeast Africa.

Similar issues are being addressed in other imperial contexts, for example in Roman archaeology where many debates about 'Romanisation' and the creation of Roman identities have begun to shift away from a focus on political and socio-economic organisation more towards religion and ideology (e.g. Derks 1998). The imperial Roman 'colonisation of consciousness' was about the introduction of a new symbolic world order in which the state ideology and the cult of the emperor figured large. Amongst the colonised, however, religious cults and their communities can equally become a focus and manifestation of resistance to the Romans (Webster 1997, 1999).

In Roman Egypt, complex approaches are also required in exploring the religious transformations underway in a period that traditionally has often been characterised as one that saw the 'decline of paganism' or the 'triumph of Christianity'. Despite the decline of the economic power of the temples and the increasing restrictions imposed on their activities, it is possible to argue that at the local level 'popular religion' could assume many new forms derived from regional as well as pan-Mediterranean religious idioms. This is perhaps most visible archaeologically in the abundant terracotta figurines, of Isis, Harpocrates, Bes and other deities that are such an abundant, and intractable feature of this period. These provide very material evidence for the resilience of indigenous religion, if in new forms, which is amply attested in the same Coptic Christian texts of the period that sought to proclaim the triumph of Christianity (Frankfurter 1998; Trombley 1995).

In early medieval Europe, religion also played its part, if in varied ways, in the changes that convulsed Germanic peoples, transforming them from kinship-based societies into new forms of political communities with new identities, represented in new forms of material culture (Hedeager 1993).

Contrasting patterns can also be seen in the ways in which Christianity and traditional ('pagan') religions were implicated in these developments. In Denmark and southern Sweden, new forms of royal power were anchored to a Scandinavian ideology in which the king of the gods, Odin, played a central role, and which had its own symbolic language in the form of Scandinavian animal ornament. Further south, when the Franks adopted Roman Catholicism, they distinguished themselves from Gallo-Roman Christians in burial forms ritually anchored in earlier pagan Germanic traditions, as part of the creation of a new Frankish identity that was neither Germanic nor Roman. In the early years of their dominance in the old Roman territories, continued reference to pagan mythology remained one strategy of legitimation for the newly established Frankish elites. By the mid seventh century they had acquired a new origin myth, recorded by Fredegar, which established their descent from the Trojan prince Francion (James 1988).

By contrast, a few centuries later we are faced with another group of Scandinavians whose religious persona has left remarkably little material trace. Despite a major presence in parts of northern and eastern England, the Vikings of the ninth and tenth centuries have left a remarkably small number of cemeteries that may be associated with them. The contrast with the archaeological record associated with the Anglo-Saxons some centuries before is very striking. We do, however, have some rare cases where particular pagan religious identities appear very central to at least one group of Scandinavians, probably members of the 'Great Army' overwintering in the Midlands of England during 873–874 (Richards and Van Buren 2000: 144–9). It is there that we find a very unusual pagan tumulus cemetery at Ingleby, probably relating to one part of the 'Great Army', other members of which were buried at Repton (Biddle and Kjølbye-Biddle 1992). Only in those exceptional circumstances, amongst a large grouping of warriors in an alien land, do we see what may be a special religious bond being manifested.

## The creation of difference

The use of religion in defining different identities and creating difference is relatively commonplace in modern history, both in defining the mainstream or core national identities, and in defining minorities (e.g. Davis and Ravid 2001) that are so often also an integral part of the nation. Creating such oppositions between 'minorities' and 'majorities' has been an essential part of processes of nation-building, defining boundaries, to the extent that the question of 'Can a Muslim Be an Indian?' (Pandey 1999) has considerable power. As part of the political project to create an Indian nation, a natural home of the Hindus, an Indian Muslim 'minority' was also created while distinguishing Hindu from Indian became essentially irrelevant: they were naturally Indian. New political issues emerged for Indian politics, where they remain today, to define 'the appropriate place and appropriate status of the "minorities"' (Pandey 1999: 611).

Such examples derive a further significance over the longer term thus drawing us back to issues concerning the creation of religious identities themselves. In eastern Asia, it has been suggested, for example, that Shinto-ism only began to acquire a coherent identity in reaction to the appearance of Buddhism and Confucianism in Japan during the mid first millennium AD. One interpretation of the emergence of Hindu identities would see it as part of a process of self-definition in relation to Muslims and others, evident in Indian vernacular literature as early as the fifteenth century (Lorenzen 1999). Part of an early fifteenth-century historical romance defines some perceived differences, as well as how such differences were made apparent:

> The Hindus and the Turks live close together.
> Each makes fun of the other's religion (dhamme).
> One calls the faithful to prayer. The other recites the Vedas.
> One butchers animals by bleeding.
> The other cuts (off their heads).
> Some are called ojhās, other khājās.
> Some (read) astrological signs, others fast in Ramadan.
> Some eat from copper plates, others from pottery.
> (From the *Kirilata* in Lorenzen 1999: 651)

The interplay of religious identity and gender has been another fertile area of research, building on the growing wider interest in gender archaeology (Gilchrist 1999). One influential group of studies explicitly concerned with such (e.g. Gilchrist 1994; Graves 1989) has been particularly concerned with medieval archaeology, with a strong emphasis on architectural interpretation, on the use of space and its relation with ritual and ritualisation. The potential for such work is much greater, however, as the very androcentric nature of so much religious discourse both within and beyond archaeology is often appar-ent (MacLean 2001). Women's experience and perceptions of Hinduism have, for example, largely been 'written out' of the tradition (Flood 1996: 20). Similar issues are encountered in studies of Islam, in which gender differences are one very important aspect of often complex pictures of very heterogeneous practice and belief, particularly in areas often perceived as within the sphere of 'popular religion'. By no means solely a gender issue, such heterogeneity of practice of course also relates to the more general tensions that exist between dominant literate orthodoxy and other forms of belief and practice – tensions that are encountered within many religions.

Within many Muslim societies distinctions can be made between practices and beliefs that may be classified as religion (Arabic *dīn*) and customary practices (Arabic *'awāid*); religious rituals being predominantly the concern of men, while customary rituals are predominantly those of women (Holy 1991: 11). That women are not only a focus, but also might be especially active in the maintenance and propagation of 'heterodox' beliefs and practices also seems likely in many religious traditions, including Islam (Holy 1988).

All too often however, where it is assumed that men define local orthodoxy, women's interests and beliefs may be largely marginalised. Holy also draws attention to other potentially important distinctions between 'religion' and 'custom', in the way, for example, religious practices may be seen as linking peoples with the wider Islamic community, while their customary practices (*'awāid*), distinguish them *from* other peoples, being important marks of ethnic identity (Holy 1983: 285).

In Nubia, anthropologists and archaeologists have been interested for nearly a century in particular manifestations of what may be termed 'popular religion', which has taken the form of a landscape filled with shrines (Kennedy 1978). These shrines have also been foci for religious conflicts, with a strong gender dimension. Representing heterodox practice, in the 1960s their abundance and popularity in Egyptian Nubia tended to be associated with village women who, both by their limited engagement with formal public Islam as well as their limited contact with currents of more urban Islam in Egypt proper, tend to have been seen as more conservative in preserving traditional practice. Such associations are also very evident today in Sudanese Nubia, where informants very commonly attribute the main interest in similar shrines to 'women' and 'old women'. Just like (male) informants in Egyptian Nubia a generation earlier, they also tend to imply that such heterodox practices no longer continue, although it is quite apparent that they do. Similar representations of religious variability along gender lines can be found in accounts a century ago (Blackman 1910; see our fig. 6.4).

Religion and gender have also come together in other ways through the interplay of archaeology and contemporary political discourse, for example in interpretations of prehistoric religion in which the figure of the Mother Goddess looms large, both as symbol of ancient European matriarchy and as a modern religious cult. Building on Gimbutas' work, various feminist positions have used a range of archaeological data to support their claims. As Lynn Meskell (1995; see also Conkey and Tringham 1995) has argued, many of Gimbutas' ideas have an obvious appeal for certain forms of eco-feminism and 'New Age' ideologies.

## Religion and power

Religion may also be implicated in the development of political power (fig. 6.5). One element of Parker Pearson's recent work (1999) highlights the widespread development of what may be termed ancestor cults in later prehistory. These in turn formed the basis on which developed new religious systems in which certain ancestors, heroes and rulers could be elevated to divine status, reflecting emerging political hierarchies, most obviously in the early states of Egypt and Mesopotamia.

In addition to the more general problems encountered in conceptualising religion, we also need to consider societies in which forms of role differentiation, including the religious, may be ordered very differently from in the

*Figure 6.4* Religion and custom. Islamic shrine in Sudanese Nubia amongst rocks named after the Safa and al-Marwa hills of Mecca. (Photograph by David N. Edwards.)

West. Economic status has, for example, emerged to be the most valued status criteria within Western (capitalist) societies. By contrast it has often been observed that political specialisation has enjoyed a much more prominent role than economic specialisation in African societies. In turn, political roles and political power are often inextricably bound up with ritual power. This may of course take many forms. Cult associations and secret societies may control property and other resources. Their control of ritual knowledge and technology brings ritual power as well as commanding payment, and may provide them with access to political power.

Ritual power can also allow a qualitatively different order of power in providing a way of transcending other, often fundamentally weak political mechanisms (Netting 1972). Societies may be encountered in which social relations, and social identities are organised through numerous forms of both vertical and horizontal associations. Many Africanists will be familiar with a

*Figure 6.5* The ritual power of Meroitic kings (Musawwarat es-Sufra, Sudan). (Photograph by David N. Edwards.)

plethora of horizontal associations or sodalities, including age sets and age grades, cult associations, title groups and secret societies, many of which have an explicit religious dimension (McIntosh 1999).

This potential importance of religion in the development of political centralisation raises many issues for archaeologists with a predisposition to equate materially 'rich' displays, in burial for example, with political status, where essentially religious roles may be being signalled. As anthropologists such as Evans-Pritchard (1965) found, even when able to meet people face-to-face it may be difficult to distinguish between a 'chief' and a 'priest' and there are rich ethnohistorical data on the interrelationship between religious and political power (Johnson 1990, 1994). A classic case in West African archaeology is found in the possible ways of interpreting the extraordinarily rich burial and deposits of ritual bronzes at Igbo Ukwu in Nigeria (Shaw 1977). Rather than being the burial of a 'chief', the burial could equally be interpreted as that of a major title-holder in a non-hierarchically organised society; its wealth of artefacts deriving from the ritual and ceremonial objects of his *obu* shrine.

Religion has also been central to the development and definition of new forms of political communities and identities, from Greek city-states (De

Polignac 1995) to imperial powers in Meso- and South America (e.g. Conrad and Demarest 1984) or Rome. The central role of religious legitimation in complex pre-capitalist societies is well recognised (Rowlands 1987: 52). As Southall suggested, the sacral power of kingship, often linked to ensuring fertility or making rain, may be an exceptional power source, especially in what he termed 'segmentary state' forms (1988: 63). That its reach might be far more extensive than that of other forms of power, shading off into a 'ritual hegemony', is also of considerable importance when attempting to assess the spatial exercise of power. The prominence and ubiquity of such powers form the basis of the generalised notions of 'Divine Kingship' that have figured widely in studies of African kingship (Vansina 1962).

In Greece, new attitudes towards the sacred can be identified during the eighth century BC, which were manifested in new material forms, new under-standings of sacred space and above all, through the emerging sanctuaries, social bodies adhering to the same religious territory. Common participation in religious rituals may have been central to constituting the first civic space that underlay the emergence of stable political institutions. The interaction of the increasingly organised religious cults and the urban aristocracies was to lay the foundations for the creation of the *polis* (De Polignac 1995: 153–4).

In the history of Roman expansion during the archaic and mid Republican periods, archaeology can hint at potentially similar roles, supplementing later literary sources. The spread of Roman cults during the Middle Republic, archaeologically traceable in the diffusion of anatomical ex-votos, should be seen in terms of *civic* religion, that is the concern only of citizens. As such, religious Romanisation could only follow the extension of citizenship, for example in its early colonies, while local cults of newly incorporated towns were maintained in a new category of 'municipal cults' (De Cazanove 2000).

In later imperial periods we can also see that conventional distinctions between religion and politics may not be helpful in understanding the Greek cults of the Roman emperors that emerged in Asia Minor. Rather, the incorporation of the emperor into the traditional religious system, relating their ruler to their own dominant symbolic system and representing the emperor to themselves in terms of divine power, was a way of 'making sense of an otherwise incomprehensible intrusion of authority into their world' (Price 1985: 247).

## Conclusion

Archaeologists face considerable problems in developing coherent approaches to the archaeology of religion and religious identities. Narrower definitions of religion, based essentially on a restricted range of Western experience, are unlikely to be helpful in dealing with the wider range of human experience. Many key aspects of peoples' lives and social personas are embedded within, framed by and organised around forms of ritual practice and symbolic struc-tures that, if challenging to Western notions of what can be defined as 'religious', cannot easily be accommodated within other categories of activity. At one end of a continuum we may perceive relatively intangible structuring principles of social life in terms of the 'habitus', embedded in and reproducing the 'habitual forms of social existence' (Comaroff and Comaroff 1989: 272). At the other end, we can see highly elaborated, structured and overt practices and displays that may become integral elements of such peculiar political projects as the ethnic nation-state. Religious identities can be constructed and manipulated as any other, inclusive or exclusive, building community or constructing boundaries. We should also be extremely wary of essentialist and normative approaches to religion that assume, or presume, the existence of correct or authentic belief or practice. The peculiar Western experience of post-Enlightenment rationalism and movements of secularisation has left us poorly equipped to appreciate the breadth of past religious experience.

# Bibliography

Abu Lughod, L. (1989) 'Zones of theory in the anthropology of the Arab world', *Annual Review of Anthropology* 18: 267–306.

Adams, W.Y. (1977) *Nubia, Corridor to Africa*, London: Allen Lane.

Alexander, J. (1979) 'The archaeological recognition of religion: the examples of Islam in Africa and the Urnfields in Europe', in B. Burnham and J. Kingsbury (eds) *Space, Hierarchy and Society*, BAR International Series 59, Oxford: British Archaeological Reports, 215–28.

Althusser, L. (1984) *Essays on Ideology*, London: Verso.

Amory, P. (1994) 'Names, ethnic identity and community in fifth and sixth-century Burgundy', *Viator* 25: 1–30.

Amoss, P. and S. Harrell (1981) 'Introduction: an anthropological perspective on aging', in P. Amoss and S. Harrell (eds) *Other Ways of Growing Old*, Stanford: Stanford University Press, 1–24.

Anderson, B. (1991) *Imagined Communities: Reflections on the Origin and Spread of Nationalism*, London: Verso, 2nd edition.

Appadurai, A. (1986) 'Introduction: commodities and the politics of value', in A. Appadurai (ed.) *The Social Life of Things: Commodities in Cultural Perspective*, Cambridge: Cambridge University Press, 3–63.

Ariès, P. (1962) *Centuries of Childhood*, London: Jonathan Cape.

Arnold, B. (1991) 'The deposed princess of Vix: the need for an engendered European prehistory', in I.D. Walde and N.D. Willows (eds) *The Archaeology of Gender*, Calgary: The University of Calgary, 366–74.

Arsenault, D. (1991) 'The representation of women in Moche iconography', in I.D. Walde and N.D. Willows (eds) *The Archaeology of Gender*, Calgary: The University of Calgary, 313–26.

Arwill-Nordbladh, E. (1989) 'Oscar Montelius and the liberation of women: An example of archaeology, ideology and the early Swedish women's movement', in T.B. Larsson and H. Lundmark (eds) *Approaches to Swedish Prehistory: A Spectrum of Problems and Perspectives in Contemporary Research*, BAR International Series 500, Oxford: British Archaeological Reports, 131–42.

Asad, T. (1986) *The Idea of an Anthropology of Islam*, Occasional papers Series, Centre for Contemporary Arab Studies, Georgetown: Georgetown University Press.

Asad, T. (1993) *Genealogies of Religion: Discipline and Reason of Power in Christianity and Islam*, Baltimore: Johns Hopkins University Press.

Ashmore, W. and A.B. Knapp (eds) (1999) *Archaeologies of Landscape: Contemporary Perspectives*, Oxford: Blackwell.

Atkinson, J.A., I. Banks and J. O'Sullivan (eds) (1996) *Nationalism and Archaeology*, Glasgow: Cruithne Press.

Aubet, M.E. (1993) *The Phoenicians and the West: Politics, Colonies and Trade*, Cambridge: Cambridge University Press.

Aykroyd, R.G., D. Lucy, A.M. Pollard and C.A. Roberts (1999) 'Nasty, brutish, but not necessarily short: a reconsideration of the statistical methods used to calculate age at death from adult human skeletal and dental age indicators', *American Antiquity* 64: 55–70.

Babić, S. (2001) 'Headgear of the Early Iron Age tribal chieftains: social and symbolic aspects', *Recueil du Musée Nationel – Archéologie* 17(1): 83–93.

Babić, S. (2002) ' "Princely graves" of the central Balkans – a critical history of research', *European Journal of Archaeology* 5(1): 70–88.

Banks, I. (1996) 'Archaeology, nationalism and ethnicity', in J.A. Atkinson, I. Banks and J. O'Sullivan (eds) *Nationalism and Archaeology*, Glasgow: Cruithne Press, 1–11.

Banks, M. (1999) *Ethnicity: Anthropological Constructions*, London Routledge.

Bapty, I. and T. Yates (eds) (1990) *Archaeology after Structuralism: Post-Structuralism and the Practice of Archaeology*, London: Routledge.

Barfield, L. and C. Chippindale (1997) 'Meaning in the later Prehistoric rock-engravings of Mont Bégo, Alpes-Maritimes, France', *Proceedings of the Prehistoric Society* 63: 103–28.

Barnard, A. and J. Spencer (1996) *Encyclopedia of Social and Cultural Anthropology*, London: Routledge.

Barndon, R. (1999) 'Iron working and social control: the use of anthropomorphic symbols in recent and past East African contexts', *K.A.N.* 22–23: 59–76.

Barnes, G. (1995) Special issue on Buddhist Archaeology (edited by G. Barnes), *World Archaeology* 27(2).

Barrett, J.C. (1988) 'Fields of discourse: reconstituting a social archaeology', *Critique of Anthropology* 7(3): 5–16.

Barrett, J.C. (2000) 'A thesis on agency', in M.-A. Dobres and J. Robb (eds) *Agency in Archaeology*, London: Routledge, 61–8.

Barrett, J.H., R.P. Beukens and R.A. Nicholson (2001) 'Diet and ethnicity during the Viking colonization of northern Scotland: evidence from fish bones and stable carbon isotopes', *Antiquity* 75: 145–54.

Barth, F. (1969) 'Introduction', in F. Barth (ed.) *Ethnic Groups and Boundaries: The Social Organization of Culture Difference*, Oslo: Universitetsforlaget, 9–38.

Bauer, B.S. (1998) *The Sacred Landscape of the Inca: The Cusco Ceque System*, Austin: The University of Texas Press.

Beausang, E. (2000) 'Childbirth in prehistory: an introduction', *European Journal of Archaeology* 3(1): 69–87.

Becker, M.J. (2000) 'Reconstructing the lives of South Etruscan women', in A.E. Rautman (ed.) *Reading the Body: Representations and Remains in the Archaeological Record*, Philadelphia: University of Pennsylvania Press, 55–67.

Bell, C. (1992) *Ritual Theory: Ritual Practice*, Oxford: Oxford University Press.

Benedict, R. (1935) *Patterns of Culture*, London: Routledge and Kegan Paul.

Benn, S.I. and G.F. Gauss (1983) 'The public and the private: concepts and action', in S.I. Benn and G.F. Gauss (eds) *Public and Private in Social Life*, New York: St Martin's Press, 3–27.

Bentley, G. (1987) 'Ethnicity and practice', *Comparative Studies in Society and History* 29: 24–55.

Bentley, R.A., L. Chikhi and T.D. Price (2003) 'The Neolithic transition in Europe: broad scale genetic and local scale isotopic evidence', *Antiquity* 77: 63–5.

Bergquist, A. (2001) 'Ethics and the archaeology of world religions', in T. Insoll (ed.) *Archaeology and World Religion*, London: Routledge, 182–91.

Bergsvik, K.A. (2003) 'Mesolithic ethnicity – too hard to handle?', in L. Larsson, H. Kindgren, K. Knutsson, D. Leoffler and A. Akerlund (eds) *Mesolithic on the Move: Papers Presented at the Sixth International Conference on the Mesolithic in Europe, Stockholm 2000*, Oxford: Oxbow, 290–301.

Bernal, F.V. (1997) 'When painters execute a murderess: the representation of Clytemnestra on Attic vases', in A.O. Koloski-Ostrow and C.L. Lyons (eds) *Naked Truths: Women, Sexuality and Gender in Classical Art and Archaeology*, London: Routledge, 93–107.

Bevan, L. (1997) 'Skin scrapers and pottery makers? "Invisible" women in prehistory', in J. Moore and E. Scott (eds) *Invisible People and Processes: Writing Gender and Childhood into European Archaeology*, Leicester: Leicester University Press, 81–7.

Biddle, M. and B. Kjølbye-Biddle (1992) 'Repton and the Vikings', *Antiquity* 66: 36–51.

Bideau, A., B. Desjardins and H. Pérez Brignoli (eds) (1997) *Infant and Child Mortality in the Past*, Oxford: Clarendon Press.

Biehl, P.F., A. Gramsch and A. Marciniak (2002) *Archäologien Europas/Archaeologies of Europe: Geschichte, Methoden und Theorien/History, Methods and Theories*, Tübingen Archäologische Taschenbücher 3, Münster; New York; München; Berlin: Waxman.

Binford, L.R. (1965) 'Archaeological systematics and the study of culture process', *American Antiquity* 31: 203–10.

Binford, L.R. (1968) 'Archaeological perspectives', in S.R. Binford and L.R. Binford (eds) *New Perspectives in Archaeology*, Chicago: Aldine, 1–32.

Binford, L.R. (1972) *An Archaeological Perspective*, New York: Seminar Press.

Binford, L.R. (1973) 'Interassemblage variability – the Mousterian and the "functional" argument', in C. Renfrew (ed.) *The Explanation of Culture Change: Models in Prehistory*, London: Duckworth, 227–54.

Binford, L.R. (1983) *In Pursuit of the Past*, London, New York: Thames & Hudson.

Bintliff, J. (ed.) (1984) *European Social Evolution: Archaeological Perspectives*, Bradford: University of Bradford Press.

Bird, C.F.M. (1993) 'Woman the toolmaker: evidence for women's use and manufacture of flaked stone tools in Australia and New Guinea', in H. duCros and L. Smith (eds) *Women in Archaeology: A Feminist Critique*, Canberra: The Australian National University, 22–30.

Blackman, A.M. (1910) 'Some Egyptian and Nubian notes', *Man* 11: 25–9.

Blair, J. and C. Pyrah (eds) (1996) *Church Archaeology: Research Directions for the Future*, York: Council for British Archaeology.

Blake, E. (1999) 'Identity-mapping in the Sardinian Bronze Age', *European Journal of Archaeology* 2(1): 35–55.

Boast, R. (1997) 'A small company of actors: a critique of style', *Journal of Material Culture* 2(2): 173–98.

Boddy, J. (1995) 'Managing tradition: superstition and the making of national identity among Sudanese women refugees', in W. James (ed.) *The Pursuit of Certainty: Religious and Cultural Formulations*, London: Routledge, 17–44.

Bodenhorn, B. (1993) 'Gendered spaces, public places: public and private revisited on the North Slope of Alaska', in B. Bender (ed.) *Landscape: Politics and Perspectives*, Oxford: Berg, 169–203.

Boesch-Achermann, H. and C. Boesch (1994) 'Hominization in the rainforest: the chimpanzee's piece of the puzzle', *Evolutionary Anthropology* 3(1): 9–16.

Boissevain, J. (1994) 'Towards an anthropology of European communities?', in V.A. Goddard, J.R. Llobera and C. Shore (eds) *The Anthropology of Europe: Identities and Boundaries in Conflict*, Oxford: Berg, 41–56.

Boivin, N. (2000) 'Life rhythms and floor sequences: excavating time in rural Rajasthan and Neolithic Çatalhöyuk', *World Archaeology* 31(3): 367–88.

Bolen, K.M. (1991) 'Changing gender roles at the gatherer-hunter transition to farmer', in I.D. Walde and N.D. Willows (eds) *The Archaeology of Gender*, Calgary: The University of Calgary, 400–405.

Bolen, K.M. (1992) 'Prehistoric construction of mothering', in C. Claassen (ed.) *Exploring Gender Through Archaeology: Selected Papers from the 1991 Boone Conference*, Monograph in World Archaeology 11, Madison: Prehistory Press, 49–62.

Bonnischen, R. (1973) 'Millie's Camp: an experiment in archaeology', *World Archaeology* 4: 277–91.

Bordes, F. (1973) 'On the chronology and contemporaneity of different palaeolithic cultures in France', in C. Renfrew (ed.) *The Explanation of Culture Change: Models in Prehistory*, London: Duckworth, 217–26.

Bosch Gimpera, P. (1922) *Ensayo de una Reconstrucción de la Etnología Prehistórica de la Península Ibérica*, Santander: Boletín de la Biblioteca Menéndez Pelayo.

Boswell, J. (1988) *The Kindness of Strangers: The Abandonment of Children in Western Europe from Late Antiquity to the Renaissance*, London: Allen Lane.

Bourdieu, P. (1977) *Outline of a Theory of Practice*, Cambridge: Cambridge University Press.

Bourdieu, P. (1984) *Distinction: A Social Critique of the Judgement of Taste*, Cambridge: Harvard University Press.

Bray, T.L. (ed.) (2001) *The Future of the Past: Archaeologists, Native Americans and Repatriation*, New York: Garland.

Bridges, P.S. (1989) 'Changes in activities with the shift to agriculture in the southeastern United States', *Current Anthropology* 30: 385–94.

Brothwell, D.R. (1981) *Digging up Bones*, Oxford: Oxford University Press, 3rd edition.

Brown, J.A. (1981) 'The search for rank in prehistoric burials', in R. Chapman, I. Kinnes and K. Randsborg (eds) *The Archaeology of Death*, Cambridge: Cambridge University Press, 25–37.

Brown, J.K. (1970) 'A note on the sexual division of labor by sex', *American Anthropologist* 72: 1073–8.

Brück, J. (1999) 'Ritual and rationality: some problems of interpretation in European archaeology', *European Journal of Archaeology* 2(3): 313–44.

Bruhns, K.O. (1991) 'Sexual activities: some thoughts on the sexual division of labor and archaeological interpretation', in I.D. Walde and N.D. Willows (eds) *The Archaeology of Gender*, Calgary: The University of Calgary, 420–29.

Brumfiel, E.M. (1991) 'Weaving and cooking: women's production in Aztec Mexico', in J. Gero and M.W. Conkey (eds) *Engendering Archaeology*, Oxford: Blackwell, 224–54.

Brumfiel, E.M. (1992) 'Distinguished lecture in archaeology: breaking and entering the ecosystem – gender, class, and faction steal the show', *American Anthropologist* 94(3): 551–67.

Brumfiel, E.M. (1996a) 'Figurines and the Aztec state: testing the effectivenes of ideological domination', in R.P. Wright (ed.) *Gender and Archaeology*, Philadelphia: University of Pennsylvania Press, 143–66.

Brumfiel, E.M. (1996b) 'The quality of tribute cloth: the place of evidence in archaeological argument', *American Antiquity* 61(3): 453–62.

Buchli, V. (1995) 'Interpreting material culture: the trouble with text', in I. Hodder, M. Shanks, A. Alexandri, V. Buchli, J. Carman, J. Last and G. Lucas (eds) *Interpreting Archaeology: Finding Meanings in the Past*, London: Routledge, 181–93.

Buchli, V. (1999) *An Archaeology of Socialism*, Oxford: Berg.

Buchli, V. (2002) 'Architecture and the domestic sphere', in V. Buchli (ed.) *The Material Culture Reader*, Oxford: Berg, 207–214.

Budd, P., A. Millard, C. Chenery, S. Lucy and C. Roberts (2004) 'Investigating population movement by stable isotope analysis: a report from Britain', *Antiquity* 78: 127–41.

Bukach, D. (2003) 'Exploring identity and place: an analysis of the provenance of passage grave stones on Guernsey and Jersey in the Middle Neolithic', *Oxford Journal of Archaeology* 22: 23–33.

Bunzl, M. (1996) 'Franz Boas and the Humboldtian tradition: From Volksgeist and Nationalcharakter to an anthropological concept of culture', in G.W.J. Stocking (ed.) *Volksgeist as Method and Ethic: Essays on Boasian Ethnography and the German Anthropological Tradition*, History of anthropology 8, Madison: University of Wisconsin Press, 17–78.

Burnham, B.C. and J. Kingsbury (eds) (1979) *Space, Hierarchy and Society: Interdisciplinary Studies in Social Area Analysis*, BAR International Series 59, Oxford: British Archaeological Reports.

Camille, M. (1994) 'The image and the self: unwriting late medieval bodies', in S. Kay and M. Rubin (eds) *Framing Medieval Bodies*, Manchester: Manchester University Press, 62–99.

Campbell, E. (2001) 'Were the Scots Irish?', *Antiquity* 75: 285–92.

Carmichael, D.L., J. Hubert, B. Reeves and A. Schanche (eds) (1994) *Sacred Sites, Sacred Places*, One World Archaeology 23, London: Routledge.

Chakrabarti, D. (2001) 'The archaeology of Hinduism', in T. Insoll (ed.) *Archaeology and World Religion*, London: Routledge, 33–60.

Chamberlain, A. (1997) 'Commentary: missing stages of life – towards the perception of children in archaeology', in J. Moore and E. Scott (eds) *Invisible People and Processes*, Leicester: Leicester University Press, 248–50.

Chamberlain, A. (2000) 'Minor concerns: a demographic perspective on children in past societies', in J. Sofaer Derevenski (ed.) *Children and Material Culture*, London: Routledge, 206–12.

Champion, T.C. and J.V.S. Megaw (1985) *Settlement and Society: Aspects of West European Prehistory in the First Millennium BC*, Leicester: Leicester University Press.

Chapa, T. (2003) 'La percepción de la infancia en el mundo ibérico', *Trabajos de Prehistoria* 60(1): 115–38.

Chapman, J. (1997) 'Changing gender relations in the later prehistory of Eastern Hungary', in J. Moore and E. Scott (eds) *Invisible People and Processes*, Leicester: Leicester University Press, 131–49.

Chapman, J. (2002) 'Theoretical archaeology in Britain in the late 20th century: an overview', in P.F. Biehl, A. Gramsch and A. Marciniak (eds) *Archäologien Europas/ Archaeologies of Europe: Geschichte, Methoden und Theorien/History, Methods and Theories*, Tübingen Archäologische Taschenbücher 3, Münster; New York; München; Berlin: Waxman, 225–38.

Chapman, R., I. Kinnes and K. Randsborg (eds) (1981) *The Archaeology of Death*, Cambridge: Cambridge University Press.

Childe, V.G. (1927) 'The Danube thoroughfare and the beginnings of civilization in Europe', *Antiquity* 1: 79–91.

Childe, V.G. (1928) 'The Lausitz Culture', *Antiquity* 2: 37–42.

Childe, V.G. (1929) *The Danube in Prehistory*, Oxford: Clarendon Press.

Childe, V.G. (1933) 'Races, peoples and cultures in prehistoric Europe', *History* 18: 193–203.

Childe, V.G. (1935) 'Changing methods and aims in prehistory', Presidential Address for 1935, *Proceedings of the Prehistoric Society* 1: 1–15.

Childe, V.G. (1951) *Man Makes Himself*, New York: New American Library, 2nd edition.

Claassen, C.P. (1992) 'Questioning gender: an introduction', in C.P. Claassen (ed.) *Exploring Gender Through Archaeology: Selected Papers from the 1991 Boone Conference*, Monograph in World Archaeology 11, Madison: Prehistory Press, 1–10.

Claassen, C.P. (1991) 'Gender, shellfishing, and the Shell Mound Archaic', in J. Gero and M.W. Conkey (eds) *Engendering Archaeology*, Oxford: Blackwell, 276–300.

Clarke, D.L. (1968) *Analytical Archaeology*, London: Methuen.

Clarke, G. (1939) *Archaeology and Society*, London: Methuen.

Cohen, A. (1994) *Self Consciousness: An Alternative Anthropology of Identity*, London: Routledge.

Cohen, M.N. and S. Bennett (1998 [1993]) 'Skeletal evidence for sex roles and gender hierarchies in prehistory', in K. Hays-Gilpin and D.S. Whitley (eds) *Reader in Gender Archaeology*, London: Routledge, 297–318.

Cokayne, K. (2003) *Experiencing Old Age in Ancient Rome*, London: Routledge.

Coles, J.M. and A.F. Harding (1979) *The Bronze Age in Europe: An Introduction to the Prehistory of Europe c. 2000–700 BC*, London: Methuen.

Colley, L. (1992) *Britons: Forging the Nation 1707–1837*, New Haven: Yale University Press.

Collier, J. and M. Rosaldo (1981) 'Politics and gender in simple societies', in S. Ortner and H. Whitehead (eds) *Sexual Meanings*, Cambridge: Cambridge University Press, 275–329.

Collier, J.F. and S.J. Yanagisako (eds) (1987) *Gender and Kinship: Essays Towards a Unified Analysis*, Stanford: Stanford University Press.

Collins, J. and R. Blot (2003) *Literacy and Literacies: Texts, Power and Identity*, Cambridge: Cambridge University Press.

Collis, J. (2003) *Celts: Origins, Myths and Inventions*, Stroud: Tempus.

Comaroff, J. and J. Comaroff (1986) 'Christianity and colonialism in South Africa', *American Ethnologist* 13(1): 1–20.

Comaroff, J. and J. Comaroff (1989) 'The colonization of consciousness in South Africa', *Economy and Society* 18(3): 267–95.

Comaroff, J. and J. Comaroff (1991) *Christianity, Colonialism, and Consciousness in South Africa*, Chicago: Chicago University Press.

Comaroff, J. and J. Comaroff (1992) *Ethnography and the Historical Imagination*, Boulder: Westview Press.

Conkey, M.W. (1986) 'Paleovisions: Interpreting the imagery of Ice Age Europe', in S.C. Scott (ed.) *The Art of Interpreting: Papers in Art History*, Philadelphia: Pennsylvania State University, 10–29.

Conkey, M.W. (1990) 'Experimenting with style in archaeology: some historical and theoretical issues', in M.W. Conkey and C. Hastorf (eds) *The Uses of Style in Archaeology*, Cambridge: Cambridge University Press, 5–17.

Conkey, M.W. (1991) 'Contexts of action, contexts from power: material culture and gender in the Magdalenian', in J. Gero and M.W. Conkey (eds) *Engendering Archaeology*, Oxford: Blackwell, 57–92.

Conkey, M.W. and J. Gero (1991) 'Tensions, pluralities, and engendering archaeology: an introduction to women in prehistory', in J. Gero and M.W. Conkey (eds) *Engendering Archaeology*, Oxford: Blackwell, 1–30.

Conkey, M.W. and J. Spector (1984) 'Archaeology and the study of gender', in M.B. Schiffer (ed.) *Advances in Archaeological Method and Theory 7*, New York: Academic Press, 1–38.

Conkey, M.W. and R. Tringham (1995) 'Archaeology and the Goddess: exploring the contours of feminist archaeology', in D.C. Stanton and A.J. Stewart (eds) *Feminisms in the Academy*, Ann Arbor: University of Michigan Press, 199–247.

Connell, R.W. (1987) *Gender and Power: Society, the Person, and Sexual Politics*, Cambridge: Polity Press.

Conrad, G.W. and A.A. Demarest (1984) *Religion and Empire: The Dynamics of Aztec and Inca Expansionism*, Cambridge: Cambridge University Press.

Conroy, L. (1993) 'Female figurines of the Upper Palaeolithic and the emergence of gender', in H. duCros and L. Smith (eds) *Women in Archaeology: A Feminist Critique*, Canberra: The Australian National University, 153–60.

Costin, C.L. (1996) 'Exploring the relationship between gender and craft in complex societies: methodological and theoretical issues of gender attribution', in R.P. Wright (ed.) *Gender and Archaeology*, Philadelphia: University of Pennsylvania Press, 111–42.

Crass, B.A. (2000) 'Gender in Inuit burial practices', in A.E. Rautman (ed.) *Reading the Body: Representations and Remains in the Archaeological Record*, Philadelphia: University of Pennsylvania Press, 68–76.

Crawford, S. (1993) 'Children, death and the afterlife in Anglo-Saxon England', *Anglo-Saxon Studies in Archaeology and History* 6: 83–91.

Crawford, S. (1999) *Childhood in Anglo-Saxon England*, Stroud: Sutton.

Crist, T.A.J. (1995) 'Bone chemistry analysis and documentary archaeology: dietary patterns of enslaved African Americans in the South Carolina low country', in A.L. Grauer (ed.) *Bodies of Evidence: Reconstructing History through Skeletal Analysis*, New York: Wiley and Sons, 125–40.

Cunningham, H. (1995) *Children and Childhood in Western Society since 1500*, London: Longman.

Curta, F. (2001) 'Pots, Slavs and "Imagined Communities": Slavic archaeologies and the history of the early Slavs', *European Journal of Archaeology* 4(3): 367–84.

Damm, C. (1991) 'From burials to gender roles: problems and potentials in post-processual archaeology', in I.D. Walde and N.D. Willows (eds) *The Archaeology of Gender*, Calgary: The University of Calgary, 130–35.

Davis, R. and B. Ravid (eds) (2001) *The Jews of Early Modern Venice*, Baltimore: Johns Hopkins University Press.

De Cazanove, O. (2000) 'Some thoughts on the "Religious Romanisation" of Italy before the Social War', in E. Bispham and C. Smith (eds) *Religion in Archaic and Republican Rome and Italy*, Edinburgh: Edinburgh University Press, 71–6.

De Polignac, F. (1995) *Cults, Territory and the Origins of the Greek City-State*, Chicago: University of Chicago Press.

DeCorse, C.R. (1989) 'Material aspects of Limba, Yalunka and Kuranko ethnicity: archaeological research in northeastern Sierra Leone', in S.J. Shennan (ed.) *Archaeological Approaches to Cultural Identity*, London: Unwin Hyman, 125–40.

Dehejia, V. (ed.) (1997) *Representing the Body: Gender Issues in Indian Art*, New Delhi: Kali for Women.

Demos, J. (1983) 'The changing faces of fatherhood: a new exploration in family history', in F.S. Kessel and A.W. Siegel (eds) *The Child and Other Cultural Inventions*, New York: Praeger, 158–81.

Demoule, J.-P. (1999) 'Ethnicity, culture and identity: French archaeologists and historians', *Antiquity* 73(279): 190–97.

Derks, T. (1998) *Gods, Temples and Ritual Practices*, Amsterdam: Amsterdam University Press.

Díaz-Andreu, M. (1996) 'Constructing identities through *culture*: the past in the forging of Europe', in P. Graves-Brown, S. Jones and C. Gamble (eds) *Cultural Identity and Archaeology*, London: Routledge, 48–61.

Díaz-Andreu, M. (1998a) 'Ethnicity and Iberians: The archaeological crossroads between perception and material culture', *European Journal of Archaeology* 2(2): 199–218.

Díaz-Andreu, M. (1998b) 'Iberian post-palaeolithic art and gender: discussing human representations in Levantine art', *Journal of Iberian Archaeology* 0 [sic]: 33–51.

Díaz-Andreu, M. (2001a) 'An all-embracing universal hunter-gatherer religion? Discussing shamanism and Levantine rock-art', in H.-P. Francfort and R. Hamayon (in collaboration with Paul Bahn) (eds) *The Concept of Shamanism: Uses and Abuses*, Bibliotheca Shamanistica, vol. 10, Budapest: Akadémiai Kiadó, 117–34.

Díaz-Andreu, M. (2001b) 'Ethnic identity/ethnicity and archaeology', in N.J. Smelser and P.B. Baltes (eds) *International Encyclopedia of the Social and Behavioral Sciences*, Oxford: Elsevier Science, 4817–21.

Díaz-Andreu, M. (2003) 'Rock art and ritual landscape in Central Spain: the rock carvings of La Hinojosa (Cuenca)', *Oxford Journal of Archaeology* 59(1): 35–51.

Díaz-Andreu, M. and T. Champion (eds) (1996) *Nationalism and Archaeology in Europe*, London: UCL Press.

Díaz-Andreu, M. and A. Smith (eds) (2001) *Nationalism and Archaeology: Nations and Nationalism 7.4*, London: Association for the Study of Ethnicity and Nationalism.

Díaz-Andreu, M. and T. Tortosa (1998) 'Gender, symbolism and power in Iberian societies', in P.P. Funari, M. Hall and S. Jones (eds) *Historical Archaeology: Back from the Edge*, London: Routledge, 99–121.

Dietler, M. and I. Herbich (1998) 'Habitus, techniques, style: an integrated approach to the social understanding of material culture and boundaries', in M.T. Stark (ed.) *The Archaeology of Social Boundaries*, Washington: Smithsonian Books, 232–63.

Dobres, M.-A. (1995) 'Gender and prehistoric technology: on the social agency of technical strategies', *World Archaeology* 27(1): 51–66.

Dobres, M.-A. and J. Robb (eds) (2000) *Agency in Archaeology*, London: Routledge.

Dodd, P. (1999) 'Englishness and the national culture', in D. Boswell and J. Evans (eds) *Representing the Nation: A Reader. Histories, Heritage and Museums*, London: Routledge, 87–108.

Donley-Reid, L.W. (1990) 'The power of Swahili porcelain, beads, and pottery', in S.M. Nelson and A.B. Kehoe (eds) *Powers of Observation: Alternative Views in Archaeology*, Papers of the American Anthropological Association 2, Washington: American Anthropological Association, 47–60.

Donlon, D. (1993) 'Imbalance in the sex ratio in collections of Australian Aboriginal skeletal remains', in H. duCros and L. Smith (eds) *Women in Archaeology: A Feminist Critique*, Canberra: The Australian National University, 98–103.

Donlon, D. (1998) 'Mortuary practices and the sex ratio of Australian Aboriginal skeletal remains in the Sydney Basin, coastal New South Wales, Australia', in M. Casey, D. Donlon, J. Hope and S. Wellfare (eds) *Redefining Archaeology: Feminist Perspectives*, Canberra: The Australian National University, 221–6.

Doucette, D.L. (2001) 'Decoding the gender bias: inferences of atlatls in female mortuary contexts', in B. Arnold and N.L. Wicker (eds) *Gender and the Archaeology of Death*, Walnut Creek: Altamira Press, 159–78.

Douglas, M. (ed.) (1966) *Purity and Danger: An Analysis of Concepts of Pollution*, New York: Praeger.

Douglas, M. (1970) *Natural Symbols*, Harmondsworth: Penguin.

Douglas, M. (ed.) (1975) *Implicit Meanings*, London: Routledge and Kegan Paul.

Dowdall, K.M. and O.O. Parrish (2003) 'A meaningful disturbance of the earth', *Journal of Social Archaeology* 3(1): 99–133.

Dowden, K. (2000) *European Paganism*, London: Routledge.

Dowson, T. (1998) 'Homosexualitat, teoria *queer* i arqueologia', *Cota Zero* 14: 81–7.

Drinkall, G. and M. Foreman (1998) *The Anglo-Saxon Cemetery at Castledyke South, Barton-on-Humber*, Sheffield: Sheffield Academic Press.

Dube, S. (1998) *Untouchable Pasts: Religion, Identity, and Power Among a Central Indian Community, 1780–1950*, Albany: State University of New York Press.

Durkheim, E. (1947 [1912]) *The Elementary Forms of Religious Life*, New York: Free Press.

Earle, T. (ed.) (1991) *Chiefdoms: Power, Economy, and Ideology*, Cambridge: Cambridge University Press.

Earle, T. (1997) *How Chiefs Come to Power: The Political Economy in Prehistory*, Stanford: Stanford University Press.

Eco, U. (1962) *Opera aperta*, Milano: Bompiani.

Edelstein, W. (1983) 'Cultural constraints on development and the vicissitudes of progress', in F.S. Kessel and A.W. Siegel (eds) *The Child and Other Cultural Inventions*, New York: Praeger, 48–81.

Edmonds, M. (1990) 'Description, understanding and the Chaîne Opératoire', *Archaeological review from Cambridge* 9(1): 55–70.

Edwards, D.N. (1996) 'Sorghum, beer and Kushite society', *Norwegian Archaeological Review* 29(2): 65–77.

Eliade, M. (1958) *Patterns in Comparative Religion*, New York: New American Library.

Elwert, G. (1997) 'Boundaries, cohesion and switching: on we-groups in ethnic, national and religious forms', in H.-R. Wicker (ed.) *Rethinking Nationalism and Ethnicity: The Struggle for Meaning and Order in Europe*, Oxford: Berg, 251–71.

Engelstad, E. (2001) 'Gender, feminism and sexuality in archaeological studies', in

N.J. Smelser and P.B. Baltes (eds) *International Encyclopedia of the Social and Behavioral Sciences. Vol. 8*, Oxford: Elsevier Science, 6002–6.

Enloe, C. (1980) 'Religion and ethnicity', in P. Sugar (ed.) *Ethnic Diversity and Conflict in Eastern Europe*, Santa Barbara: ABC-Clio, 350–60.

Ennew, J. (1986) *The Sexual Exploitation of Children*, Cambridge: Polity Press.

Epstein, A.L. (1978) *Ethos and Identity: Three Studies in Ethnicity*, London: Tavistock Publications.

Eriksen, T.H. (1991) 'The cultural contexts of ethnic differences', *Man* 26: 127–44.

Eriksen, T.H. (1993) *Ethnicity and Nationalism: Anthropological Perspectives*, London: Pluto.

Estioko-Griffin, A. and P.B. Griffin (1981) 'Woman the hunter: the Agta', in F. Dahlberg (ed.) *Woman the Gatherer*, New Haven: Yale University Press, 121–52.

Evans-Pritchard, E.E. (1965) *Theories of Primitive Religion*, Oxford: Clarendon Press.

Evison, M. (2000) 'All in the genes? Evaluating the biological evidence of contact and migration', in D.M. Hadley and J.D. Richards (eds) *Cultures in Contact: Scandinavian Settlement in England in the Ninth and Tenth Centuries*, Turnhout, Belgium: Brepols, 277–94.

Falk, D. (1997) 'Brain evolution in females: an answer to Mr Lovejoy', in L. Hager (ed.) *Women in Human Evolution*, London: Routledge, 114–36.

Fernández, V. (2003) 'Four thousand years in the Blue Nile: paths to inequality and ways of resistance', *Complutum* 12: 409–25.

Feuerbach, L. (1957) *The Essence of Christianity*, London: Harper & Row.

Fforde, C., J. Hubert and P. Turnbull (eds) (2002) *The Dead and their Possessions: Repatriation in Principle, Policy and Practice*, One World Archaeology 43, London: Routledge.

Fildes, V. (1988) *Wet Nursing: A History from Antiquity to the Present*, Oxford: Blackwell.

Finlay, N. (1997) 'Kid knapping: the missing children in lithic analysis', in J. Moore and E. Scott (eds) *Invisible People and Processes*, Leicester: Leicester University Press, 203–12.

Finlay, N. (2000) 'Outside of life: traditions of infant burial in Ireland from cillín to cist', *World Archaeology* 31(3): 407–22.

Flannery, K.V. (ed.) (1976) *The Early Mesoamerican Village*, New York: Academic Press.

Fletcher, R. (1997) *The Conversion of Europe: From Paganism to Christianity 371–1386 AD*, London: HarperCollins.

Flood, G. (1996) *An Introduction to Hinduism*, Cambridge: Cambridge University Press.

Fol, A., B. Nikolov and R.F. Hoddinott (1986) *The New Thracian Treasure from Rogozen, Bulgaria*, London: British Museum Press.

Foucault, M. (1977) *Discipline and Punish: The Birth of the Prison*, New York: Vintage.

Fowler, C. (2004) *The Archaeology of Personhood: An Anthropological Approach*, London: Routledge.

Frankel, D. (2000) 'Migration and ethnicity in prehistoric Cyprus: technology as *habitus*', *European Journal of Archaeology* 3(2): 167–87.

Frankenstein, S. and M.J. Rowlands (1978) 'The internal structure and regional context of early Iron Age society in South-Western Germany', *Bulletin of the Institute of Archaeology* 15: 73–112.

Frankfurter, D. (1998) *Religion in Roman Egypt: Assimilation and Resistance*, Princeton: Princeton University Press.

Frend, W.H.C. (1996) *The Archaeology of Early Christianity*, London: Geoffrey Chapman.

Fried, M.H. (1967) *The Evolution of Political Society: An Essay in Political Anthropology*, New York: Random House.

Galle, J.E. (1999) 'Haute Couture: cotton, class, and culture change in the American Southwest', in N.L. Wicker and B. Arnold (eds) *From the Ground Up: Beyond Gender Theory in Archaeology: Proceedings of the Fifth Gender and Archaeology Conference, University of Wisconsin-Milwaukee, October 1998*, British Archaeological Reports S812, Oxford: British Archaeological Reports, 125–31.

Galloway, P. (1998) 'Where have all the menstrual huts gone? The invisibility of menstrual seclusion in the Late Prehistoric Southeast', in K. Hays-Gilpin and D.S. Whitley (eds) *Reader in Gender Archaeology*, London: Routledge, 197–212.

Gardner, A. (1999) 'Military identities in Late Roman Britain', *Oxford Journal of Archaeology* 18: 403–17.

Garman, J.C. (1998) 'Rethinking "resistant accommodation": towards an archaeology of African-American lives in southern New England, 1683–1800', *International Journal of Historical Archaeology* 2(2): 133–60.

Garwood, P., P. Jennings, R. Skeates and J. Toms (eds) (1991) *Sacred and Profane*, Oxford Committee for Archaeology Monograph 32, Oxford: Oxbow.

Geary, P.J. (1983) 'Ethnic identity as a situational construct in the early middle ages', *Mitteilungen der Anthropologischen Gesellschaft in Wien* 113: 15–26.

Geary, P.J. (2002) *The Myth of Nations: The Medieval Origins of Europe*, Princeton: Princeton University Press.

Gellner, E. (1981) *Muslim Society*, Cambridge: Cambridge University Press.

Gero, J.M. (1991) 'Genderlithics: women's roles in stone tool production', in J. Gero and M.W. Conkey (eds) *Engendering Archaeology*, Oxford: Blackwell, 163–93.

Gero, J.M. and C. Scattolin. (2002) 'Beyond complementarity and hierarchy', in S.M. Nelson and M. Rosen-Ayalon (eds) *In Pursuit of Gender: Worldwide Archaeological Approaches*, Walnut Creek: AltaMira Press, 155–71.

Gibson, A. and D. Simpson (1998) *Prehistoric Ritual and Religion*, Stroud: Sutton.

Gibson, O.B. and M.N. Geselowitz (1988) 'The evolution of complex society in late prehistoric Europe: toward a paradigm', in O.B. Gibson and M.N. Geselowitz (eds) *Tribe and Polity in Late Prehistoric Europe*, New York: Plenum Press, 3–37.

Giddens, A. (1979) *Central Problems in Social Theory*, London: Macmillan.

Giddens, A. (1984) *The Constitution of Society: Outline of a Theory of Structuration*, Cambridge: Polity Press.

Gifford-Gonzalez, D. (1993) 'Gaps in zooarchaeological analyses of butchery: is gender an issue', in J. Hudson (ed.) *From Bones to Behavior: Ethnoarchaeological and Experimental Contributions to the Interpretation of Faunal Remains*, Carbondale: Southern Illinois University at Carbondale Center for Archaeological Investigations, 181–99.

Gilchrist, R. (1994) *Gender and Material Culture: The Archaeology of Religious Women*, London: Routledge.

Gilchrist, R. (1997) 'Ambivalent bodies: gender and medieval archaeology', in J. Moore and E. Scott (eds) *Invisible People and Processes*, Leicester: Leicester University Press, 42–58.

Gilchrist, R. (1999) *Gender and Archaeology: Contesting the Past*, London: Routledge.

Gillespie, R. (1997) 'On human blood, rock art and calcium oxalate: further studies on organic carbon content and radiocarbon age of materials relating to Australian rock art', *Antiquity* 71: 430–37.

Gilman, A. (1984) 'Explaining the Upper Palaeolithic revolution', in M. Spriggs (ed.) *Marxist Perspectives in Archaeology*, Cambridge: Cambridge University Press, 115–26.

Ginn, J. and S. Arber. (1995) '"Only connect": gender relations and ageing', in S. Arber and J. Ginn (eds) *Connecting Gender and Ageing: A Sociological Approach*, Buckingham: Open University Press, 1–14.

Godelier, M. (1982) *La production des grands hommes: pouvoir et domination masculine chez les Barya de Nouvelle-Guinée*, Paris: Fayard.

Godelier, M. (1988) *The Mental and the Material: Thought, Economy and Society*, London: Verso.

Godelier, M. and M. Panoff (1998) 'Introduction', in M. Godelier and M. Panoff (eds) *La production du corps: Approches anthropologique et historique*, Amsterdam: Editions des Archives Contemporaines, xi–xxv.

Golden, M. (1990) *Children and Childhood in Classical Athens*, Baltimore: Johns Hopkins University Press.

Gowland, R.L. (forthcoming) 'Ageing the past: examining age identity from funerary evidence', in R.L. Gowland and C. Knüsel (eds) *The Social Archaeology of Funerary Remains*, Oxford: Oxbow.

Gowland, R.L. and A.T. Chamberlain (2002) 'A Bayesian approach to ageing perinatal skeletal material from archaeological sites: implications for the evidence for infanticide in Roman Britain', *Journal of Archaeological Science* 29(6): 677–85.

Graham, E. (1998) 'Mission archaeology', *Annual Review of Anthropology* 17: 25–62.

Gramsci, A. (1971) *Selections from the Prison Notebooks*, New York: International Publishers.

Gräslund, A.-S. (2001) 'The position of Iron Age Scandinavian woman: evidence from graves and rune stones', in B. Arnold and N.L. Wicker (eds) *Gender and the Archaeology of Death*, Walnut Creek: Altamira Press, 81–102.

Graves, C.P. (1989) 'Social space in the English medieval parish church', *Economy and Society* 18(3): 297–322.

Graves-Brown, P. (1996) 'All things bright and beautiful? Species, ethnicity and cultural dynamics', in P. Graves-Brown, S. Jones and C. Gamble (eds) *Cultural Identity and Archaeology: The Construction of European Communities*, London: Routledge, 81–95.

Greenfield, P. (2004) *Weaving Generations Together: Evolving Creativity in the Maya of Chiapas*, Santa Fe: SAR Press.

Grimm, L. (2000) 'Apprentice flintknapping: relating material culture and social practice in the Upper Palaeolithic', in J. Sofaer Derevenski (ed.) *Children and Material Culture*, London: Routledge, 53–71.

Gutiérrez, N. (1997) 'Ethnic revivals without nation-states? The theories of E. Gellner and A.D. Smith revisited', in H.-R. Wicker (ed.) *Rethinking Nationalism and Ethnicity: The Struggle for Meaning and Order in Europe*, Oxford: Berg, 163–73.

Hachlili, R. (2001) 'The archaeology of Judaism', in T. Insoll (ed.) *Archaeology and World Religion*, London: Routledge, 96–122.

Hadley, D.M. (ed.) (1999) *Masculinity in Medieval Europe*, London: Longman.

Håland, R. (1977) 'Archaeological classification and ethnic groups: a case study from Sudanese Nubia', *Norwegian Archaeological Review* 10: 1–17.

Hall, S. (1996) 'Introduction: who needs "Identity"?', in S. Hall and P. du Gay (eds) *Questions of Cultural Identity*, London: Sage, 1–17.

Hamilakis, Y. (1999) 'Food technologies/technologies of the body: the social context of wine and olive oil production. and consumption in Bronze Age Crete', *World Archaeology* 35(1): 38–54.

Hamilakis, Y., M. Pluciennik and S. Tarlow (eds) (2002a) *Thinking Through the Body: Archaeologies of Corporeality*, New York: Kluwer Academic/Plenum.

Hamilakis, Y., M. Pluciennik and S. Tarlow. (2002b) 'Introduction: thinking through the body', in Y. Hamilakis, M. Pluciennik and S. Tarlow (eds) *Thinking Through the Body: Archaeologies of Corporeality*, New York: Kluwer Academic/Plenum, 1–21.

Hamlin, C. (2001) 'Sharing the load: gender and task division at Windover Site', in B. Arnold and N.L. Wicker (eds) *Gender and the Archaeology of Death*, Walnut Creek: Altamira Press, 119–36.

Hammond, G. and N. Hammond (1981) 'Child's play: a distorting factor in archaeological distribution', *American Antiquity* 46: 634–6.

Hanawalt, B. (1993) *Growing Up in Medieval London: The Experience of Childhood in History*, Oxford: Oxford University Press.

Harlow, M. and R. Laurence (2002) *Growing Up and Growing Old in Ancient Rome: A Life Course Approach*, London: Routledge.

Harris, M. (1977) *Cannibals and Kings: The Origins of Cultures*, New York: Random House.

Hastorf, C.A. (1991) 'Gender, space, and food in prehistory', in J. Gero and M.W. Conkey (eds) *Engendering Archaeology*, Oxford: Blackwell, 132–62.

Hastorf, C.A. (1998a) 'Cultural implications of crop introductions in Andean prehistory', in C. Gosden and J. Hather (eds) *The Prehistory of Food*, London: Routledge, 35–58.

Hastorf, C.A. (1998b) 'The cultural life of early domestic plant use', *Antiquity* 72: 773–82.

Haughton, C. And D. Powlesland (1999) *West Heslerton: The Anglian Cemetery*, Yedingham: Landscape Research Centre.

Hawkes, C. (1954) 'Archaeological theory and method: some suggestions from the Old World', *American Anthropologist* 56: 155–68.

Hawkes, C. and J. Hawkes (1943) *Prehistoric Britain*, Harmondsworth: Penguin.

Hays-Gilpin, K. and D.S. Whitley (1998) 'Introduction to part III: identifying "sexual" divisions of labor', in K. Hays-Gilpin and D.S. Whitley (eds) *Reader in Gender Archaeology*, London: Routledge, 139–43.

Hebdige, D. (1979) *Subculture: The Meaning of Style*, London: Methuen.

Hedeager, L. (1992) *Iron-Age Societies: From Tribe to State in Northern Europe, 500 BC to AD 700*, Oxford: Blackwell.

Hedeager, L. (1993) 'The creation of Germanic identity: a European origin-myth', in P. Brun, S. van der Leeuw and W. Whittaker (eds) *Frontières d'empire: Nature et signification des frontières romaines. Actes de la Table Ronde Internationale de Nemours 1992*, Mémoires du Musée de Préhistoire d'Ile-de-France 5, Nemours: Musée de Préhistoire d'Ile-de-France, 121–31.

Hendrick, H. (1997) *Children, Childhood and English Society, 1880–1990*, Cambridge: Cambridge University Press.

Heywood, C. (2001) *A History of Childhood*, Cambridge: Polity Press.

Hides, S. (1996) 'The genealogy of material culture and cultural identity', in P.

Graves-Brown, S. Jones and C. Gamble (eds) *Cultural Identity and Archaeology: The Construction of European Communities*, London: Routledge, 25–47.

Hill, J.D. (1989) 'Re-thinking the Iron Age', *Scottish Archaeological Review* 6: 16–24.

Hill, J.D. (1995) 'The pre-Roman Iron Age in Britain and Ireland (ca. 800 BC to AD 100): An overview', *Journal of World Prehistory* 9: 47–98.

Hill, J.D. (2001) 'Romanisation, gender and class', in S. James and M. Millett (eds) *Britons and Romans: Advancing an Archaeological Agenda*, Council for British Archaeology Research Report 125, York: Council for British Archaeology, 12–18.

Hills, C. (2003) *Origins of the English*, London: Duckworth.

Hjørungdal, T. (1994) 'Poles apart: have there been any male and female graves?', *Current Swedish Archaeology* 2: 141–8.

Hobsbawm, E.J. (1983) 'Introduction: inventing traditions', in E.J. Hobsbawm and T. Ranger (eds) *The Invention of Tradition*, Cambridge: Cambridge University Press, 1–14.

Hockey, J. and A. James (1993) *Growing Up and Growing Old: Ageing and Dependency in the Life Course*, London: Sage.

Hodder, I. (1978) 'Simple correlations between material culture and society: a review', in I. Hodder (ed.) *The Spatial Organisation of Culture*, London: Duckworth, 3–24.

Hodder, I. (ed.) (1982a) *Symbolic and Structural Archaeology*, Cambridge: Cambridge University Press.

Hodder, I. (1982b) *Symbols in Action: Ethnoarchaeological Studies of Material Culture*, Cambridge: Cambridge University Press.

Hodder, I. (1986) *Reading the Past*, Cambridge: Cambridge University Press.

Hodder, I. and C. Orton (1976) *Spatial Analysis in Archaeology*, Cambridge: Cambridge University Press.

Hollimon, S.E. (2000) 'Archaeology of the '*AQi*: gender sexuality in prehistoric Chumash society', in R.A. Schmidt and B.L. Voss (eds) *Archaeologies of Sexuality*, London: Routledge, 179–96.

Hollimon, S.E. (2001) 'The gendered peopling of North America: addressing the antiquity of systems of multiple genders', in N. Price (ed.) *The Archaeology of Shamanism*, London: Routledge, 123–34.

Holy, L. (1983) 'Symbolic and non-symbolic aspects of Berti space', *Man* 18(2): 269–88.

Holy, L. (1988) 'Gender and ritual in an Islamic society: the Berti of Darfur', *Man* 23(3): 469–87.

Holy, L. (1990) 'Strategies for old age among the Berti of the Sudan', in P. Spencer (ed.) *Anthropology and the Riddle of the Sphinx: Paradoxes of Change in the Life Course*, London: Routledge, 167–82.

Holy, L. (1991) *Religion and Custom in a Muslim Society*, Cambridge: Cambridge University Press.

Hopkins, E. (1994) *Childhood Transformed: Working-class Children in Nineteenth-century England*, Manchester: Manchester University Press.

Hoppa, R.D. and J.W. Vaupel (eds) (2002) *Paleodemography? Age Distributions from Skeletal Samples*, Cambridge: Cambridge University Press.

Houby-Nielsen, S. (2000) 'Child burials in ancient Athens', in J. Sofaer Derevenski (ed.) *Children and Material Culture*, London: Routledge, 151–66.

Howell, S. (1987) 'From child to human: Chewong concepts of self', in G. Jahoda and I.M. Lewis (eds) *Acquiring Culture*, London: Croom Helm, 147–68.

Humphrey, L. (2000) 'Interpretation of the growth of past populations', in J. Sofaer Derevenski (ed.) *Children and Material Culture*, London: Routledge, 193–205.

Humphreys, S.C. (1978) 'History, economics, and anthropology: the work of Karl Polanyi', in S.C. Humphreys *Anthropology and the Greeks*, London: Routledge, 31–75.

Hunter, F. (2001) 'Roman and native in Scotland: new approaches', *Journal of Roman Archaeology* 14: 289–309.

Hurcombe, L. (1997) 'A viable past in the pictorial present?', in J. Moore and E. Scott (eds) *Invisible People and Processes*, Leicester: Leicester University Press, 15–24.

Insoll, T. (1999) *Case Studies in Archaeology and World Religion*, BAR International Series 755, Oxford: British Archaeological Reports.

Insoll, T. (ed.) (2001a) *Archaeology and World Religion*, London: Routledge.

Insoll, T. (2001b) 'Introduction: the archaeology of world religion', in T. Insoll (ed.) *The Archaeology of World Religion*, London: Routledge, 1–32.

Insoll, T. (2004) *Archaeology, Ritual, Religion*, London: Routledge.

Işcan, M.Y., S.R. Loth and R.K. Wright (1984) 'Metamorphosis at the sternal rib end: a new method to estimate age at death in white males', *American Journal of Physical Anthropology* 65: 147–56.

Işcan, M.Y., S.R. Loth and R.K. Wright (1985) 'Estimation from the rib by phase analysis: white females', *Journal of Forensic Sciences* 30: 853–63.

Jackson, T.L. (1991) 'Pounding acorn: women's production as social and economic focus', in J. Gero and M.W. Conkey (eds) *Engendering Archaeology*, Oxford: Blackwell, 301–28.

James, A. (1993) *Childhood Identities: Self and Social Relationships in the Experience of the Child*, Edinburgh: Edinburgh University Press.

James, A. (1998) 'From the child's point of view', in C. Panter-Brick (ed.) *Biosocial Perspectives on Children*, Cambridge: Cambridge University Press, 45–65.

James, A., C. Jenks and A. Prout (1998) *Theorizing Childhood*, Cambridge: Polity Press.

James, E. (1988) *The Franks*, Oxford: Blackwell.

James, E. (1989) 'The origins of barbarian kingdoms: the continental evidence', in S. Bassett (ed.) *The Origins of Anglo-Saxon Kingdoms*, Leicester: Leicester University Press, 40–52.

James, S. (1999) *The Atlantic Celts: Ancient People or Modern Invention?* London: British Museum Press.

James, W. and D. Johnson (eds) (1988) *Vernacular Christianity*, Oxford: JASO.

Jarvenpa, R. and H.J. Brumbach (1995) 'Ethnoarchaeology and gender: Chipewyan woman as hunters', *Research in Economic Anthropology* 16: 39–82.

Jenkins, R. (1990) 'Dimensions of adulthood in Britain: long-term unemployment and mental handicap', in P. Spencer (ed.) *Anthropology and the Riddle of the Sphinx: Paradoxes of Change in the Life Course*, London: Routledge, 131–46.

Jenkins, R. (1994) 'Rethinking ethnicity: identity, categorization and power', *Ethnic and Racial Studies* 17(2): 197–223.

Jenkins, R. (1997) *Rethinking Ethnicity: Arguments and Explorations*, London: Sage.

Jenks, C. (1982) 'Introduction: constituting the child', in C. Jenks (ed.) *The Sociology of Childhood: Essential Readings*, London: Batsford, 9–24.

Jenks, C. (1993) *Culture*, London: Routledge.

Jenks, C. (1996) *Childhood: Key Ideas*, London: Routledge.

Jiao, T. (2001) 'Gender studies in Chinese Neolithic archaeology', in B. Arnold and N.L. Wicker (eds) *Gender and the Archaeology of Death*, Walnut Creek: Altamira Press, 51–63.

Johnson, D. (1990) 'Fixed shrines and spiritual centres in the Upper Nile', *Azania* 25: 41–56.

Johnson, D. (1994) *Nuer Prophets: A History of Prophecy from the Upper Nile in the Nineteenth and Twentieth Centuries*, Oxford: Clarendon Press.

Johnson, M.H. (1989) 'Conceptions of agency in archaeological interpretation', *Journal of Anthropological Archaeology* 8: 189–211.

Johnson, M.H. (1999) *Archaeological Theory: An Introduction*, Oxford: Blackwell.

Jones, P. and N. Pennick (1995) *The History of Pagan Europe*, London: Routledge.

Jones, R. (1992) 'Philosophical time travellers', *Antiquity* 66: 744–57.

Jones, S. (1996) 'Discourses of identity in the interpretation of the past', in P. Graves-Brown, S. Jones and C. Gamble (eds) *Cultural Identity and Archaeology: The Construction of the Past*, London: Routledge.

Jones, S. (1997) *The Archaeology of Ethnicity*, London: Routledge.

Jones, S. (1998) 'Historical categories and the praxis of identity: the interpretation of ethnicity in historical archaeology', in P.P. Funari, M. Hall and S. Jones (eds) *Historical Archaeology: Back from the Edge*, London: Routledge, 219–32.

Jones, S. and P. Graves-Brown (1996) 'Introduction: archaeology and cultural identity in Europe', in P. Graves-Brown, S. Jones and C. Gamble (eds) *Cultural Identity and Archaeology*, London: Routledge, 1–24.

Joyce, R.A. (1992) 'Images of gender and labor organization in classic Maya society', in C.P. Claassen (ed.) *Exploring Gender Through Archaeology: Selected Papers from the 1991 Boone Conference*, Monograph in World Archaeology 11, Madison: Prehistory Press, 63–70.

Joyce, R.A. (2000) 'Male sexuality among the ancient Maya', in R.A. Schmidt and B.L. Voss (eds) *Archaeologies of Sexuality*, London: Routledge, 263–83.

Kamp, K.A., N. Timmerman, G. Lind, J. Graybill and I. Natowsky (1999) 'Discovering childhood: Using fingerprints to find children in the archaeological record', *American Antiquity* 64(2): 309–15.

Kane, S. (ed.) (2003) *Politics of Archaeology and Identity in a Global Context*, Colloquia and Conference Papers 7, Boston: Archaeological Institute of America.

Karp, I. (1980) 'Beer drinking and social experience in an African society', in I. Karp and C.S. Bird (eds) *Explorations in African Systems of Thought*, Bloomington: Indiana University Press, 83–119.

Katz, D. and J.M. Suchey (1986) 'Age determination of the male os pubis', *American Journal of Physical Anthropology* 69: 427–35.

Kehoe, A.B. (2000) 'Mississippian weavers', in A.E. Rautman (ed.) *Reading the Body: Representations and Remains in the Archaeological Record*, Philadelphia: University of Pennsylvania Press, 132–8.

Kemp, B. (1995) 'How religious were the Ancient Egyptians?', *Cambridge Archaeological Journal* 5: 25–54.

Kennedy, J. (ed.) (1978) *Nubian Ceremonial Life*, Berkeley: University of California Press.

Kessel, F.S., M.H. Bornstein and A.J. Sameroff (eds) (1991) *Contemporary Constructions of the Child: Essays in Honour of William Kessen*, Hillsdale: Lawrence Erlbaum Associates.

Kessel, F.S. and A.W. Siegel (eds) (1983) *The Child and Other Cultural Inventions*, New York: Praeger.

Kessler, S. (1998) *Lessons from the Intersexed*, New Brunswick: Rutgers University Press.

Keuls, E.C. (1985) *The Reign of the Phallus: Sexual Politics in Ancient Athens*, Berkeley: University of California Press.

Kimmel, M. (ed.) (1987) *Changing Men: New Directions in Research on Men and Masculinity*, California: Sage.

Knapp, A.B. (1998) 'Boys will be boys: masculinist approaches to a gendered archaeology', in K. Hays-Gilpin and D.S. Whitley (eds) *Reader in Gender Archaeology*, London: Routledge, 365–73.

Kohl, P.L. and C. Fawcett (eds) (1995) *Nationalism, Politics, and the Practice of Archaeology*, Cambridge: Cambridge University Press.

Koloski-Ostrow, A.O. (1997) 'Violent stages in two Pompeian houses: Imperial taste, aristocratic response, and messages of male control', in A.O. Koloski-Ostrow and C.L. Lyons (eds) *Naked Truths: Women, Sexuality and Gender in Classical Art and Archaeology*, London: Routledge, 243–66.

Kopytoff, I. (1986) 'The cultural biography of things: commoditization as process', in A. Appadurai (ed.) *The Social Life of Things: Commodities in Cultural Perspective*, Cambridge: Cambridge University Press, 64–91.

Kossinna, G. (1911) *Die Herkunft der Germanen. Zür Methode der Siedlungsarchäologie*, Würzburg: Mannus-Bibliothek 6.

Kus, S. (1992) 'Toward an archaeology of body and soul', in J.-C. Gardin and C. Peebles (eds) *Representations in Archaeology*, Bloomington: Indiana University Press, 168–77.

La Fontaine, J.S. (1985) *Initiation*, Manchester: Manchester University Press.

Lane, P. (1998) 'Engendered spaces bodily practices in the Iron Age of Southern Africa', in S. Kent (ed.) *Gender in African Prehistory*, Walnut Creek: Altamira Press, 179–204.

Lane, P. (1999) 'Archaeology, nonconformist missions and the "colonisation of consciousness" in Southern Africa, *c.*1820–1900', in T. Insoll (ed.) *Case Studies in Archaeology and World Religion*, BAR International Series 755, Oxford: British Archaeological Reports, 153–65.

Larick, R. (1986) 'Age grading and ethnicity in the style of Loikup (Samburu) spears', *World Archaeology* 18: 269–83.

Laslett, P. (1995) 'Necessary knowledge: age and ageing in the societies of the past', in D.I. Kertzer and P. Laslett (eds) *Ageing in the Past: Demography, Society and Old Age*, Berkeley: University of California Press, 3–77.

Laurence, R. (2000) 'Metaphors, monuments and texts: the life course in Roman culture', *World Archaeology* 31(3): 442–55.

Laurence, R. and J. Berry (eds) (1998) *Cultural Identity in the Roman Empire*, London: Routledge.

Lawrence, S. (2003) *Archaeologies of the British: Explorations of Identity in Great Britain and its Colonies 1600–1945*, One World Archaeology 46, London: Routledge.

Layton, R. (ed.) (1989a) *Conflict in the Archaeology of Living Traditions*, One World Archaeology 8, London: Unwin Hyman.

Layton, R. (ed.) (1989b) *Who Needs the Past?*, One World Archaeology 5, London: Unwin Hyman.

Layton, R. (1997) *An Introduction to Theory in Anthropology*, Cambridge: Cambridge University Press.

Lee, K.A. (1994) 'Attitudes and prejudices towards infanticide: Carthage, Rome and today', *Archaeological Review from Cambridge* 13(2): 65–79.

Leeds, E.T. (1913) *The Archaeology of the Anglo-Saxon Settlements*, Oxford: Clarendon Press.

Lemonnier, P. (1993) 'Introduction', in P. Lemonnier (ed.) *Technological Choices: Transformation in Material Cultures since the Neolithic*, London: Routledge, 1–35.

Leone, M.P. (1973) 'Archaeology as the science of technology: Mormon town plans and fences', in C.L. Redman (ed.) *Research and Theory in Current Archaeology*, New York: Wiley and Sons, 125–50.

Leone, M.P. (1984) 'Interpreting ideology in historical archaeology: the William Paca garden in Annapolis, Maryland', in D. Miller and C. Tilley (eds) *Ideology, Power and Prehistory*, Cambridge: Cambridge University Press, 25–37.

Lesnick-Oberstein, K. (1998) 'Childhood and textuality: culture, history, literature', in K. Lesnick-Oberstein (ed.) *Children in Culture: Approaches to Childhood*, London: Macmillan, 1–28.

Levine, H.B. (1999) 'Reconstructing ethnicity', *Journal of the Royal Anthropological Institute* 5(2): 165–80.

Levine, R. (1998) 'Child psychology and anthropology: an environmental view', in C. Panter-Brick (ed.) *Biosocial Perspectives on Children*, Cambridge: Cambridge University Press, 102–30.

Levy, J.E. (1999) 'Gender, power, and heterarchy in the middle-level societies', in T.L. Sweely (ed.) *Manifesting Power: Gender and the Interpretation of Power in Archaeology*, London: Routledge, 62–78.

Lewis, I.M. (1983) 'The past and the present in Islam: the case of African "survivals"', *Temenos* 19: 55–67.

Lillehammer, G. (1989) 'A child is born: the child's world in an archaeological perspective', *Norwegian Archaeological Review* 22: 91–105.

Linde-Laursen, A. (1993) 'The nationalization of trivialities: how cleaning becomes an identity marker in the encounter of Swedes and Danes', *Ethnos* 3–4: 275–93.

Lorenzen, D.N. (1999) 'Who invented Hinduism?', *Comparative Studies in Society and History* 41(4): 630–59.

Lovejoy, C.O., R.S. Meindl, T.R. Pryzbeck and R.P. Mensforth (1985) 'Chronological metamorphosis of the auricular surface of the ilium: a new method of determining adult age at death', *American Journal of Physical Anthropology* 68: 15–28.

Lucas, G.M. (1996) 'Of death and debt: a history of the body in Neolithic and Early Bronze Age Yorkshire', *Journal of European Archaeology* 4: 99–118.

Lucy, S. (1994) 'Children in Early Medieval cemeteries', *Archaeological Review from Cambridge* 13(2): 21–34.

Lucy, S. (1997) 'Housewives, warriors and slaves? Sex and gender in Anglo-Saxon burials', in J. Moore and E. Scott (eds) *Invisible People and Processes*, Leicester: Leicester University Press, 150–68.

Lucy, S. (1998) *The Early Anglo-Saxon Cemeteries of East Yorkshire: An Analysis and Reinterpretation*, BAR British Series 272, Oxford: British Archaeological Reports.

Lucy, S. (2000a) *The Anglo-Saxon Way of Death*, Stroud: Sutton.

Lucy, S. (2000b) 'Early medieval burials in East Yorkshire: reconsidering the evidence', in H. Geake and J. Kenny (eds) *Early Deira: Archaeological Studies of the East Riding in the Fourth to Ninth centuries AD*, Oxford: Oxbow, 11–18.

Luhmer, K. (1990) 'Moral education in Japan', *Journal of Moral Education* 19(3): 172–82.

Lustig, J. (1997) 'Kinship, gender and age in Middle Kingdom tomb scenes and texts', in J. Lustig (ed.) *Anthropology and Egyptology: A Developing Dialogue*, Monographs in Mediterranean Archaeology 8, Sheffield: Sheffield Academic Press, 43–65.

Lyons, C.L. and J.K. Papadopoulos (eds) (2002) *The Archaeology of Colonialism*, Los Angeles: Getty Research Institute.

Lyons, D. (1991) 'The construction of gender, time and space', in D. Walde and N.D. Willows (eds) *The Archaeology of Gender*, Calgary: The University of Calgary, 108–14.

Lyons, D. (1996) 'The politics of house shape: round vs. rectilinear domestic structures in Déle compounds, northern Cameroon', *Antiquity* 70(268): 351–67.

McBrearty, S. and M. Moniz (1991) 'Prostitutes or providers? Hunting, tool use, and sex roles in earliest *Homo*', in I.D. Walde and N.D. Willows (eds) *The Archaeology of Gender*, Calgary: The University of Calgary, 71–82.

McCafferty, G. and S.D. McCafferty (1999) 'The metamorphosis of Xochiquetzal: a window on womanhood in pre-and post-conquest Mexico', in T.L. Sweely (ed.) *Manifesting Power: Gender and the Interpretation of Power in Archaeology*, London: Routledge, 103–25.

McCafferty, S. and G. McCafferty (1991) 'Spinning and weaving as female gender identity in post-Classical Central Mexico', in M. Schevill, J.C. Berlo and E.B. Dwyer (eds) *Textile Traditions of Mesoamerica and the Andes*, New York: Garland, 19–48.

McCafferty, S.D. and G.G. McCafferty (1988) 'Powerful women and the myth of male dominance in Aztec Society', *Archaeological Review from Cambridge* 7(1): 45–59.

McCafferty, S.D. and G.G. McCafferty (1998 [1991]) 'Spinning and weaving as female gender identity in post-Classic Mexico', in K. Hays-Gilpin and D.S. Whitley (eds) *Reader in Gender Archaeology*, London: Routledge, 213–30.

McGuire, K.R. and W.R. Hildebrandt (1994) 'The possibilities of women and men: gender and the California milling stone horizon', *Journal of California and Great Basin Archaeology* 16(1): 41–59.

McGuire, R. (1991) 'Building power in the cultural landscape of Broome County, New York, 1880–1940', in R. McGuire and R. Paynter (eds) *The Archaeology of Inequality*, Oxford: Blackwell, 102–24.

McGuire, R.H. (1982) 'The study of ethnicity in historical archaeology', *Journal of Anthropological Archaeology* 1: 159–78.

McIntosh, S.K. (ed.) (1999) *Beyond Chieftains: Pathways to Complexity in Africa*, Cambridge: Cambridge University Press.

McKell, S.M. (1993) 'An axe to grind: More ripping yarns from Australian Prehistory', in H. duCros and L. Smith (eds) *Women in Archaeology: A Feminist Critique*, Canberra: The Australian National University, 115–20.

Maceachern, S. (1998) 'Scale, style and cultural variation: technological traditions in the North Mandara Mountains', in M.T. Stark (ed.) *The Archaeology of Social Boundaries*, Washington: Smithsonian Books, 107–31.

MacGaffey, W. (1972) 'Comparative analysis of Central African religions', *Africa* 42(1): 21–31.

MacGaffey, W. (1980) 'African religion: types and generalisations', in I. Karp and

C.S. Bird (eds) *Explorations in African Systems of Thought*, Bloomington: Indiana University Press, 301–28.

MacKenzie, M.A. (1991) *Androgynous Objects: String Bags and Gender in Central New Guinea*, Reading: Harwood Academic Publishers.

MacLean, R. (1998) 'Gendered technologies and gendered activities in the Interlacustrine Early Iron Age', in S. Kent (ed.) *Gender in African Prehistory*, Walnut Creek: Altamira Press, 163–78.

MacLean, R. (2001) 'Gender in the archaeology of world religion?', in T. Insoll (ed.) *Archaeology and World Religion*, London: Routledge, 193–202.

Malina, J. and Z. Vasícek (1990) *Archaeology Yesterday and Today: The Development of Archaeology in the Sciences and Humanities*, Cambridge: Cambridge University Press.

Marshall, Y. (1985) 'Who made the Lapita pots? A case study in gender archaeology', *Journal of the Polynesian Society* 94(3): 205–33.

Martin, M.K. and B. Voorhies (1975) *Female of the Species*, New York: Columbia University Press.

Marucci, G. (1999) 'Women's ritual sites in the interior of British Columbia: an archaeological model', in N.L. Wicker and B. Arnold (eds) *From the Ground Up: Beyond Gender Theory in Archaeology: Proceedings of the Fifth Gender and Archaeology Conference, University of Wisconsin-Milwaukee, October 1998*, British Archaeological Reports S812, Oxford: British Archaeological Reports, 75–82.

Matthews, K. (1994) 'An archaeology of homosexuality? Perspectives from the Classical world', in S. Cottam, D. Dungworth, S. Scott and J. Taylor (eds) *TRAC 94: Proceedings of the Fourth Annual Theoretical Roman Archaeology Conference, Durham 1994*, Oxford: Oxbow, 118–32.

Mauss, M. (1979 [1950]) 'Body techniques', in G. Gurwich (ed.) *Sociology and Anthropology*, London: Routledge, 97–123.

Mays, S. (1998) *The Archaeology of Human Bones*, London: Routledge.

Mazo Karras, R. (2003) *From Boys to Men: Formations of Masculinity in Late Medieval Europe*, Philadelphia: University of Pennsylvania Press.

Mead, M. (1973 [1928]) *Coming of Age in Samoa: A Psychological Study of Primitive Youth for Western Civilisation*, New York: Morrow.

Meinander, C.F. (1981) 'The concept of culture in European archaeological literature', in G. Daniel (ed.) *Towards a History of Archaeology*, London and New York: Thames & Hudson, 100–11.

Meindl, R.S. and C.O. Lovejoy (1985) 'Ectocranial suture closure: a revised method for the determination of skeletal age at death based on the lateral-anterior sutures', *American Journal of Physical Anthropology* 68: 57–66.

Memon, M.U. (1976) *Ibn Taimiya's Struggle against Popular Religion*, The Hague: Mouton.

Meskell, L. (1995) 'Goddesses, Gimbutas and "New Age" Archaeology', *Antiquity* 69: 74–86.

Meskell, L. (ed.) (1998) *Archaeology Under Fire: Nationalism, Politics and Heritage in the Eastern Mediterranean and Middle East*, London: Routledge.

Meskell, L. (ed.) (1999) *Archaeologies of Social Life: Age, Sex, Class Etcetera in Ancient Egypt*, Oxford: Blackwell.

Meskell, L. (2001) 'Archaeologies of identity', in I. Hodder (ed.) *Archaeological Theory Today*, Cambridge: Polity Press, 187–213.

Miles, A.E.W. (1963) 'The dentition in the assessment of individual age in skeletal material', in D.R. Brothwell (ed.) *Dental Anthropology*, Oxford: Pergamon, 191–209.

Millard, A.R. and R.L. Gowland (2002) 'A Bayesian approach to the estimation of age from tooth development and wear in humans', *Archaeologia e Calcolatori* 13: 197–210.

Miller, D. (1987) *Material Culture and Mass Consumption*, London: Blackwell.

Miller, D. (1989) 'The limits of dominance', in D. Miller, M. Rowlands and C. Tilley (eds) *Domination and Resistance*, London: Unwin Hyman, 63–78.

Miller, D. (1994) *Modernity: An Ethnographic Approach – Dualism and Mass Consumption in Trinidad*, Oxford: Berg.

Miller, D. (1995) 'Consumption studies as the transformation of anthropology', in D. Miller (ed.) *Acknowledging Consumption: A Review of New Studies*, London: Routledge, 264–95.

Miller, D. (2002) 'Consumption', in V. Buchli (ed.) *The Material Culture Reader*, Oxford: Berg, 237–43.

Miller, D., M. Rowlands and C. Tilley (1989) 'Introduction', in D. Miller, M. Rowlands and C. Tilley (eds) *Domination and Resistance*, London: Unwin Hyman, 1–26.

Miller, D. and C. Tilley (1984) 'Introduction', in D. Miller and C. Tilley (eds) *Ideology, Power, and Prehistory*, Cambridge: Cambridge University Press, 1–15.

Milner, N., O.E. Craig, G.N. Bailey, K. Pedersen and S.H. Andersen (2004) 'Something fishy in the Neolithic? A re-evaluation of stable isotope analysis of Mesolithic and Neolithic coastal populations', *Antiquity* 78: 9–22.

Minois, G. (1989) *History of Old Age: From Antiquity to the Renaissance*, Cambridge: Polity Press.

Mirza, M.N. and D.B. Dungworth (1995) 'The potential misuse of genetic analyses and the social construction of "race" and "ethnicity"', *Oxford Journal of Archaeology* 14(3): 345–54.

Mitchell, P.J. and I. Plug (1997) 'Ritual mutilation in Southern Africa: gender and ethnic identities and the possibilities of archaeological recognition', in L. Wadley (ed.) *Our Gendered Past: Archaeological Studies in Southern Africa*, Johannesburg: Witwatersrand University Press, 135–66.

Mitterauer, M. (1992) *A History of Youth*, Oxford: Blackwell.

Mohen, J.-P., A. Duval and C. Eluère. (1987) *Les trésors des princes celtes*, Paris: Éditions de le Réunion des Musées Nationaux.

Molleson, T. (1994) 'The eloquent bones of Abu Hureyra', *Scientific American* 217(2): 60–5.

Molleson, T. and M. Cox (1993) *The Spitalfields Project, Volume 2: The Anthropology: The Middling Sort*, CBA Research Report 86, York: Council for British Archaeology.

Moore, H.L. (1986) *Space, Text and Gender: An Anthropological Study of the Marakwet of Kenya*, Cambridge: Cambridge University Press.

Moore, J. and E. Scott (eds) (1997) *Invisible People and Processes: Writing Gender and Childhood into European Archaeology*, Leicester: Leicester University Press.

Moore, J.H. (1994) 'Putting anthropology back together again: the ethnogenetic critique of cladistic theory', *American Anthropologist* 96(4): 925–48.

Moreland, J. (2000) 'Ethnicity, power and the English', in W.O. Frazer and A. Tyrrell (eds) *Social Identity in Early Medieval Britain*, Leicester: Leicester University Press, 23–51.

Morgan, L.H. (1877) *Ancient Society*, New York: World Publishing.

Morris, B. (1987) *Anthropological Studies of Religion: An Introductory Text*, Cambridge: Cambridge University Press.

Morris, I. (1987) *Burial and Ancient Society: The Rise of the Greek City-State*, Cambridge: Cambridge University Press.

Morris, I. (1992) *Death-Ritual and Social Structure in Classical Antiquity*, Cambridge: Cambridge University Press.

Murdock, G.P. and C. Provost (1973) 'Factors in the division of labour by sex: A cross-cultural analysis', *Ethnology* 12: 203–25.

Nanda, S. (1993) 'Neither man nor woman: the Hirjas of India', in C.B. Brettell and C.F. Sargent (eds) *Gender in Cross-Cultural Perspective*, New York: Prentice Hall, 175–9.

Nanda, S. (1994) 'Hirjas: an alternative sex and gender role in India', in G. Herdt (ed.) *Third Sex, Third Gender: Beyond Sexual Dimorphism in Culture and History*, New York: Zone Books, 373–418.

Nelson, S.M. (1997) *Gender in Archaeology: Analyzing Power and Prestige*, Walnut Creek: Altamira Press.

Nelson, S.M. and M. Rosen-Ayalon (2002) 'Introduction', in S.M. Nelson and M. Rosen-Ayalon (eds) *In Pursuit of Gender: Worldwide Archaeological Approaches*, Walnut Creek: Altamira Press, 1–7.

Netting, R. (1972) 'Sacred power and centralization', in B. Spooner (ed.) *Population Growth: Anthropological Implications*, Cambridge: MIT Press, 219–44.

Niles, J.D. (1997) 'Appropriations: a concept of culture', in A.J. Frantzen and J.D. Niles (eds) *Anglo-Saxonism and the Construction of Social Identity*, Gainesville: University Press of Florida, 202–28.

Oakley, A. (1972) *Sex, Gender, and Society*, London: Temple Smith and New Society.

O'Brien, O. (1994) 'Ethnic identity, gender and life cycle in North Catalonia', in V.A. Goddard, J.R. Llobera and C. Shore (eds) *The Anthropology of Europe: Identities and Boundaries in Conflict*, Oxford: Berg, 191–207.

Olsen, B. and Z. Kobylínski (1991) 'Ethnicity in anthropological and archaeological research: a Norwegian-Polish Perspective', *Archaeologia Polona* 29: 5–28.

Orme, N. (2001) *Medieval Children*, New Haven: Yale University Press.

Ortner, S.B. and H. Whitehead (eds) (1981) *Sexual Meanings: The Cultural Construction of Gender and Sexuality*, Cambridge: Cambridge University Press.

Otto, R. (1950) *The Idea of the Holy*, Oxford: Oxford University Press.

Pandey, G. (1999) 'Can a Muslim be an Indian?', *Comparative Studies in Society and History* 41: 608–29.

Panter-Brick, C. (1998) 'Biological anthropology and child health: context, process and outcome', in C. Panter-Brick (ed.) *Biosocial Perspectives on Children*, Cambridge: Cambridge University Press, 66–101.

Park, L. (1998) 'Size counts: the miniature archaeology of childhood in Inuit societies', *Antiquity* 72: 269–81.

Parker Pearson, M. (1984) 'Economic and ideological change: cyclical growth in the pre-state societies of Jutland', in D. Miller and C. Tilley (eds) *Ideology, Power and Prehistory*, Cambridge: Cambridge University Press, 99–114.

Parker Pearson, M. (1999) *The Archaeology of Death and Burial*, Stroud: Sutton.

Parker Pearson, M. (2001) 'Death, being, and time', in T. Insoll (ed.) *Archaeology and World Religion*, London: Routledge, 203–20.

Parker, R. (1984) *The Subversive Stitch: Embroidery and the Making of the Feminine*, London: The Women's Press.

Parkin, T.G. (1992) *Demography and Roman Society*, Baltimore: Johns Hopkins University Press.

Parkin, T.G. (2002) *Old Age in the Roman World: A Cultural and Social History*, Baltimore: Johns Hopkins University Press.

Parkington, J. (2002) 'Men, women, and eland: hunting and gender among the San of Southern Africa', in S.M. Nelson and M. Rosen-Ayalon (eds) *In Pursuit of Gender: Worldwide Archaeological Approaches*, Walnut Creek: Altamira Press, 93–117.

Pateman, C. (1983) 'Feminist critiques of the public/private dichotomy', in S.I. Benn and G.F. Gauss (eds) *Public and Private in Social Life*, New York: St Martin's Press, 281–303.

Peebles, C.S. and S.M. Kus (1977) 'Some archaeological correlates of ranked societies', *American Antiquity* 42(3): 421–48.

Peterson, J.D. (2000) 'Labor patterns in the Southern Levant in the Early Bronze Age', in A.E. Rautman (ed.) *Reading the Body: Representations and Remains in the Archaeological Record*, Philadelphia: University of Pennsylvania Press, 38–54.

Pettitt, P.B. (2000) 'Neanderthal lifecycles: developmental and social phases in the lives of the last archaics', *World Archaeology* 31(3): 351–66.

Pilcher, J. (1995) *Age and Generation in Modern Britain*, Oxford: Oxford University Press.

Platt, C. (1987) Special issue on Archaeology of the Christian Church (edited by C. Platt), *World Archaeology* 18(3): all.

Pluciennik, M. (1996a) 'Genetics, archaeology and the wider world', *Antiquity* 70: 13–14.

Pluciennik, M. (1996b) 'A perilous but necessary search: archaeology and European identities', in J.A. Atkinson, I. Banks and J. O'Sullivan (eds) *Nationalism and Archaeology*, Glasgow: Cruithne Press, 35–58.

Pohl, W. (1998) *Strategies of Distinction: The Construction of Ethnic Communities, 300–800*, Leiden: Brill.

Polet, C. and M.A. Katzenberg (2003) 'Reconstruction of the diet in a medieval monastic community from the coast of Belgium', *Journal of Archaeological Science*, 30, (5): 525–33.

Pollock, L. (1983) *Forgotten Children: Parent–Child Relations from 1500 to 1900*, Cambridge: Cambridge University Press.

Pollock, S. and R. Bernbeck (2000) 'And they said, let us make gods in our image: gendered ideologies in ancient Mesopotamia', in A.E. Rautman (ed.) *Reading the Body: Representations and Remains in the Archaeological Record*, Philadelphia: University of Pennsylvania Press, 150–64.

Poole, F.J. (1994) 'Socialization, enculturation and the development of personal identity', in T. Ingold (ed.) *Companion Encyclopedia of Anthropology*, London: Routledge, 831–60.

Price, N. (ed.) (2001) *The Archaeology of Shamanism*, London: Routledge.

Price, S.R.F. (1985) *Rituals and Power: The Roman Imperial Cult in Asia Minor*, Cambridge: Cambridge University Press.

Price, T.D., A. Bentley, J. Lüning, D. Graonenborn and J. Wahl (2001) 'Prehistoric human migration in the *Linearbandkeramik* of Central Europe', *Antiquity* 75: 593–603.

Prine, E. (2000) 'Searching for third genders: towards a prehistory of domestic space in Middle Missouri Villages', in R.A. Schmidt and B.L. Voss (eds) *Archaeologies of Sexuality*, London: Routledge, 197–219.

Privat, K.L., T.C. O'Conell and M.P. Richards (2002) 'Stable isotope analysis of human and faunal remains from the Anglo-Saxon cemetery at Berinsfield, Oxfordshire: dietary and social implications', *Journal of Archaeological Science* 29(7): 779–90.

Prout, A. and A. James (1990) 'A new paradigm for the sociology of childhood? Provenance, promise and problems', in A. James and A. Prout (eds) *Constructing and Reconstructing Childhood: Contemporary Issues in the Sociological Study of Childhood*, London: The Falmer Press, 7–34.

Pryor, F. (2002) *Seahenge: A Quest for Life and Death in Bronze Age Britain*, London: HarperCollins.

Ramstad, M. (1998) 'Common group identity with or without ethnicity? The Norwegian West Coast during the Late Stone Age', in A.-C. Andersson, Å. Gillberg, O.W. Jensen, H. Karlsson and M.V. Rolöf (eds) *The Kaleidoscopic Past: Proceedings of the 5th Nordic TAG Conference, Göteborg, 2–5 April 1997*, Gotarc Serie C, Arkeologiska Skrifter No. 16, Göteborg: Göteborg University, Department of Archaeology, 355–65.

Rao, N. (1999) 'Ayodhya and the ethics of archaeology', in T. Insoll (ed.) *Case Studies in Archaeology and World Religion: The Proceedings of the Cambridge Conference*, BAR International Series 755, Oxford: British Archaeological Reports, 44–7.

Redfield, R. (1956) *Peasant Society and Culture*, Chicago: Chicago University Press.

Reeve, J. and M. Adams (1993) *The Spitalfields Project, Volume 1: The Archaeology Across the Styx*, CBA Research Report 85, London.

Rega, E. (1997) 'Age, gender and biological reality in the Early Bronze Age cemetery at Mokrin', in J. Moore and E. Scott (eds) *Invisible People and Processes*, Leicester: Leicester University Press, 229–47.

Reid, A., P. Lane, E. Segobye, L. Borjeson, N. Mathibidi and P. Sekgarametso (1997) 'Tswana architecture and responses to colonialism', *World Archaeology* 28: 370–92.

Renfrew, C. (ed.) (1973) *The Explanation of Culture Change: Models in Prehistory*, London: Duckworth.

Renfrew, C. (1982) 'Socio-economic change in ranked societies', in C. Renfrew and S. Shennan (eds) *Ranking, Resource and Exchange-Aspects*, Cambridge: Cambridge University Press, 1–8.

Renfrew, C. (1985) *The Archaeology of Cult: The Sanctuary at Phylakopi*, London: British School in Athens.

Renfrew, C. (1994) 'The archaeology of religion', in C. Renfrew and E. Zubrow (eds) *The Ancient Mind*, Cambridge: Cambridge University Press, 47–54.

Renfrew, C. and S. Shennan (1982) *Ranking, Resource and Exchange: Aspects of the Archaeology of Early European Society*, Cambridge: Cambridge University Press.

Rice, P. (1991) 'Women and prehistoric pottery production', in I.D. Walde and N.D. Willows (eds) *The Archaeology of Gender*, Calgary: The University of Calgary, 436–43.

Richards, J. and M. Van Buren (2000) *Order, Legitimacy and Wealth in Ancient States*, Cambridge: Cambridge University Press.

Richards, M.P., T.D. Price and E. Koch (2003) 'The Mesolithic/Neolithic transition in Denmark: new stable isotope data', *Current Anthropology* 44: 288–94.

Riley, M.W. (1987) 'On the significance of age in sociology', *American Sociological Review* 52(1): 1–14.

Ringrose, K.M. (1994) 'Living in the shadows: eunuchs and gender in Byzantium', in G. Herdt (ed.) *Third Sex, Third Gender: Beyond Sexual Dimorphism in Culture and History*, New York: Zone Books, 85–110.

Robb, J. (1993) 'A social prehistory of European languages', *Antiquity* 67: 747–60.

Robb, J. (1997) 'Intentional tooth removal in Neolithic Italian women', *Antiquity* 71: 659–69.

Robb, J.E. (2001) 'Island identities: ritual, travel and the creation of difference in Neolithic Malta', *European Journal of Archaeology* 4(2): 175–202.

Roosevelt, A.C. (2002) 'Gender in human evolution: sociobiology revisited and revised', in S.M. Nelson and M. Rosen-Ayalon (eds) *In Pursuit of Gender: Worldwide Archaeological Approaches*, Walnut Creek: Altamira Press, 355–76.

Roscoe, W. (1994) 'How to become a Berdache: toward a unified analysis of gender', in G. Herdt (ed.) *Third Sex, Third Gender: Beyond Sexual Dimorphism in Culture and History*, New York: Zone Books, 329–72.

Rosenthal, J.T. (1996) *Old Age in Late Medieval England*, Philadelphia: University of Pennsylvania Press.

Roth, A.M. (2000) 'Father Earth, Mother Sky: ancient Egyptian beliefs about conception and fertility', in A.E. Rautman (ed.) *Reading the Body: Representations and Remains in the Archaeological Record*, Philadelphia: University of Pennsylvania Press, 187–201.

Roveland, B. (1997) 'Archaeology of children', *Anthropology Newsletter (American Anthropological Association)* 38(4): 14.

Roveland, B. (2000) 'Footprints in the clay: Upper Palaeolithic children in ritual and secular contexts', in J. Sofaer Derevenski (ed.) *Children and Material Culture*, London: Routledge, 29–38.

Rowlands, M.J. (1987) 'Power and moral order in pre-colonial West-Central Africa', in E. Brumfiel and T. Earle (eds) *Specialisation, Exchange and Complex Societies*, Cambridge: Cambridge University Press, 52–63.

Rowlands, M.J. (1989) 'A question of complexity', in D. Miller, M. Rowlands and C. Tilley (eds) *Domination and Resistance*, London: Unwin Hyman, 29–40.

Rowlands, M.J. (1998) 'Consumption and ethnicity in the interpretation of cultural form', in M. Pearce and M. Tosi (eds) *Papers from the EAA Third Annual Meeting at Ravenna 1997, Volume I: Pre- and Protohistory*, BAR International Series 717, Oxford: British Archaeological Reports, 261–3.

Rubin, G. (1975) 'The traffic in women: notes on the "Political economy" of sex', in R. Reiter (ed.) *Toward an Anthropology of Women*, New York: Monthly Press, 157–210.

Russell, A.E. (1997) 'Material culture and African-American spirituality at the Hermitage', *Historical Archaeology* 31(2): 63–80.

Russell, P. (1991) 'Men only? The myths about European Palaeolithic artists', in D. Walde and N.D. Willows (eds) *The Archaeology of Gender*, Calgary: The University of Calgary, 346–51.

Sackett, J.R. (1977) 'The meaning of style in archaeology', *American Antiquity* 42: 369–80.

Sackett, J.R. (1990) 'Style and ethnicity in archaeology: the case for isochretism', in M.W. Conkey and C.A. Hastorf (eds) *The Use of Style in Archaeology*, Cambridge: Cambridge University Press, 32–43.

Sahlins, M. (2000) '"Sentimental pessimism" and ethnographic experience or, why culture is not a disappearing "object"', in L. Daston (ed.) *Biographies of Scientific Objects*, Chicago: University of Chicago Press, 158–202.

Savage, S.H. (2000) 'The status of women in Predynastic Egypt as revealed through mortuary analysis', in A.E. Rautman (ed.) *Reading the Body: Representations and Remains in the Archaeological Record*, Philadelphia: University of Pennsylvania Press, 77–94.

Saxe, A. (1970) *Social Dimensions of Mortuary Practices*, PhD Dissertation, University of Michigan.

Schildkrout, E. (1978) 'Age and gender in Hausa society: socio-economic roles of children in urban Kano', in J.S. La Fontaine (ed.) *Sex and Age as Principles of Social Differentiation*, New York: Academic Press, 109–37.

Schlegel, A. (1995) 'A cross-cultural approach to adolescence', *Ethos* 23(1): 15–32.

Schmidt, P. (1998) 'Reading gender in the ancient iron technology of Africa', in S. Kent (ed.) *Gender in African Prehistory*, Walnut Creek: Altamira Press, 139–62.

Schülke, A. (1999) 'On Christianization and grave finds', *European Journal of Archaeology* 2: 77–106.

Schultz, J.A. (1995) *The Knowledge of Childhood in the German Middle Ages 1100–1350*, Philadelphia: University of Pennsylvania Press.

Schurr, M.R. (1992) 'Isotopic and mortuary variability in a Middle Mississippian population', *American Antiquity* 57: 300–320.

Scott, E. (1992) 'Images and contexts of infants and infant burials: some thoughts on some cross-cultural evidence', *Archaeological Review from Cambridge* 11(1): 77–92.

Scott, E. (1997) 'Introduction: on the incompleteness of archaeological narratives', in J. Moore and E. Scott (eds) *Invisible People and Processes*, Leicester: Leicester University Press, 1–12.

Scott, E. (2001) 'Killing the female? Archaeological narratives of infanticide', in B. Arnold and N.L. Wicker (eds) *Gender and the Archaeology of Death*, Walnut Creek: Altamira Press, 1–22.

Sen, A. (1992) *Inequality Reexamined*, New York: Russel Sage Foundation.

Service, E.R. (1962) *Primitive Social Organization: An Evolutionary Perspective*, New York: Random House.

Service, E.R. (1971) *Cultural Evolutionism: Theory in Practice*, New York: Holt, Rinehart and Winston.

Service, E.R. (1975) *Origins of the State and Civilisation: The Process of Cultural Evolution*, New York: Norton.

Shafter, B.S., K.M. Gardner and J.F. Powell (2000) 'Prehistoric and ethnographic Pueblo gender roles: continuity of lifeways from the eleventh to the early twentieth century', in A.E. Rautman (ed.) *Reading the Body: Representations and Remains in the Archaeological Record*, Philadelphia: University of Pennsylvania Press, 139–49.

Shahar, S. (1990) *Childhood in the Middle Ages*, London: Routledge.

Shahar, S. (1997) *Growing Old in the Middle Ages*, London: Routledge.

Shaw, C.T. (1977) *Unearthing Igbo Ukwu*, Oxford: Oxford University Press.

Sheehan, M. (ed.) (1990) *Aging and the Aged in Medieval Europe*, Toronto: Pontifical Institute of Mediaeval Studies.

Shennan, S. (1978) 'Archaeological "cultures": an empirical investigation', in I. Hodder (ed.) *The Spatial Organisation of Culture*, London: Duckworth, 113–39.

Shennan, S. (ed.) (1989a) *Archaeological Approaches to Cultural Identity*, London: Unwin Hyman.

Shennan, S. (1989b) 'Introduction: archaeological approaches to cultural identity', in S. Shennan (ed.) *Archaeological Approaches to Cultural Identity*, London: Unwin Hyman, 1–32.

Shennan, S. (1991) 'Some current issues in the archaeological identification of past peoples', *Archaeologia Polona* 29: 29–38.

Shipek, F.C. (1989) 'An example of intensive plant husbandry: the Kumeyaay of southern California', in D.R. Harris and G.C. Hillman (eds) *Foraging and Farming: The Evolution of Plant Exploitation*, London: Unwin Hyman, 159–70.

Shoolongdej, R. (2002) 'Gender roles depicted in rock art: a case from Western Thailand', in S.M. Nelson and M. Rosen-Ayalon (eds) *In Pursuit of Gender: Worldwide Archaeological Approaches*, Walnut Creek: Altamira Press, 187–206.

Sillar, R. (1994) 'Playing with God: cultural perceptions of children, play and miniatures in the Andes', *Archaeological Review from Cambridge* 13(2): 47–63.

Silverblatt, I. (1988) 'Women in states', *Annual Review of Anthropology* 17: 427–60.

Sims-Williams, P. (1998) 'Genetics, linguistics and prehistory: thinking big and thinking straight', *Antiquity* 72: 505–27.

Singleton, T.A. (1995) 'The archaeology of slavery in North America', *Annual Review of Anthropology* 24: 119–40.

Small, D.B. (1991) 'Initial study of the structure of women's seclusion in the archaeological past', in I.D. Walde and N.D. Willows (eds) *The Archaeology of Gender*, Calgary: The University of Calgary, 336–44.

Smart, N. (1998) *The World's Religions*, Cambridge: Cambridge University Press.

Smith, A.D. (1984) 'National identity and myths of ethnic descent', *Research in Social Movements, Conflict and Change* 7: 95–130.

Smith, A.D. (1986) *The Ethnic Origin of Nations*, Oxford: Blackwell.

Smith, C. (1991) 'Female artists: the unrecognized factor in sacred rock art production', in P. Bahn and A. Rosenfeld (eds) *Rock Art and Prehistory: Papers Presented to Symposium G of the AURA Congress, Darwin 1988*, Oxbow Monograph 10, Oxford: Oxbow, 45–52.

Smith, W.C. (1962) *The Meaning and End of Religion*, New York: Mentor Books.

Sofaer Derevenski, J. (1994a) 'Where are the children? Accessing children in the past', *Archaeological Review from Cambridge* 13(2): 7–20.

Sofaer Derevenski, J. (1994b) 'Editorial', *Archaeological Review from Cambridge* 13(2): 1–5.

Sofaer Derevenski, J. (1997a) 'Age and gender at the site of Tiszapolgár-Basatanya, Hungary', *Antiquity* 71: 875–89.

Sofaer Derevenski, J. (1997b) 'Engendering children, engendering archaeology', in J. Moore and E. Scott (eds) *Invisible People and Processes*, Leicester: Leicester University Press, 192–202.

Sofaer Derevenski, J. (1997c) 'Linking age and gender as social variables', *Ethnographisch-Archäologischen Zeitschrift* 38: 485–93.

Sofaer Derevenski, J. (ed.) (2000a) *Children and Material Culture*, London: Routledge.

Sofaer Derevenski, J. (2000b) 'Material culture shock: confronting expectations in the material culture of children', in J. Sofaer Derevenski (ed.) *Children and Material Culture*, London: Routledge, 3–16.

Sofaer Derevenski, J. (2000c) 'Rings of life: the role of early metalwork in mediating the gendered life course', *World Archaeology* 31(3): 389–406.

Soffer, O., J.M. Adovasio and D.C. Hyland (2000) 'Textiles, basketry, gender, and status in the Upper Paleolithic', *Current Anthropology* 31(4): 511–38.

Sokal, R.R., G.M. Jaquez, N.L. Oden, D. DiGiovanni, A.B. Falsetti, E. McGee and B.A. Thomson (1993) 'Genetic relationships of European populations reflect their ethnohistorical affinities', *American Journal of Physical Anthropology* 91: 55–70.

Sommerville, C.J. (1992) *The Discovery of Childhood in Puritan England*, Athens, Ga.: University of Georgia Press.

Sørensen, M.L.S. (1996) 'Women as/and metalworkers', in A. Devonshire and B. Wood (eds) *Women in Industry and Technology: From Prehistory to the Present: Current Research and the Museum Experience*, London: Museum of London, 45–52.

Sørensen, M.L.S. (1992) 'Gender archaeology and Scandinavian Bronze Age studies', *Norwegian Archaeological Review* 25(1): 31–49.

Sørensen, M.L.S. (1997) 'Reading dress: the construction of social categories and identities in Bronze Age Europe', *Journal of European Archaeology* 5(1): 93–114.

Sørensen, M.L.S. (2000) *Gender Archaeology*, Cambridge: Polity Press.

Southall, A. (1988) 'The segmentary state in Africa and Asia', *Comparative Studies in Society and History* 30: 52–82.

Sparkes, B. (1998) 'Sex in Classical Athens', in B. Sparkes (ed.) *Greek Civilization: An Introduction*, Oxford: Blackwell, 248–62.

Spector, J.D. (1991) 'What this awl means: toward a feminist archaeology', in J. Gero and M.W. Conkey (eds) *Engendering Archaeology*, Oxford: Blackwell, 388–406.

Spencer, H. (1876) *The Principles of Sociology*, London: Williams and Norgate.

Spencer, P. (1990) 'The riddled course: theories of age and its transformations', in P. Spencer (ed.) *Anthropology and the Riddle of the Sphinx: Paradoxes of Change in the Life Course*, London: Routledge, 1–34.

Spencer-Wood, S.M. (1991) 'Toward a feminist historical archaeology of the construction of gender', in D. Walde and N.D. Willows (eds) *The Archaeology of Gender*, Calgary: The University of Calgary, 234–44.

Spencer-Wood, S.M. (1999) 'Gendering power', in T.L. Sweely (ed.) *Manifesting Power: Gender and the Interpretation of Power in Archaeology*, London: Routledge, 175–83.

Spengler, O. (1991 [1918–22]) *The Decline of the West*, New York: Oxford University Press.

Stahl, A.B. and M.d.D. Cruz (1998) 'Men and women in a market economy: gender and craft production in West Central Ghana *c.* 1775–1995', in S. Kent (ed.) *Gender in African Prehistory*, Walnut Creek: Altamira Press, 205–26.

Stalsberg, A. (1991) 'Women as actors in Northern European Viking Age trade', in R. Samson (ed.) *Social Approaches to Viking Studies*, Glasgow: Cruithne Press, 75–83.

Stalberg, A. (2001), 'Visible women made invisible: interpreting Varansian women in Old Russia', in B. Arnold and N.L. Wicker (eds) *Gender and the Archaeology of Death*, Walnut Creek: Altamira Press, 65–80.

Stephens, S. (1995) 'Introduction: children and the politics of culture in "late capital-ism"', in S. Stephens (ed.) *Children and the Politics of Culture*, Princeton: Princeton University Press, 3–48.

Stoller, R. (1968) *Sex and Gender*, New York: Science House.

Suthrell, C. (2004) *Unzipping Gender: Sex, Cross-Dressing and Culture*, Oxford: Berg.

Sweely, T.L. (1999a) 'Gender, space, people, and power at Cerén, El Salvador', in T.L. Sweely (ed.) *Manifesting Power: Gender and the Interpretation of Power in Archaeology*, London: Routledge, 155–172.

Sweely, T.L. (ed.) (1999b) *Manifesting Power: Gender and the Interpretation of Power in Archaeology*, London: Routledge.

Sykes, B. (2001) *The Seven Daughters of Eve*, London: Bantam.

Tainter, J.A. (1977) 'Modeling change in prehistoric social systems', in L.R. Binford (ed.) *For Theory Building in Archaeology*, New York: Academic Press, 327–52.

Tainter, J.A. (1978) 'Mortuary practices and the study of prehistoric social systems', in M.B. Schiffer (ed.) *Advances in Archaeological Method and Theory, Vol. 1*, New York: Academic Press, 106–41.

Talbot, C. (1995) 'Inscribing the other, inscribing the self: Hindu-Muslim identities in pre-Colonial India', *Comparative Studies in Society and History* 37(4): 692–722.

Tambiah, J. (1979) 'A performative approach to ritual', *Proceedings of the British Academy* 65: 113–69.

Tcherkezoff, S. (1993) 'The illusion of dualism in Samoa: "Brothers-and-sisters" are not "men-and-women"', in T. del Valle (ed.) *Gendered Anthropology*, London: Routledge, 54–87.

Thane, P. (2000) *Old Age in English History: Past Experiences, Present Issues*, Oxford: Oxford University Press.

Thomas, J. (2000a) 'Introduction: the polarities of post-processual archaeology', in J. Thomas (ed.) *Interpretive Archaeology: A Reader*, Leicester: Leicester University Press, 1–18.

Thomas, J. (2000b) 'Reconfiguring the social, reconfiguring the material', in M.B. Schiffer (ed.) *Social Theory in Archaeology*, Salt Lake City: University of Utah Press, 143–55.

Thomason, S.G. and T. Kaufman (1988) *Language Contact, Creolization and Genetic Linguistics*, Berkeley: University of California Press.

Tilley, C. (1989) 'Discourse and power: the genre of the Cambridge Inaugural Lecture', in D. Miller, M. Rowlands and C. Tilley (eds) *Domination and Resistance*, London: Unwin Hyman, 41–63.

Tilley, C. (ed.) (1990) *Reading Material Culture*, Oxford: Blackwell.

Tilley, C. (1999) *Metaphor and Material Culture*, Oxford: Blackwell.

Tilley, C. (2002) 'Metaphor, materiality and interpretation', in V. Buchli (ed.) *The Material Culture Reader*, Oxford: Berg, 23–6.

Tougher, S.F. (1997) 'Byzantine Eunuchs: an overview, with special reference to their creation and origin', in L. James (ed.) *Women, Men and Eunuchs: Gender in Byzantium*, London: Routledge, 168–99.

Tougher, S.F. (1999) 'Images of effeminate men: the case of Byzantine Eunuchs', in D.M. Hadley (ed.) *Masculinity in Medieval Europe*, London: Longman.

Towler, R. (1974) *Homo Religiosus: Sociological Problems in the Study of Religion*, London: Constable.

Treherne, P. (1995) 'The warrior's beauty: the masculine body and self-identity in Bronze Age Europe', *Journal of European Archaeology* 3(1): 105–44.

Trocolli, R. (1999) 'Women leaders in native North American societies: invisible women in power', in T.L. Sweely (ed.) *Manifesting Power: Gender and the Interpretation of Power in Archaeology*, London: Routledge, 49–61.

Trombley, F.R. (1995) *Hellenic Religion and Christianization, c. 370–529, Vol. 2*, Leiden: Brill.

Turner, V. (1977) *The Ritual Process: Structure and Anti-Structure*, Ithaca: Cornell University Press.

Tylor, E.B. (1871) *Primitive Culture*, London: John Murray.

Tyrrell, A. (2000) '*Corpus Saxonum*: early medieval bodies and corporeal identity', in W.O. Frazer and A. Tyrrell (eds) *Social Identity in Early Medieval Britain*, Leicester: Leicester University Press, 137–55.

Vail, L. (1989) 'Introduction: ethnicity in South African history', in L. Vail (ed.) *The Creation of Tribalism in Southern Africa*, Berkeley: University of California Press, 1–19.

Van Gennep, A. (1960) *The Rites of Passage*, London: Routledge and Kegan Paul.

Vansina, J. (1962) 'A comparison of African kingdoms', *Africa* 32: 324–35.

Vansina, J. (1973) *The Tio Kingdom of the Middle Congo 1882–1892*, London: International African Institute.

Vasta, E. (1991) 'Gender, class and ethnic relations: the domestic and work experiences of Italian migrant women in Australia', in G. Bottomley, M. de Lepervanche and J. Martin (eds) *Intersexions: Gender/Class/Culture/Ethnicity*, London: Allen and Unwin, 159–77.

Veit, U. (1989) 'Ethnic concepts in German prehistory: a case study on the relationship between cultural identity and cultural objectivity', in S. Shennan (ed.) *Archaeological Approaches to Cultural Identity*, London: Unwin Hyman, 35–56.

Vencl, S. (1994) 'The archaeology of thirst', *Journal of European Archaeology* 2(2): 299–326.

Verdery, K. (1999) *The Political Lives of Dead Bodies: Reburial and Postsocialist Change*, New York: Columbia University Press.

Voss, B.L. and R.A. Schmidt. (2000) 'Archaeologies of sexuality: an introduction', in R.A. Schmidt and B.L. Voss (eds) *Archaeologies of Sexuality*, London: Routledge, 1–32.

Wadley, L. (1998) 'The invisible meat providers: women in the Stone Age of South Africa', in S. Kent (ed.) *Gender in African Prehistory*, Walnut Creek: Altamira Press, 69–82.

Walker, P.L. and J.M. Erlandson (1986) 'Dental evidence for prehistoric dietary change on the Northern Channel Islands, California', *American Antiquity* 51: 375–83.

Wallace, A.F.C. (1966) *Religion: An Anthropological View*, New York: Random House.

Ware, C. (2003) *The Use and Organisation of Space: Settlements in England AD 400–1000*, PhD Dissertation, University of Newcastle, UK.

Wartofsky, M. (1983) 'The child's construction of the world and the world's construction of the child: from historical epistemology to historical psychology', in F.S. Kessel and A.W. Siegel (eds) *The Child and Other Cultural Inventions*, New York: Praeger, 188–215.

Wason, P.K. (1994) *The Archaeology of Rank*, Cambridge: Cambridge University Press.

Watson, P.J. and M.C. Kennedy (1991) 'The development of horticulture in the Eastern Woodlands of North America: women's role', in J. Gero and M.W. Conkey (eds) *Engendering Archaeology*, Oxford: Blackwell, 255–75.

Weber, C.A. (1991) 'The genius of the orangery: women and eighteenth century Chesapeake gardens', in I.D. Walde and N.D. Willows (eds) *The Archaeology of Gender*, Calgary: The University of Calgary, 263–8.

Weber, M. (1958) *The Protestant Ethic and the Spirit of Capitalism*, New York: Charles Scribner.

Webster, J. (1997) 'Necessary comparisons: a post-colonial approach to religious syncretisms in the Roman provinces', *World Archaeology* 28: 339–50.

Webster, J. (1999) 'At the end of the world: Druidic and other revitalization movements in post-Conquest Gaul and Britain', *Britannia* 30: 1–20.

Welinder, S. (1998) 'The cultural construction of childhood in Scandinavia, 3500BC–1350AD', *Current Swedish Archaeology* 6: 185–204.

Welinder, S. (2001) 'The archaeology of old age', *Current Swedish Archaeology* 9: 163–78.

Wells, P. (1992) 'Tradition, identity and change beyond the Roman frontier', in E.M. Schortman and P.A. Urban (eds) *Resources, Power and Interregional Interaction*, New York: Plenum Press, 175–88.

Wells, P.S. (1999) *The Barbarians Speak: How the Conquered Peoples Shaped Roman Europe*, Princeton: Princeton University Press.

Wells, P.S. (2001) *Beyond Celts, Germans and Scythians: Archaeology and Identity in Iron Age Europe*, London: Duckworth.

Wenke, R.J. (1981) 'Explaining the evolution of cultural complexity: a review', in M.B. Schiffer (ed.) *Advances in Archaeological Method and Theory, Vol. 4*, New York: Academic Press, 79–127.

Whelan, M.K. (1991a) 'Gender and archaeology: mortuary studies and the search for the origins of gender differentiation', in I.D. Walde and N.D. Willows (eds) *The Archaeology of Gender*, Calgary: The University of Calgary, 358–65.

Whelan, M.K. (1991b) 'Gender and historical archaeology: Eastern Dakota patterns in the 19th century', *Historical Archaeology* 25: 17–32.

Whitehead, H. (1981) 'The bow and the burden strap: a new look at institutionalized homosexuality in Native North America', in S. Ortner and H. Whitehead (eds) *Sexual Meanings*, Cambridge: Cambridge University Press, 80–115.

Whitley, D.S. (1992) 'Shamanism and rock art in far western North America', *Cambridge Archaeological Journal* 2: 89–113.

Whitley, D.S. and J.D. Keyser (2003) 'Faith in the past: debating an archaeology of religion', *Antiquity* 77: 385–93.

Wicker, N. (1998) 'Selective female infanticide as partial explanation of the dearth of women in Viking Age Scandinavia', in G. Halsall (ed.) *Violence and Society in the Early Medieval West: Private, Public, and Ritual*, Woodbridge: Boydell Press, 205–22.

Wilk, R.R. (1996) *Economies and Cultures: Foundations of Economic Anthropology*, Boulder: Westview Press.

Wilkie, L.A. (1997) 'Secret and sacred: contextualizing the artifacts of African-American magic and religion', *Historical Archaeology* 31(4): 81–106.

Wilkie, L.A. (2000) 'Magical passions: sexuality and African-American archaeology', in R.A. Schmidt and B.L. Voss (eds) *Archaeologies of Sexuality*, London: Routledge, 129–42.

Willis, S. (1994) 'Roman imports into Late Iron Age British societies: towards a critique of existing models', in S. Cottam, D. Dungworth, S. Scott and J. Taylor (eds) *TRAC 94: Proceedings of the Fourth Annual Theoretical Roman Archaeology Conference, Durham*, Oxford: Oxbow, 142–5.

Wilson, A. (1980) 'The infancy of the history of childhood: an appraisal of Philippe Ariès', *History and Theory* 19(1): 132–53.

Wilson, S. (1984) 'The myth of motherhood a myth: the historical view of European child-rearing', *Social History* 9(2): 181–98.

Wobst, M. (1977) 'Stylistic behavior and information exchange', in C.E. Cleland (ed.) *Papers for the Director*, Anthropological Papers of the University of Michigan, Michigan: University of Michigan, 317–42.

Wolf, E.R. (1982) *Europe and the People Without History*, Berkeley: California University Press.

Wolf, E.R. (1990) 'Distinguished lecture: facing power – old insights, new questions', *American Anthropologist* 92: 586–96.

Wolf, E.R. (1999) *Envisioning Power–Ideologies of Dominance and Crisis*, Berkeley: University of California Press.

Wood, D. (ed.) (1994) *The Church and Childhood*, Studies in Church History 31, Oxford: Blackwell.

Woolf, G. (1998) *Becoming Roman: The Origins of Provincial Civilization in Gaul*, Cambridge: Cambridge University Press.

Wright, R.P. (1991) 'Women's labor and pottery production in prehistory', in J. Gero and M.W. Conkey (eds) *Engendering Archaeology*, Oxford: Blackwell, 194–223.

Wylie, A. (1991) 'Gender theory and the archaeological record: why is there no archaeology of gender?', in J. Gero and M.W. Conkey (eds) *Engendering Archaeology*, Oxford: Blackwell, 31–56.

Yanagisako, S.J. and J.F. Collier. (1987) 'Toward a unified analysis of gender and kinship', in J.F. Collier and S.J. Yanagisako (eds) *Gender and Kinship: Essays Towards a Unified Analysis*, Stanford: Stanford University Press, 15–44.

Yates, T. (1993) 'Frameworks for an archaeology of the body', in C. Tilley (ed.) *Interpretative Archaeology*, Oxford: Berg, 31–72.

Yentsch, A. (1996) 'The symbolic divisions of pottery: sex-related attributes of English and Anglo-American household pots', in R.W. Preucel and I. Hodder (eds) *Contemporary Archaeology in Theory: A Reader*, Oxford: Blackwell, 315–50.

Yoffee, N. (1993) 'Too many chiefs? (or, safe texts for the '90s)', in N. Yoffee and A. Sherratt (eds) *Archaeological theory: Who Sets the Agenda?*, Cambridge: Cambridge University Press, 60–78.

Yorke, B. (2000) 'Political and ethnic identity: a case study of Anglo-Saxon practice', in W.O. Frazer and A. Tyrrell (eds) *Social Identity in Early Medieval Britain*, Leicester: Leicester University Press, 69–89.

Zbarsky, I. and S. Hutchinson (1997) *Lenin's Embalmers*, London: The Harvill Press.

Zvelebil, M. (1995) 'At the interface of archaeology, linguistics and genetics: Indo-European dispersals and the agricultural transition in Europe', *Journal of European Archaeology* 3(1): 33–70.

# Index

# Related titles from Routledge

### The Archaeology of Personhood
### An Anthropological Approach
Chris Fowler

Bringing together a wealth of research in social and cultural anthropology, philosophy and related fields, this is the first book to address the contribution that an understanding of personhood can make to our interpretations of the past

Applying an anthropological approach to detailed case studies from European prehistoric archaeology, the book explores the connection between people, animals, objects, their societies and environments and investigates the relationship that jointly produces bodies, persons, communities and artefacts.

*The Archaeology of Personhood* examines the characteristics that define a person as a category of being, highlights how definitions of personhood are culturally variable and explores how that variation is connected to human uses of material culture.

Hb: 0–415–3172–15
Pb: 0–415–3172–23

Available at all good bookshops
For ordering and further information please visit:
## www.routledge.com

# Related titles from Routledge

### Archaeology, Ritual, Religion
Timothy Insoll

The archaeology of religion is a much neglected area, yet religious sites and artefacts constitute a major area of archaeological evidence. Timothy Insoll presents an introductory statement on the archaeology of religion, examining what archaeology can tell us about religion, the problems of defining and theorizing religion in archaeology, and the methodology, or how to 'do', the archaeology of religion.

This volume assesses religion and ritual through a range of examples from around the world and across time, including prehistoric religions, shamanism, African religions, death, landscape and even food. Insoll also discusses the history of research and varying theories in this field before looking to future research directions. This book will be a valuable guide for students and archaeologists, and initiate a major area of debate.

Hb: 0–415–253128
Pb: 0–415–253136

Available at all good bookshops
For ordering and further information please visit:

## www.routledge.com

# Related titles from Routledge

## Archaeology
### The Basics
Clive Gamble

'Gamble's book provides an excellent introduction to the aims and methods of archaeology, which is by no means easy within the confines of one book. But to do so in a manner which is intellectually engaged with the subject matter and which evokes the excitement and interest of archaeological work is a considerable achievement. The best short introduction to the subject I know and one which will become a standard text for any teacher of archaeology or related subject.' – *Chris Gosden, Pitt Rivers Museum, University of Oxford, UK*

'The digger boasting the worn stub of a trowel in their right back trouser pocket should feel incomplete without a copy of *Archaeology: The Basics* in the other.' – *Current Archaeology*

From archaeological jargon to interpretation, *Archaeology: the Basics* provides an invaluable overview of a fascinating subject and probes the depths of this increasingly popular discipline, presenting critical approaches to the understanding of our past.

Lively and engaging, *Archaeology: The Basics* fires the archaeological imagination whilst tackling such questions as:

* What are the basic concepts of archaeology?
* How and what do we know about people and objects from the past?
* What makes a good explanation in archaeology?
* Why dig here?

This ultimate guide for all new and would-be archaeologists, whether they are students or interested amateurs, will prove an invaluable introduction to this wonderfully infectious discipline.

Hb: 0–415–22803–4
Pb: 0–415–22153–6

Available at all good bookshops
For ordering and further information please visit:
## www.routledge.com

# Related titles from Routledge

**Archaeology**
**The Key Concepts**
Edited by Colin Renfrew and Paul Bahn

Clearly written, and easy to follow, *Archaeology: The Key Concepts* collates entries written specifically by specialists in their field. Each entry offers a definition of the term, its origins and development, and all the major figures involved in the area.

The entries include:

* thinking about landscape
* cultural evolution
* urban societies
* archaeology of gender
* experimental archaeology

* archaeology of cult and religion
* concepts of time
* the Antiquity of Man
* feminist archaeology
* multiregional evolution.

Accessibly written for even beginner students, with guides to further reading and extensive cross-referencing, this book is a superb guide for anyone studying, teaching, or with any interest in archaeology.

Hb: 0–415–31757–6
Pb: 0–415–31758–4

Available at all good bookshops
For ordering and further information please visit:
**www.routledge.com**